Whoever wishes to remember must trust to oblivion, to the risk entailed in forgetting absolutely, and to this wonderful accident that memory then becomes.

—Maurice Blanchot

I seek the crucial region of the soul where absolute Evil and fraternity clash.

—André Malraux

PART

ONE

1

THE GAZE

They stand amazed before me, and suddenly, in that terror-stricken gaze, I see myself—in their horror.

For two years, I had lived without a face. No mirrors, in Buchenwald. I saw my body, its increasing emaciation, once a week, in the shower. Faceless, that absurd body. Sometimes I gently touched the jutting bones of the eye sockets, the hollow of a cheek. I could have gotten myself a mirror, I suppose. You could find anything on the camp's black market in exchange for bread, tobacco, margarine. Even tenderness, on occasion.

But I wasn't interested in such niceties.

I watched my body grow more and more vague beneath the weekly shower. Wasted but alive: the blood still circulated, nothing to fear. It would be enough, that thinned down but available body, fit for a much dreamed of—although most unlikely—survival.

The proof, moreover: here I am.

They stare at me, wild-eyed with panic.

It can't be because of my close-cropped hair. Young recruits and country boys, among others, innocently wear short hair. It's no big deal. A louse cut never bothered anyone. Nothing frightening about it. My outfit, then? A curious one, I admit: mismatched cast-offs. But my boots are Russian, of soft leather. Across my chest hangs a German submachine gun, an obvious sign of authority these days. Authority isn't alarming; on the whole, it's even reassuring. My thinness? They must have seen worse by now. If they're following the Allied armies' drive into Germany this spring, they've already seen worse. Other camps, living corpses . . .

The stubble on my head, my worn and ill-assorted clothing—such particulars can be startling, intriguing. But these men aren't startled or intrigued. What I read in their eyes is fear.

It must be my gaze, I conclude, that they find so riveting. It's the horror of my gaze that I see reflected in their own. And if their eyes are a mirror, then mine must look like those of a madman.

They got out of the car just now, only a moment ago. Took a few steps in the sunshine, stretching their legs. Then saw me, and moved forward.

Three officers, in British uniforms.

A fourth soldier, the driver, stayed near the automobile, a large gray Mercedes still bearing its German license plates.

The men came toward me.

Two of them are about thirty, blond, rather pink-complexioned. The third one is younger, darker, wearing a badge with a cross of Lorraine on which is written the word "France."

I remember the last French soldiers I saw, in June 1940. From the regular army, of course. Because after that I'd seen irregulars, guerrillas—plenty of them. Enough for me to have remembered them, in any case.

In the Tabou, for example, a Burgundian *maquis* between Laignes and Larrey.

But the last regular soldiers of the French Army—that was in June 1940, in the streets of Redon: wretched men falling back in disorder, in shame and misfortune, gray with dust and defeat. Five years later, in the April sunlight, the man in front of me doesn't look defeated. He wears a badge of France over his heart, over the left pocket of his uniform jacket.

Triumphantly, or at least joyfully.

He must be my age, a few years older. I could try being friendly.

He stares at me, bewildered by fright.

"What's the matter?" I ask irritably, and doubtless harshly. "You're surprised to find the woods so quiet?"

He looks around at the trees encircling us. The other men do the same. Listening. No, it's not the silence. They hadn't noticed, hadn't heard the silence. I'm what's scaring them, obviously, and nothing else.

"No birds left," I continue, pursuing my idea. "They say the smoke from the crematory drove them away. Never any birds in this forest. . . ."

They listen closely, straining to understand.

"The smell of burned flesh, that's what did it!"

They wince, glance at one another. In almost palpable distress. A sort of gasp, a heave of revulsion.

"A strange smell," wrote Léon Blum.

Deported in April 1943, with Georges Mandel, Blum lived for two years at Buchenwald. He was confined outside the actual perimeter of the camp, however, in one of the villas provided for SS officers, beyond the electrified barbed wire. He never left the house; no one ever entered it except the soldiers on guard. He was taken to the dentist two or three times, but that was by car, at night, along deserted roads through the forest of beeches. In his memoirs, he noted that the SS patrolled constantly with submachine guns slung across their shoulders and dogs on leashes, making endless rounds on the narrow path between the villa and the barbed-wire fence. "Like mute and impassive shadows," wrote Léon Blum.

The strictness of this confinement explains his ignorance. Blum did not even know where he was, to what part of Germany he had been deported. He spent two years in a villa in the SS quarters of Buchenwald completely unaware of the adjacent concentration camp, even though it was so close by.

"The first indication of it we had," he wrote afterward, "was a strange smell that often reached us in the evening, through the open windows, and haunted us all night long when the wind held steady: it was the smell of the crematory ovens."

One can imagine Léon Blum, on those evenings. In the spring, probably: windows open to the first mild breath of the season, the fragrance of nature. Moments of nostalgia, of vague yearning, in the aching uncertainty of this renewal. And suddenly, borne on the breeze, the curious odor: sweetish, cloying, with a bitter and truly nauseating edge to it. The peculiar odor that would later prove to be from the crematory ovens.

A strange and haunting smell indeed.

I'd need only close my eyes, even today. It wouldn't take any effort—on the contrary, the slightest distraction of a memory brimful of trifles, of petty joys, would be enough to summon that ghost. Distraction from the shimmering opacity of life's offerings. Only a moment would suffice, at any moment. Distraction from oneself, from the existence that inhabits and possesses us, stubbornly, obtusely: the obscure desire to go on living, to persevere in this obstinacy for whatever reason, or unreason. It would take only a single instant of distraction from oneself, from others, from the world, an instant of nondesire, of quietude this side of life, an instant when the truth of that long-ago, primal event would rise to the surface, and the strange smell would drift over the hillside of the Ettersberg, that foreign homeland to which I always return.

It would take only a moment, any moment, unguarded, at random, out of the blue, at point-blank range. Or just the opposite: a carefully considered decision.

The strange smell would immediately invade the reality of memory. I would be reborn there; I would die if returned to life there. I would embrace and inhale the muddy, heady odor of that estuary of death.

When those three officers appeared, however, I felt more like laughing. Like gamboling in the sunshine, yelling my head off (what would that sound like?), running from tree to tree through the beech wood.

All things considered, it felt rather good to be alive.

The day before, toward noon, a warning siren had sounded, and a hoarse, panicky voice had crackled over the loudspeakers: *"Feindalarm, Feindalarm!"* We'd been awaiting this signal for several days, ever since life in the camp had been paralyzed by the approach of General Patton's armored divisions.

No more dawn departures for the outside *Kommandos*. April 3 saw the last general roll call of deportees. No more work, aside from maintenance duty within the camp. Buchenwald was tense with expectation. The SS command had strengthened surveillance, doubled the guard in the watchtowers. Patrols circled the perimeter more and more frequently, outside the electrified barbed-wire fence.

A week like that, waiting. The sounds of battle were drawing nearer. From Berlin came the order to evacuate the camp, but this order was only partly carried out. The clandestine International Committee promptly organized a passive resistance. Deportees ignored the summons for assignment to their departure groups. SS detachments were then sent deep into the camp, armed to the teeth but intimidated by the immensity of Buchenwald. By the determined and overwhelming mass of tens of thousands of still able-bodied men. Sometimes the SS fired blindly, in great bursts, trying to force the deportees to gather on the roll-call square.

But how can you terrorize men made resolute by despair, who have already crossed the threshold of death?

Out of fifty thousand detainees in Buchenwald, the SS managed to evacuate barely half: the oldest, the weakest, the least organized. Or those who, like the Poles, had chosen collectively to try their luck on the evacuation routes rather than wait for an uncertain fate. For a probable last-minute massacre. We knew that SS teams equipped with flamethrowers had arrived at Buchenwald.

I'm not going to tell you the story of our lives, as I haven't the time. At least not enough to go into detail, which is what gives a story its spice. Because the three officers in British uniform are right in front of me with their eyes popping out of their heads.

I don't know what they're waiting for, but they're holding their ground.

So, to wrap this up: the day before, on April 11, shortly before noon, the warning siren had begun wailing in short blasts, insistently repeated.

Feindalarm, Feindalarm!

The enemy was at the gates: freedom.

Combat units assembled at their appointed places. At three o'clock, the clandestine Military Committee gave the order for action. Men suddenly appeared with their arms full of weapons. Automatic rifles, submachine guns, a few stick-grenades, automatic pistols. And some bazookas—*Panzerfaust,* in German. Weapons stolen from the SS barracks, in particular during the panic and confusion of the bombing raids in August 1944. Weapons abandoned by guards on the trains that brought Jewish survivors from Auschwitz in the dead of winter. Weapons smuggled out of the Gustloff Works, part by part, then assembled in the secret workshops of the camp.

Weapons patiently collected over long years for this improbable day. Today.

In the Big Camp, the Spanish shock troops were gathered in a ground-floor wing of my block, number 40. French prisoners were housed next door in Block 34, and in the alley between the buildings Palazón now appeared at a run, followed by the men carrying our weapons.

"Grupos, a formar!" yelled Palazón, the military leader of the Spanish contingent.

We shouted, too, as we leaped through the open windows.

We each knew which weapon to grab, where to go, what to do. Unarmed, mingling with the haggard, starving, disoriented crowd on Sunday afternoons, we had already rehearsed these actions, covered this ground, until our momentum had become pure reflex.

By three-thirty, the control tower and the watchtowers had been occupied. The German Communist Hans Eiden, one of the oldest veterans of Buchenwald, was able to address the other prisoners over the camp's loudspeakers.

Still later, we marched on Weimar. We were overtaken on the road after nightfall by Patton's armored combat vehicles, whose crews were at first astonished, then wildly excited—after our explanations—by these strange armed bands of ragged soldiers. We exchanged words of greeting and recognition in every language of *la vieille Europe,* there on the slopes of the Ettersberg.

Not a single one of us would ever have dared dream of this. No one had been alive enough to dream, to risk imagining a future. Standing in the snow at roll call, assembled by the thousands in perfectly straight lines to witness the hanging of a comrade, none of us would have defiantly carried such a dream to this conclusion: rising up in arms and marching on Weimar by night.

Simply dreaming of surviving—even crippled, destitute, defeated—would already have been crazy enough.

Nobody would have dared cherish such a dream, it's true. Yet suddenly, as in a dream, it was true.

I'm laughing, laughing to find myself alive.

The springtime, the sun, my companions, the pack of Camels given to me that night by a young American soldier from New Mexico who spoke a lilting Castilian Spanish—it's all rather amusing to me.

Perhaps I shouldn't have laughed. Perhaps laughter is indecent, given what I must look like. Judging from the expressions of the British officers, laughter doesn't much suit me at the moment.

And it seems my face is no laughing matter, either.

They're standing silently a few steps away. They avoid looking at me. One officer's mouth has gone dry, I can tell. The other Britisher has a twitching eyelid. Nerves. As for the Frenchman, he's looking for something in a pocket of his military jacket, which allows him to avert his gaze.

I laugh again—too bad if it's out of place.

"The crematory shut down yesterday," I tell them. "No more smoke over the countryside, ever again. Maybe the birds will come back."

They wince, vaguely nauseated.

But they can't really understand. They probably know what the words mean. Smoke: you know what that is, you think you know. Throughout historic memory, there have been smoking chimneys. Sometimes country hearths, domestic firesides: the smoke of household gods.

This smoke, however, is beyond them. And they will never

really understand it. Not these people, that day. Nor all the others, afterward. They will never know—they cannot imagine, whatever their good intentions may be.

Ever-present, billowing or spiraling over the squat smoke-stack of the crematory of Buchenwald, not far from the administrative offices of the Labor Service, the *Arbeitsstatistik,* where I was assigned during that last year.

I had only to bend over a little, without leaving my duties at the central card index, and look out one of the windows facing the forest. There was the crematory, massive, surrounded by a high palisade, crowned with smoke.

Or flames, at night.

When the Allied aircraft flew deep into the heart of Germany on night bombing runs, the SS ordered that the fire in the crematory ovens be extinguished. The flames, which actually shot out of the chimney, were an ideal landmark for the English and American pilots.

"Krematorium, ausmachen!" A curt, impatient shout would crackle over the camp loudspeakers.

"Crematory, shut down!"

Sleeping, we would awaken to the hollow voice of the SS officer on duty in the control tower. Or rather: the voice would first become a part of our slumber, reverberating through our dreams, before waking us. In Buchenwald, while our bodies and our souls struggled blindly, during the brief nights, to return to life with a tenacious and carnal yearning belied by reason in the returning light of day, these two words—*Krematorium, ausmachen!*—exploded over and over in our dreams, filling them with echoes, bringing us back to the reality of death. Tearing us away from the dream of life.

Later, after we had returned from that absence, whenever we heard them (not necessarily during a nightmare: in a daydream or an idle moment, even in the midst of a friendly conversatio it makes no difference), these two German words—and it is always these two words, only these, that ring out: *Krematorium, ausmachen!*—would still bring us back to reality.

And so, in the jolt of awakening, or of returning self-awareness, we sometimes suspected that life had been only a dream, albeit occasionally a pleasant one, since our release from Buchenwald. A dream from which these two words would jar us awake, plunging us into a strangely serene despair. For it wasn't the reality of death, suddenly recalled, that was anguishing. It was the dream of life, even a peaceful one, even one filled with little joys. It was the fact of being alive, even in a dream, that was alarming.

"To leave by the chimney," "to go up in smoke": common expressions in Buchenwald slang, in the slang spoken in all the camps—there's ample evidence. These expressions were used at every turn and in every tone, including the rasp of sarcasm. The sarcastic edge even predominated, among ourselves, at least. The SS and the civilian foremen, the *Meisters,* always adopted a threatening manner or a tone of dire prediction.

They cannot understand, not really, these three officers. They'd have to be told the story of the smoke: sometimes dense, a sooty black against the variable sky. Or light and gray, almost vaporous, drifting with the winds over the assembled living like a portent, a farewell.

Smoke for a shroud as vast as the heavens, the last trace of the passing, body and soul, of our companions.

It would take hours, entire seasons, an eternity of telling to come close to accounting for them all.

There will be survivors, of course. Me, for example. Here I am, the survivor on duty, appearing opportunely before these three Allied officers to tell them of the crematory smoke, the smell of burned flesh hanging over the Ettersberg, the roll calls out in the falling snow, the murderous work details, the exhaustion of life, the inexhaustibility of hope, the savagery of the human animal, the nobility of man, the fraternity and devastation in the naked gaze of our comrades.

But can the story be told? Can anyone tell it?

From that first moment, I'm filled with misgivings.

It's April 12, 1945, the day after the liberation of Buchenwald. Recent history, in a word. No need to tax our memories. No need for trustworthy, verified documentation, either. Death is still a thing of the present. It happens right before our eyes, just look around. They go on dying by the hundreds, the starving inhabitants of the Little Camp, the Jewish survivors of Auschwitz.

All you have to do is begin. The reality is there, waiting. And the words as well.

Yet I start to doubt the possibility of telling the story. Not that what we lived through is indescribable. It was unbearable, which is something else entirely (that won't be hard to understand), something that doesn't concern the form of a possible account, but its substance. Not its articulation, but its density. The only ones who will manage to reach this substance, this transparent density, will be those able to shape their evidence into an artistic object, a space of creation. Or of re-creation. Only the artifice of a masterly narrative will prove capable of conveying some of the truth of such testimony. But there's nothing exceptional about this: it's the same with all great historical experiences.

In short, you can always say everything. The "ineffable" you hear so much about is only an alibi. Or a sign of laziness. You can always say everything: language contains everything. You can speak of the most desperate love, the most terrible cruelty.

You can speak of evil, its poisonous pleasures, its poppy flavor. You can speak of God, and that's saying a lot. You can speak of the rose, the dewdrop, the span of a morning. You can speak of tenderness, and the infinite succor of goodness. You can speak of the future, where poets venture with closed eyes and wagging tongues.

You can tell all about this experience. You have merely to think about it. And set to it. And have the time, of course, and the courage, for a boundless and probably never-ending account, illuminated (as well as enclosed, naturally) by that possibility of going on forever. Even if you wind up repeating yourself. Even if you remain caught up in it, prolonging death, if necessary—reviving it endlessly in the nooks and crannies of the story. Even if you become no more than the language of this death, and live at its expense, fatally.

But can people hear everything, imagine everything? Will they be able to understand? Will they have the necessary patience, passion, compassion, and fortitude? I begin to doubt it, in that first moment, that first meeting with men from *before,* from the *outside,* emissaries from life—when I see the stunned, almost hostile, and certainly suspicious look in the eyes of the three officers.

They're speechless, unable to face me.

I've seen myself for the first time in two years in their horrified gaze. These three jokers have spoiled this first morning for me. I thought I'd made it out alive. Made it back to life, in any case. Guess not. Imagining what my eyes must look like from what I see in theirs, I would say that I haven't left death all that far behind.

I'm struck by the idea, if one can call it an idea (that tonic flash of warmth, that rush of blood, that pride in the bodily knowledge of something vital), struck by the sudden overwhelming feeling, in any case, that I have not escaped death, but passed through it. Rather: that it has passed through me. That I have, in a way, lived through it. That I have come back from it the way you return from a voyage that has transformed and—perhaps—transfigured you.

I have abruptly understood that these soldiers are right to be afraid, to avoid looking into my eyes. Because I have not really survived death. I have not avoided it. I have not escaped it. I have, instead, crossed through it, from one end to the other. I have wandered along its paths, losing and finding my way in this immense land streaming with absence. All things considered, I am a ghost.

Frightening things, ghosts.

Suddenly, I am intrigued, even thrilled: death is no longer on the horizon, somewhere straight ahead, like the unpredictable end-all of fate, drawing me on toward its indescribable certainty. Death is already in my past, worn down to the nub, drained to the dregs, its breath on my neck growing fainter and farther away with each passing day.

On this splendid April morning, it is exciting to imagine that thenceforward, growing old will not bring me closer to death, but quite on the contrary, carry me away from it.

Perhaps I have not simply survived death, but been resurrected from it. Perhaps, from this moment on, I am immortal. It's an indefinite reprieve, at least. As though I'd swum to the other side of the River Styx.

This feeling did not vanish amid the rituals and routines of the return to life, during the summer of that return. I was not only sure I was alive, but convinced I was indestructible. Out of reach, in any case. I'd been through everything: nothing else could ever happen to me. Except life, which I would hungrily embrace. It was with this confidence that I later spent ten years in the Spanish underground.

Every morning during that clandestine period, before plunging into the daily adventure of meetings and appointments sometimes set up weeks in advance, rendezvous to which Franco's police might have been tipped off by some slipup or an informer, I would prepare myself for possible arrest. For certain torture. Every morning, though, I shrugged my shoulders after that spiritual exercise: nothing could happen to me. I'd already paid the price, spent that mortal part I carried within me. I was invulnerable, temporarily deathless.

When the time comes, when the studied disorder of this narrative permits, or rather, demands it, I will reveal when, why, and how death ceased to be in my past, my ever-receding past. When and why, on what occasion, death loomed up once again in my future, cunning and inevitable.

Sometimes the confidence I felt at having passed through death would vanish, however, with evil effect. That passage then became the sole conceivable reality, the only true experience. Everything since then had been simply a dream, a futile adventure, at best, even when enjoyable. Despite my daily actions and their efficacy, despite the evidence of my senses, which allowed me to orient myself in a labyrinth of perspectives, a multitude of people and things, I would then have the precise and crushing impression of living only in a dream. Of being a dream myself. Before dying in Buchenwald, before drifting away in smoke across the Ettersberg, I'd dreamed of this future life, this deceptive incarnation.

But I haven't reached that point yet.

I'm still caught in the shocked gaze of the three officers in British uniform.

For almost two years, I'd seen a fraternal spirit gleaming in the eyes of those around me—when the light in their eyes hadn't gone out altogether. Most of the deportees had dead eyes. Their gaze had been clouded, extinguished, blinded by the crude glare of death. Their lives were winding down, and the look in their eyes was the guttering glimmer of a dead star.

They passed by, shuffling like automatons, subdued, adjusting their stride, counting their steps, except at those times of the day when they had to step out smartly, in soldierly fashion, during the morning and evening inspection by the SS, at roll call, at the departure and return of the labor squads. They walked with their eyes half closed, to protect themselves from the brutal radiance of the world, sheltering the tiny, vacillating flame of their vitality from icy drafts.

But whatever light still survived in their gaze was a fraternal one. From being nourished on so much death, probably. Nourished on such huge portions.

On Sundays I went over to Block 56 in the Little Camp, a second enclosure within the camp perimeter, reserved for the quarantine of new arrivals. Reserved for invalids—Block 56 in particular—and all the deportees who had not yet been integrated into the labor system of Buchenwald.

I'd go over on Sunday afternoons, on every afternoon that spring, in 1944, after the noon roll call and the Sunday noodle soup. I'd say hello to Nicolai, my Russian pal, the young barbarian. I'd chat with him a bit. It was better to have him on good terms with you. Well, to be on good terms with him, actually. He was the head of the *Stubendienst,* the barracks orderlies in Block 56. He was also one of the leaders of the gangs of young Russian thugs who ran things in the Little Camp and controlled the black market there.

Nicolai liked me. He'd walk me over to the bunk where Halbwachs and Maspero were rotting away.

Week after week, I'd watched the black light of death dawning in their eyes. We shared it, that certainty, like a morsel of bread. Death was approaching, veiling their eyes, and we shared it like a piece of bread: a sign of brotherhood. The way one shares what remains of one's life. Death, a bit of bread, a kind of brotherhood. Death concerned us all, was the substance of our relations. We were nothing else, nothing more—nothing less, either—than that approaching death. The only difference among us was the time we still had left, the distance yet to cover.

I placed a hand (lightly, gently) on the emaciated shoulder of Maurice Halbwachs: the bone was almost crumbly, on the verge of breaking. I talked to him about the classes he used to teach at the Sorbonne. In the past, elsewhere, outside, in another life: life. I spoke of his course on the custom of potlatch. Dying, he would smile, fixing his eyes on me like a brother. I would have long talks with him about his books.

Those first Sundays, Maurice Halbwachs could still speak. He was anxious to hear how things were going, to have news of the war. He asked me—the last pedagogical concern of the professor whose student I had been at the Sorbonne—if I was already on the right track, if I'd found my vocation. I replied that history interested me. He nodded; why not? Perhaps that's why Halbwachs then told me about Marc Bloch and their meeting at the University of Strasbourg after World War I.

Soon, however, he no longer had the strength to utter a single word. He could only listen to me, and only at the cost of superhuman effort. Which is, moreover, the nature of man.

He listened; I spoke of spring drawing to a close, and passed on good news from the battlefields, and reminded him of what he had written in his books, the lessons of his teaching.

Dying, he would smile, gazing at me like a brother.

On the last Sunday, Maurice Halbwachs did not even have the strength to listen. Barely enough to open his eyes.

Nicolai accompanied me to the wretched bunk where Halbwachs lay next to Henri Maspero.

"Your Mr. professor's going up the chimney this very day," he murmured.

Nicolai was in a particularly jovial mood that Sunday. He'd intercepted me cheerfully the moment I crossed the threshold and plunged into the unbreathable fetor of Block 56.

I could tell that things were going well for Nicolai. He must have pulled off some big deal.

"You get a look at my cap?" he asked me.

He took off his cap, held it out to me. I couldn't help seeing it. A Soviet army officer's cap, that's what it was.

Nicolai ran his finger softly, caressingly, along the blue piping of his beautiful cap.

"Did you see?" he insisted.

I'd seen, and so what?

"It's a NKVD cap!" he exclaimed triumphantly. "A real one! I organized it just today!"

I'd nodded, not quite comprehending.

I knew what "organizing" meant in camp slang. It was the equivalent of stealing, or of getting something on the black market through some fiddle, barter, or extortion. I also knew what the NKVD was, of course. First it had been the Cheka, then the Ogpu, and now it was the NKVD, the People's Commissariat for Internal Affairs. It was around that time, by the way, that the people's commissariats disappeared, turning into plain old ministries.

In short, I knew that the NKVD was the police, but I didn't understand the importance that Nicolai obviously attached to wearing a policeman's cap.

The explanation was not long in coming.

"Now," he exclaimed, "you see right away that I'm a master!"

I watched him put his cap back on. He held himself proudly, like a soldier, no doubt. You could tell he was a master.

Nicolai had said *Meister.* This Russian youth was fluent, even chatty, in a rather basic but expressive German. If he couldn't find the right word, he improvised, making one up from the

German prefixes and verb forms he already knew. Whenever we'd spoken, during my Sunday visits to Maurice Halbwachs, we'd spoken in German.

But the word *Meister* sent a chill up my spine. That's what we called the petty bosses, the German civilian overseers who were harder than the SS themselves, harder than the *Wehrmacht* guys anyway; these foremen ruled with shouts and cudgel blows over the brutal forced labor of the deportees in the factories of Buchenwald. *Meister:* taskmaster, slave master.

I told Nicolai that I wasn't thrilled with the word *Meister.*

He laughed savagely, swearing something in Russian about fucking my mother. A frequent suggestion in Russian profanity, actually.

Then he tapped me condescendingly on the shoulder.

"You'd rather I said *Führer* instead of *Meister,* for example? All the German words for 'boss' are sinister!"

This time, he'd used *Kapo* for "boss." All the German words for *Kapo,* he'd said.

He was still laughing.

"And in Russian? You think the Russian words for *Kapo* are funny?"

I shook my head; I didn't know Russian.

Suddenly, however, he stopped laughing. His gaze was troubled by a strange uneasiness that quickly faded away.

He placed his hand on my shoulder again.

The first time I'd seen Nicolai, he'd been less familiar with me. He hadn't yet acquired his NKVD cap with the blue piping, but he already had the look of a gang leader.

He'd rushed over to me.

"Where do you think you're going?"

He'd planted himself in the middle of the aisle between the tall rows of bunks in Block 56, barring my way into his territory. I could see the highly polished leather of his riding boots glistening in the dim light. For although he wasn't yet wearing the special forces cap of the People's Commissariat for Internal Affairs, he was already sporting riding boots and breeches, and an elegantly tailored fatigue jacket.

All in all, the perfect little boss.

I had to put him in his place right away, or I'd be in big trouble. Two months in camp had taught me that.

"And you?" I shot back. "Looking for a fight? Do you happen to know where I've just been?"

He paused for a moment, studying my outfit. I was wearing a blue jacket, almost new. Gray woolen pants and leather boots in perfect condition. Enough to make him hesitate, naturally. Or at least think things over.

But his eyes kept coming back to the registration number sewn on my chest, and above it, the letter *S* in a triangle of red cloth.

This clue to my nationality (*S* for *Spanier*, Spanish) didn't seem to impress him. Quite the contrary. What Spaniard had ever belonged to any privileged group in Buchenwald, or ever wielded any power in the camp? No, after all, that *S* on my chest just made him smile.

"Pick a fight? With you?" he said haughtily.

So I called him an *Arschloch*, an asshole, barking out my words, and ordered him to fetch me his block leader. I worked at the *Arbeitsstatistik*, I told him; did he want to find himself on a transport list?

I saw myself doing this, heard myself shouting all that at him, and felt rather foolish. Even rather ashamed, to be threatening to make trouble for him. But that was the name of the game at Buchenwald, and I wasn't the one who'd set up the rules.

Anyway, the mention of the *Arbeitsstatistik* had worked a miracle. That was the camp administrative office where assignments were made to the different labor *Kommandos* as well as to the outlying subcamps, which were generally even harsher than Buchenwald. Nicolai had figured out that I wasn't bluffing, that I really did work in the office. He'd softened his tone immediately.

Ever since that first day, I'd been in his good graces.

So: he placed his hand on my shoulder.

"Believe me," he said curtly, sternly. "You'd better wear a NKVD cap if you want to look like a Russian *Kapo!*"

I didn't get all of what he meant by that. What I did get was rather disconcerting. But I didn't ask him any questions. And he wasn't saying anything further, that was clear. He turned on his heel and was walking me to Maurice Halbwachs's bunk.

"Dein Herr Professor," he whispered, *"kommt heute noch durch's Kamin!"*

I took the hand of the dying man, who hadn't the strength to open his eyes. In answer, I felt only the lightest pressure from his fingers, an almost imperceptible message.

Professor Maurice Halbwachs had arrived at the limit of human resistance. He was slowly emptying out, having reached the last stage of the dysentery that was carrying him off in a fearful stench.

A little later, when I was rambling on to him, just so that he would hear the sound of a friendly voice, he suddenly opened his eyes. In them I saw unspeakable misery, and shame over his disintegrating body, but also a gleam of dignity, of vanquished yet undiminished humanity. The immortal light of a gaze fixed upon the approach of death, the look of someone who knows where he stands, who's seen everything death has to offer and faces it squarely, weighing the risks and the stakes, freely, with sovereign power.

Then, seized with panic, not knowing whether I might call upon some god to accompany Maurice Halbwachs, yet aware of the need for a prayer, trying to control my voice and pitch it properly despite the lump in my throat, I recited a few lines by Baudelaire. It was the only thing I could think of.

Ô mort, vieux capitaine, il est temps, levons l'ancre . . .
[O death, old captain, it's time, let's weigh anchor . . .]

His eyes brightened slightly, as though with astonishment.
I continued to recite. When I reached the line

nos cœurs que tu connais sont remplis de rayons . . .
[our hearts, which you know, are filled with light . . .]

a delicate tremor passed over the lips of Maurice Halbwachs.
Dying, he smiled, gazing at me like a brother.

There were the SS as well, naturally.

But it was hard to catch their eye. They were so distant: lofty, above it all, beyond reach. Our eyes could never meet. They passed by, busy, arrogant, crisply outlined against the pale sky of Buchenwald and the drifting smoke from the crematory.

Sometimes, however, I managed to look into the eyes of *Obersturmführer* Schwartz.

You had to stand at attention, take off your cap, click your heels properly, and in a loud voice, clearly, distinctly, an- nounce—no, shout—your identification number. While staring off into space, preferably. While staring at the sky with its lazy ribbons of crematory smoke, preferably. Then, with a bit of stealth and daring, you could try to look him in the face. How- ever briefly I would manage to look into Schwartz's eyes, I never saw anything there but hatred.

An obtuse hatred, it's true, gnawed at by perceptible dismay. As with Nicolai under different circumstances, but for similar motives, Schwartz's attention was riveted by the *S* of my national identification. He, too, must have wondered how a Spanish Red had made it to the top of the internal administration hierarchy in Buchenwald.

It was reassuring, though, it warmed my heart, this hatred in *Obersturmführer* Schwartz's eyes, no matter how much bafflement I saw in them as well. It was a reason to live, even to try to survive.

And so, paradoxically (at least at a first, quick glance), the look in my companions' eyes, no matter how fraternal (because it was, on the whole), reflected the image of death. Death was the substance of our brotherhood, the key to our destiny, the sign of our membership in the community of the living. Together we lived that experience of death, that compassion. This defined our being: to be with one another as death advanced upon us—or rather, ripened in us, spreading through us like a luminous poison, like an intense light that would obliterate us. All we who were going to die had chosen the fraternity of this death through a love of freedom.

That is what I learned from the gaze of Maurice Halbwachs, as he lay dying.

Whereas the gaze of the SS officer, brimming with anxious hatred . . . that death-dealing gaze returned me to life. To the insane desire to last, to survive, to survive *him*. It instilled in me a ferocious will to endure.

But today, in this April sunshine, now that the winter of Europe is over, after the rain of fire and iron, what is reflected back at me by the frightened gaze of the three officers in their British uniforms?

What horror, what madness?

2

KADDISH

All of a sudden, a voice, behind us.

A voice? More like a bestial moan. The inarticulate groaning of a wounded animal. A bloodcurdling wail of lamentation.

We froze on the threshold of the hut, just as we were stepping back out into the fresh air, Albert and I. Standing stock-still at the boundary between the stinking murkiness inside and the April sunlight outdoors. In front of us, blue sky, faintly streaked with fleecy clouds. Around us, the mostly green mass of the forest, beyond the huts and tents of the Little Camp. Off in the distance, the mountains of Thuringia. In short, the timeless landscape Goethe and Eckermann must have contemplated during their walks on the Ettersberg.

It really was a human voice, though: an eerie, guttural humming.

Albert and I were still standing there, petrified.

Albert was a Hungarian Jew, stocky, indefatigable, always cheerful. Or at least optimistic. I was accompanying him, that day, on a last tour of inspection. For the past two days we had been regrouping the Jewish survivors of Auschwitz and the other camps in Poland. Children and adolescents, in particular, had been gathered together in a building in the SS section.

Albert was in charge of this rescue operation.

We went back into the unspeakable gloom, in icy apprehension. Where was the inhuman voice coming from? Because we had just determined that no one in there was still alive. We had just walked the entire length of the central aisle in that hut. Faces were turned toward us, as we passed by. The wasted bodies, covered in rags, lay on three tiers of bunks aligned in rows. The corpses were all mixed up with one another, and sometimes stiffened into a ghastly immobility. They stared out at us, into the center aisle; often they'd had to twist their necks violently around. Dozens of protruding eyes had watched us pass.

Watched without seeing us.

There had been no more survivors in that hut in the Little Camp. The wide-open eyes, their dilated pupils glaring inscrutably at the abomination of the world, were lifeless, their light snuffed out.

We had passed by, Albert and I, choked with emotion, walking as lightly as possible in the viscous silence where death was in its element, setting off the stone-cold fireworks of all those eyes gazing at the hellish scene, the underside of the world.

From time to time, Albert—I myself hadn't had the courage—had drawn closer to the jumbled bodies piled on the bare planks of the bunks. The corpses would move all of a piece, like tangled roots on a tree stump. Albert shoved this deadwood aside with a firm hand. He peered into the hollows, the interstices between the bodies, still hoping to find life.

But there hadn't seemed to be any survivors there that day, on April 14, 1945. All who could must have fled the hut upon hearing that the camp had been liberated.

I can be certain of that date, April 14, and speak of it with confidence, yet the period of my life between the liberation of Buchenwald and my return to Paris is confused, my memory clouded by forgetfulness. By vagueness, in any case.

I've often tallied up the days and nights. I always obtain a disconcerting result. Between the liberation of Buchenwald and my return to Paris, eighteen days passed: that much is certain. I have very few memories of this time, however. The rare images are startlingly clear, it's true, and bathed in a bleak radiance, but they're surrounded by a thick halo of shadowy mist. I remember enough to fill a few short hours in a life, no more.

It's easy to establish the date at the beginning of this period. It's in the history books: April 11, 1945, the day Buchenwald was liberated. It's possible to figure out when I arrived in Paris, but I'll spare you the data behind my calculations. It was two days before May Day, which makes it April 29. In the afternoon, to be absolutely precise. It was on the afternoon of April 29 that I arrived in Paris, on the Rue de Vaugirard, with a convoy of the repatriation mission carried out by the Abbé Rodhain.

I provide all these facts, which are probably superfluous and even silly, to show that my memory is fine, that it's not because of failing powers of remembrance that I have more or less forgotten those two long weeks of existence before my return to life, to what is called life.

Nevertheless, there it is: I have only a few scattered recollections of this period, barely enough to fill several hours out of those two long weeks. Memories that shine with a garish light, to be sure, but which are enveloped in the grayish haze of nonbeing. Of something almost impossible to pin down, at any rate.

So the day in question was April 14, 1945.

That morning I'd reflected that the date was an important one in my childhood: Spain was declared a republic on that same day in 1931. Crowds poured in from the outlying neighborhoods, heading for the center of Madrid beneath a rippling forest of flags. "We've changed regimes without breaking a single window!" announced the leaders of the republican parties triumphantly—and in some amazement. History caught up with itself five years later in a long and bloody civil war.

But on April 14, 1945, there hadn't been any survivors in that hut in the Little Camp at Buchenwald.

There had been only dead eyes, wide open on the horror of the world. The corpses, which were as contorted as the figures of El Greco, seemed to have used their last reserves of strength to crawl across the planks to the edge of the bunks nearest to the center aisle, where their last hope of rescue might finally have appeared. Their glazed eyes, dulled by the agony of waiting, had no doubt watched until the end for some sudden salvation. The despair visible in those eyes bespoke the torment of that vigil, of the violence of their last hope.

I abruptly understood the mistrustful, fearful astonishment of the three Allied officers of the previous day. If my gaze reflected, in fact, even a mere hundredth part of the terror discernible in the dead eyes we had contemplated, Albert and I, then it was no wonder the three officers in British uniform had been appalled.

"You hear that?" murmured Albert.

It wasn't really a question. How could I not hear it? I listened to that inhuman voice, that crooned sobbing, that strangely rhythmic death rattle, that rhapsody from the great beyond.

I turned back toward the outdoors: the balmy April breeze, the blue sky. I took a deep draught of spring.

"What is it?" asked Albert in a low, toneless voice.

"Death," I told him. "Who else?"

Albert made a gesture of irritation.

It was death that was humming, no doubt, somewhere amid the heaps of corpses. The life of death, in other words, making itself heard. The agony of death, its shining and mournfully loquacious presence. But why point out the obvious? That's what Albert's gesture seemed to say. Why bother, indeed?

I kept quiet.

The crematory furnace had been shut down three days earlier. When the camp's International Committee and the American military authorities had restored the essential services of Buchenwald in order to feed, clothe, care for, and reorganize the several tens of thousands of survivors, no one had considered restarting the crematory. It was truly unthinkable. The smoke from the crematory had to disappear forever: there was no question of seeing it drift across the landscape ever again. Even though we no longer went up in smoke, however, that didn't mean that death had taken a holiday. The end of the crematory wasn't the end of death, which had merely ceased hovering overhead, in dense clouds or ragged wisps, depending on the circumstances. Death was no longer smoke that was sometimes almost immaterial, a practically impalpable fall of gray ash upon the countryside. Death had become carnal again, incarnate once more in the dozens of tortured, emaciated bodies that still constituted its daily harvest.

To avoid risking an epidemic, the American military authorities had decided to collect and identify the corpses and then bury them in common graves. Which was why Albert and I were making one final sweep through the Little Camp that day, hoping to find some last survivors too enfeebled to have rejoined, on their own, the communal life of Buchenwald since its liberation.

Albert's face went livid. He strained to hear, and suddenly became frantic, squeezing my arm painfully.

"Yiddish!" he shouted. "It's speaking Yiddish!"

So, death spoke Yiddish.

Albert was more able than I was to glean this information from the guttural (and to me, meaningless) sounds of that ghostly singsong.

After all, it was hardly surprising that death spoke Yiddish. Now, there was a language it had certainly been forced to learn over the last few years. If indeed it hadn't already known it from the very beginning.

But Albert has grabbed my arm and is clutching it tightly. He drags me back into the hut.

We take a few steps down the center aisle, and stop. We listen hard, trying to determine where the voice is coming from.

Albert is panting.

"It's the prayer for the dead," he whispers.

I shrug. Of course it's a funeral chant. No one expects death to serenade us with funny songs. Or words of love, either.

We let ourselves be guided by that prayer for the dead. Sometimes we have to wait, motionless, holding our breath. Death has fallen silent, leaving us no way to locate the source of that monotonous threnody. But it always starts up again: inexhaustible, the voice of death. Immortal.

Suddenly, as we grope around in a short lateral aisle, I feel we're almost there: now the voice—hoarse, mumbling—is quite near.

Albert rushes over to the bunk where the voice is rattling faintly.

Two minutes later, we have extracted from a heap of corpses the dying man through whose mouth death is singing to us. Reciting its prayer to us, actually. We carry the man out in front of the hut, into the April sunshine. We lay him down on a pile of rags that Albert has collected. The man doesn't open his eyes, but he hasn't stopped singing, in a rough, barely audible voice.

I have never seen a human face that more closely resembled that of the crucified Christ. Not the stern but serene countenance of a Roman Jesus, but the tormented face of a Spanish Gothic Jesus. Of course, Christ on the Cross does not usually intone the Jewish prayer for the dead, but this is a minor detail. There is nothing from a theological point of view, I presume, to prevent Christ from chanting the Kaddish.

"Wait for me here," says Albert firmly. "I'll dash over to the *Revier* for a stretcher!"

He takes a few steps, then comes back to me.

"You'll take care of him, right?"

That strikes me as so stupid, so outrageous, even, that I blow up.

"What is it you think I should do for him? We could have a little chat? How about if I sing him a song? 'La Paloma,' maybe?"

But Albert doesn't lose control.

"Just stay with him, that's all!"

And he runs off to the camp infirmary.

I turn back toward the man. Eyes closed, he lies there, still singing faintly. More and more faintly, it seems to me.

I had mentioned "La Paloma" just like that, out of nowhere. But it reminds me of something I can't remember. Reminds me that I ought to remember something, anyway. Something I could remember, if I tried. "La Paloma"? The beginning of the song pops into my mind . . . and strange as it may seem, the words are in German.

Kommt eine weisse Taube zu Dir geflogen . . .

I mutter the beginning of "La Paloma," in German. Now I know what story I could remember.

I really think back, deliberately, since I'm going to have to remember it anyway.

The German was young, he was tall, and he was blond. He was the absolute embodiment of the German ideal: all in all, a perfect German. This was a year and a half earlier, in 1943. It was autumn, in the area of Semur-en-Auxois. At a bend in the river, there was a kind of natural dam, and there the surface of the water was almost completely still: a liquid looking-glass beneath the autumn sun. Shadows of trees moved upon this translucent, silvery mirror.

The German had appeared on the crest of the riverbank. His motorcycle rumbled softly as he guided it along the path leading down to the water's edge.

We were waiting for him, Julien and I.

That is to say, we weren't waiting for that particular German. That blond, blue-eyed youth. (Watch out—I'm fabricating: I wasn't able to see the color of his eyes at that point. Not until later, when he was dead. But he certainly looked like the blue-eyed type to me.) We were waiting for a German, for some Germans. No matter which ones. We knew that the soldiers of the *Wehrmacht* had taken to coming in groups, toward the end of the afternoon, to refresh themselves at that spot. Julien and I had come to study the terrain, to see if it would be possible to stage an ambush with the help of the local Resistance fighters.

This German appeared to be alone, however. No other motorcycle, no other vehicle had appeared behind him on the road at the top of the riverbank. Admittedly, it wasn't the soldiers' usual visiting time, either. It was around midmorning.

He went down to the water, got off his bike, and parked it on its kickstand. There he stood, breathing the mild air of the French countryside. He unfastened the collar of his jacket. He was relaxed, obviously. He hadn't let down his guard, though: he had a machine gun slung across his chest, hanging from a strap around his neck.

Julien and I looked at each other. The same idea occurred to us. We had our Smith and Wessons, and the German was alone, within easy range. There was a motorcycle for the taking, and a machine gun.

We were on the lookout, under cover. We had a perfect target. So the same thought came into our minds.

But the young German soldier suddenly looked up at the sky and began to sing.

Kommt eine weisse Taube zu Dir geflogen . . .

Startled, I almost gave us away by knocking the barrel of my Smith and Wesson against the rock that concealed us. Julien gave me a furious look.

Perhaps that song meant nothing to him. Perhaps he didn't even know that it was "La Paloma." Even if he'd known that, perhaps the song wouldn't have brought back any memories for him. Childhood, the maids singing in the pantry, music from the bandstands in shady village squares . . . "La Paloma"! How could I not have started when I heard that song?

The German went on singing, in a lovely blond voice. My hand began to shake. It had become impossible for me to shoot at that young soldier singing "La Paloma." As though singing that melody from my childhood, that refrain so full of nostalgia, had suddenly made him innocent. Not personally innocent, which perhaps he was, in any case, whether he'd ever sung "La Paloma" or not. Maybe he had nothing to reproach himself for, this young soldier, nothing besides having been born a German in the time of Adolf Hitler. No—it was as though he'd just become innocent in a completely different way. Innocent not only of being born a German under Hitler, of belonging to an army of occupation, of involuntarily embodying the brute force of Fascism. But fundamentally innocent, in the fullness of his existence, because he was singing "La Paloma." It was absurd, and I knew it. Still, I was incapable of shooting at this young German singing "La Paloma," with his face turned to the sky in the candid enjoyment of an autumn morning, utterly immersed in the mellow beauty of a French countryside.

I lowered the long barrel of my Smith and Wesson, brightly painted with red lead to keep it from rusting.

Julien had seen me hesitate, and he lowered his arm as well.

Now he looks at me anxiously, doubtless wondering what's happening to me.

"La Paloma" is happening to me, that's all: my Spanish childhood, right in the face.

But the young soldier has turned around and is walking slowly back to where his bike waits motionless on its kickstand.

Then I grab my weapon with both hands. Aiming at the German's back, I squeeze the trigger of the Smith and Wesson. I hear the reports of Julien's revolver beside me: he, too, has fired several times.

The German soldier leaps forward, as though pushed violently from the back. Because he actually has been pushed from the back, by the brutal impact of the bullets.

He falls full length.

I collapse, with my face in the cool grass, and pound my fist furiously on the flat rock that had concealed us.

"Shit, shit, shit!"

I shout louder and louder, frightening Julien.

He shakes me, screaming that now is not the moment to go into hysterics—we have to get out of there. Take the motorcycle, and the German's machine gun, and beat it.

He's right. There's nothing else to do.

We get up and cross the river, scrambling over the rocks that block the watercourse. Julien takes the dead man's gun, after turning over his body. And it's true: the German does have blue eyes, wide open with surprise.

We flee on the motorcycle, which starts up on the first kick.

But that is a story I have told before.

Not the one about the Jewish survivor we found, Albert and I, because he was chanting the prayer for the dead in Yiddish. This is the first time I've ever related that particular story. It's one of the stories I haven't told before. It would take me several lifetimes to tell about all that death. Telling the story of that death right through to the end would be an endless task.

The story about the German is one I've told before. The young German soldier, blond and handsome, whom we shot down, Julien and I, in the vicinity of Semur-en-Auxois. I don't remember the name of the river; perhaps I never knew it. I recall that it was in September, and that it was September as far as the eye could see. I remember the mildness of September, the sweetness of a landscape so in harmony with peaceful pleasures, with the horizon of human labor. I remember that the scenery made me think of Jean Giraudoux, of his feeling for the beauty of France.

I told that story about the German soldier in a short novel called *L'évanouissement* [*The Disappearance*]. It's a book that had hardly any readers. No doubt that's why I decided to tell once again the story of the young German who sang "La Paloma." But that wasn't the only reason. I also wanted to correct the first version, which wasn't altogether truthful. What I mean is, the story is all true, even in its first version, the one in *L'évanouissement*. The river is true, the town of Semur-en-Auxois isn't some invention of mine, the German really did sing "La Paloma," and we did shoot him down.

But I was with Julien, when all that happened with the German soldier, and not with Hans. In *L'évanouissement,* my companion was Hans, a fictional character I'd substituted for a real person. Julien was someone real: a young Burgundian who always referred to the Resistance forces as "the patriots." This living remnant of Jacobin language delighted me. Together, Julien and I roamed the *maquis,* the local scrub land, distributing weapons dropped in by parachute for the network to which I belonged, "Jean-Marie Action," which was run by Henri Frager. Julien drove the front-wheel-drive cars and motorcycles along the roads of the Yonne and the Côte-d'Or at breakneck speed, and it was a joy to share the emotions of those night rides with him. With Julien, you could tie the patrols of the *Feld* up in knots. But then Julien was caught in a trap. He defended himself like the very devil, and with the last bullet in his Smith and Wesson, he shot himself in the head.

Hans Freiberg, on the other hand, is a fictional character. I'd invented Hans Freiberg—whom Michel and I called Hans von Freiberg zu Freiberg in *Le grand voyage* [*The Long Voyage*], with a nod to Giraudoux's *Ondine*—in order to have a Jewish friend. I'd had Jewish pals at that time of my life, so I wanted to have one in the novel as well. And the reasons behind that invention of Hans, the fictional Jewish pal who stood in for my real ones, are suggested in *L'évanouissement.*

"We invented Hans," I wrote there,

> as the image of ourselves: the purest image, the one closest to our dreams. He wound up German because we were internationalists: we weren't aiming at the foreigner in each German soldier we cut down in ambush, but at the most blatant and murderous essence of our own bourgeoisies, in other words, of those class structures we wanted to change in our own societies. He turned out to be Jewish because we wanted to liquidate all oppression and because the

Jew—even passive, even resigned—was the intolerable embodiment of the oppressed.

That's why I invented Hans, why I placed him at my side, that
day when the German soldier sang "La Paloma." But it was
Julien who was there, in reality. Julien was a Burgundian and he
called the *maquisards* "the patriots." He shot himself in the head
to avoid being taken alive by the *Feldgendarmerie.*

That's the truth of it, the whole truth behind this story,
which was already a truthful account.

As for the moribund Jew chanting the prayer for the dead, he's
quite real. So real that he's dying right before my eyes.

I can't hear the Kaddish anymore. I no longer hear death
singing in Yiddish. I've been lost among my memories, not paying any attention. How long ago did he stop his chanting? Did
he really die, just now, sneaking off while my thoughts were
elsewhere for a moment?

I lean over him, listening to his heart. I think I hear something, still beating inside his sunken chest. Something quite
muffled, and very far off: a sigh that's fading away, running out of
breath. A heart that's stopping, that's what it sounds like to me.

It's pretty pathetic.

I look around for help. There is none. There's no one. The
Little Camp was cleared the day after the liberation of Buchenwald. The survivors were installed in the most comfortable buildings of the main camp, or else in the barracks formerly used by
the SS *Totenkopf* Division.

I look around: no one. There is only the sound of the wind
blowing, as always, on this slope of the Ettersberg. In spring or
winter, mild breeze or icy blast, there is always the wind on the
Ettersberg. A wind for all seasons on Goethe's hillside, stirring
the smoke from the crematory.

We're behind the hut of the collective latrines of the Little Camp, which is located at the foot of the Ettersberg, where it joins the fertile green plain of Thuringia. And the camp spreads out all around these collective latrines, because the barracks in the Little Camp don't have any latrines or washrooms. During the day, the huts were usually empty, since all the deportees in quarantine—while awaiting departure to an outlying subcamp or employment within the internal organization of Buchenwald—were assigned various tasks that were usually exhausting, as they had a pedagogical (i.e., punitive) function: "Just you wait and see!"

Work in the quarry, for example: *Steinbruch*. And *Gärtnerei*, gardening—a euphemism, because it was probably the worst labor of all. It consisted of carrying, two by two (and the pairing up of these porters, for those who didn't quickly see to it themselves, was done by the *Kapos*, who were generally longtime prisoners, embittered and therefore sadistic, who would make the most ill-assorted types work as partners—a short fat guy and a tall skinny one, for example, or a great hulking fellow and a runt—in order to create, aside from the practical difficulty of the job itself under such conditions, an almost inevitable animosity between two people of such different physical capacities and endurance)—of carrying in pairs, as I was saying, at a run and while being beaten with clubs, poles from which hung heavy wooden tubs filled to the brim with night soil (hence the familiar name of "shit duty") intended for the vegetable gardens of the SS.

So at dawn or before curfew, whatever the weather, prisoners had to leave their huts in the quarantine camp, the Little Camp, and go to the latrine building, a kind of bare hall with a rough concrete floor that became a sea of mud with the first rains of autumn. Along the length of this hall on either side ran zinc basins and cold-water taps for the obligatory morning ablutions. The SS authorities were obsessed with the danger of epidemics: a big poster of repellent realism hung in the huts, proclaiming the SS slogan of cleanliness in several languages beneath a huge blowup of a threatening louse: *Eine Laus, dein Tod!* "One louse, your death!" Down the center of the hall, from end to end, stretched the collective cesspool, a ditch surmounted along its entire length by two wooden beams, barely rough-planed, that served as seating for innumerable defecations, which were thus made by prisoners sitting back-to-back in endless rows.

Yet despite the mephitic vapor and pestilential odor that constantly clung to the building, the latrines of the Little Camp were a convivial place, a kind of refuge where you could meet your compatriots, friends from your neighborhood or the underground; it was a spot to share news, a few shreds of tobacco, memories, laughter, a bit of hope—some life, in short. In the Little Camp, the revolting latrines were a place of freedom: the SS and the *Kapos* naturally shunned the building and its nauseating stench, thus making it the area of Buchenwald where one felt the most free of the tyranny inherent in the very operation of the concentration-camp world.

By day, during working hours, the latrines were used only by invalids or those in the quarantine blocks who were too ill to work. Later, however, between the evening roll call and curfew, the latrines became not just a privy, but a marketplace of hopes and illusions, a souk where the most unusual things could be traded for a slice of black bread or a few butts of *makhorka* tobacco, an agora for the exchange of words: the currency of a discourse of fraternity, of resistance.

And so it was in the latrine building that I met some of my best friends in the quarantine camp: Serge Miller, Yves Darriet, Claude Francis-Boeuf, for example. We were all in the same block, number 62, having arrived together during the mass deportations of January 1944 that emptied the French prisons and the camp at Compiègne. Following a rather revealing military tradition, these two successive operations were given poetic code names, *Meerschaum* and *Frülingswind:* "Sea Foam" and "Spring Wind."

In the haggard crowd of Block 62, liable to every kind of forced labor, disoriented by the shocking reality of life in Buchenwald, with its absolutely inexplicable but absolutely compulsive rules, we were unable to recognize one another, to discover the common ties binding us to the same cultural and moral universe. It was in the collective latrines, in this unhealthy atmosphere reeking of urine, shit, feverish sweat, and acrid *makhorka,* that we found one another, literally brought together by huddling around the same cigarette butt, sharing the same caustic attitude as well, the same combative and fraternal curiosity about the chances of our unlikely survival.

Or, more likely, the death we would share.

It was there, one memorable night, that Darriet and I, taking delicious drags on the same cigarette end, discovered a mutual taste for jazz and poetry. Shortly afterward, when the first whistle blasts signaling curfew had already sounded in the distance, Miller came over to join us. We'd been trading poems: Darriet had just recited some Baudelaire for me; I was giving him Paul Valéry's "La fileuse." Miller laughed and called us chauvinists. He recited some verse by Heine, in German. And then, to the great joy of Darriet, who marked time to our performance by waving his hands around like an orchestra conductor, Serge Miller and I together declaimed the song of the Lorelei.

Ich weiss nicht, was soll es bedeuten
Dass ich so traurig bin . . .

We screamed out the end of the poem amid the deafening roar of dozens of pairs of wooden clogs galloping off to the huts at the very last minute before final curfew.

Und das hat mit ihrem Singen
Die Lorelei getan . . .

After which, we ran off at top speed as well, heading for Block 62 in a kind of thrilling, unutterable happiness.

Kneeling next to the dying Jew, I have no idea how to keep him alive, my Christ of the Kaddish. I speak softly to him. Finally I take him in my arms, as carefully as possible, afraid he might break at my touch. Don't do this to me, I beg him—Albert would never forgive me.

I had taken Maurice Halbwachs in my arms, too, that last Sunday. He was lying in the middle level of the three tiers of bunks, just at chest height to me. I slipped an arm under his shoulders and leaned over his face, to speak to him as closely, as gently as I could. I had just recited to him that poem by Baudelaire, the way one says a prayer for the dying. Halbwachs was no longer able to speak. He had gone even farther into death than that unknown Jew over whom I am now bending, who still has the strength—the unimaginable strength—to recite for himself the prayer for the dying, to accompany his own passing with words that celebrate death. That make it immortal, at least. Halbwachs no longer had the strength for this. Or the weakness, who knows? He no longer had the opportunity, in any case. Or the desire. Death is doubtless the exhaustion of all desire, including that of dying. It's only from life, from the knowledge of life, that one can have the desire to die. Such a death wish is still a reflex of life.

Maurice Halbwachs, however, was obviously past all desire, even the desire to die. He had clearly gone beyond all that, into the pestilential eternity of his decomposing body.

I took him in my arms; I drew my face close to his; I was enveloped in the fetid, fecal smell of death, which was growing in him like a carnivorous plant with a poisonous flower, rotting splendidly away. I told myself—in a moment of deliberate sarcasm intended to help me bear this unbearable moment, or simply live through it, not with bathos, but with an austere, unsentimental compassion—I told myself . . . that at least I would have learned this, in Buchenwald: to identify the many smells of death. The smell of the crematory smoke, the smell of the invalids' block and the huts of the *Revier*. The smell of leather and cologne on the SS *Sturmführer*. I told myself that this was pertinent knowledge—but was it useful? Who could swear to the contrary?

Maurice Halbwachs did not die in my arms. On that Sunday, the last Sunday, I'd been obliged to leave him, to abandon him to the solitude of his death, because the curfew whistles had forced me to return to my block in the Big Camp. It was only two days later that I saw his name in the report detailing the movements of the deportees: arrivals, departures in transports, deaths. His name appeared on the list of daily deaths. So he had held on two more days, another forty-eight hours of eternity.

After curfew had forced me to abandon Halbwachs in the Little Camp that Sunday, I'd rinsed myself with ice-cold water, bare-chested, in the washroom adjoining the dormitory in C wing, upstairs in Block 40 in the Big Camp, where I lived. But no matter how I splashed and rubbed, I still breathed the foul odor of death, which seemed to have seeped into my lungs. I stopped washing my chest, my arms, my shoulders. I went off to sleep in the stifling promiscuity of the dormitory, with my soul permeated by the smell of death, yet still pledged to hope.

And so it was two days later that I saw Halbwachs's name on the daily list of those who had died. I removed the folder with his identification number on it from the central card index in the *Arbeitsstatistik*. I took out the index card with Maurice Halbwachs's name on it, and I erased that name: a living person would now be able to take the dead man's place. By a living person, I mean: a future corpse. I did everything necessary. I carefully erased his family name, Halbwachs, and his first name, Maurice—all his signs of identity. I held the rectangular card in the palm of my hand. It had become blank and white once more, ready for another life to be written on it, and a new death. I stared at that blank white index card for a long time, probably without seeing it. Probably seeing nothing at that moment but the absent face of Halbwachs, my last sight of that face: the waxen mask, the closed eyes, the otherworldly smile.

I was overwhelmed by a kind of physical sadness. I sank into the sorrow of my body, a carnal distress that made me uninhabitable to myself. Time had passed, Halbwachs had died. I had experienced the death of Halbwachs.

But I did not want to experience the death of that Hungarian Jew I held in my arms, a few months later, on an April day in 1945. At least, I assumed he was Hungarian. In any case, his identification number, barely visible on his tattered, striped jacket, suggested that he had arrived in the convoys of Jews from Hungary. Because of my work as a file clerk in the *Arbeitsstatistik*, I was fairly knowledgeable about what the sets of numbers assigned to new arrivals meant: which country of origin, what period of Buchenwald's operation.

Even if he hadn't been Hungarian, I wouldn't have wanted to live the death of that Jew. Even if he hadn't been Jewish, I should add. However, the fact that on top of everything else, he was Jewish, this anonymous survivor Albert and I had discovered mixed in with a heap of real corpses, only made the situation more desperate. What I mean is, it only made me more desperate to save him. Only made my desperation more solemn, more anguished. It would have been truly absurd—no, intolerable—for him to have survived all that death, to have lived that death right to the end, to such a limit of solitude, with such stubborn, visceral strength, only to succumb to it now.

I could easily imagine his itinerary, these last few years. His deportation, his arrival in Auschwitz, the chance selection that sent him to the side of survival, the equally perilous life that followed, the evacuation of the camp before the advance of the Red Army, the endless voyage across wintry Germany, the pangs of hunger, the frostbite from the bitter cold. He had arrived at Buchenwald at the most dramatic moment of the camp's long history, when prisoners were piling up in the blocks and barracks because of overpopulation. Daily rations had just been reduced again. And in the Little Camp, where the Jewish survivors of Auschwitz were dumped, things were worst of all. Living in the Little Camp of Buchenwald, that last winter of the war, was a nightmare. Surviving there was something of a miracle.

Spring had returned, liberty was restored, and as I tried to keep alive the Hungarian Jew I held in my arms, I had no trouble imagining the long agony he had endured. The ebbing strength, the growing difficulty of moving about, each step becoming a torture, requiring superhuman effort. I'd seen them, him, his fellows, his brothers, in the barracks of the Little Camp, in the tents and sheds they'd set up that winter in an effort to relieve the overcrowding. I'd seen them in the latrine building, in the wards of the infirmary: gaunt, living cadavers, half naked, moving with infinite slowness on their impossibly long, skeletal legs, clinging to the bunk posts to shuffle along, step by step, with the imperceptible movements of sleepwalkers.

Never afterward, a whole lifetime afterward, even beneath the sun of Saint-Paul-de-Vence, in a lovely and orderly landscape bearing the invigorating imprint of human labor, never, on the terrace of the Fondation Maeght, in the patch of sky and cypress trees within Sert's walls of pink brick, never could I ever contemplate the figures of Giacometti without recalling the strange shufflers of Buchenwald, those walking corpses in the dim, bluish light of the Contagious Ward, the immemorial cohorts gathered about the latrines in the Little Camp, stumbling on the stony ground that turned muddy at the first rain and flooded when the snow melted, wraiths advancing with measured steps—oh, how that banal, ready-made expression, slipping casually into the text, takes on a meaning here, a meaning fraught with anxiety: measuring steps, indeed, counting them one by one to save strength, so as not to take one too many (and pay a heavy price for it), stepping in someone else's footsteps, wrenching the clogs free of the mud, of the weight of the world that pulls on your legs, miring you in nothingness!—advancing with measured steps toward the latrine building in the Little Camp, a place of possible encounters, conversation, strangely welcoming in spite of the repulsive reek of urine and excrement, a last haven of humanity.

Never afterward, a whole lifetime afterward, could I avoid that surge of emotion (I'm not speaking of feelings aroused by the beauty of these figures, feelings so obvious they need no explanation), an emotion that is retrospective, moral, not simply aesthetic, an emotion that Giacometti's *promeneurs* would arouse anywhere: those sinewy figures gazing indifferently at endless, unsettled skies, strolling tirelessly, in dizzying stillness, toward an uncertain future, with no other perspective or depth beyond what their own blind yet obstinate steps might create. They would always remind me insidiously—whatever the circumstances, however joyous the occasion—of those figures of the past, in Buchenwald.

But I don't want to experience the death of this anonymous (perhaps Hungarian) Jew. I hold him in my arms; I speak softly in his ear. I tell him the story of the young German soldier who sang "La Paloma" and whom we shot down, Julien and I. I don't mention Julien, however, but Hans. At that very moment I begin to invent Hans Freiberg—my imaginary Jewish friend, my Jewish Resistance fighter—as company for this dying man, this anonymous Jew I would like to see survive his own death. So: I tell him the story of Hans, whom I have just invented, to help him live.

And here's Albert now. Arriving on the double, with two stretcher bearers from the *Revier.*

An hour later, we're sitting in the sun, in the little wood behind the *Revier.* We look out at the plain of Thuringia beneath the April sunshine. Thanks to the man's registration number, Albert has identified the Kaddish singer we left in the hands of a French doctor in the infirmary. He's a Jew from Budapest. And it's not impossible that he might pull through, the French doctor had said.

Albert is thrilled to have perhaps saved one of his countrymen.

"You know who André Malraux is, Albert?" I ask him. "A writer—"

He turns on me, glaring, with a gesture of indignation. He interrupts me angrily.

"Is that supposed to be some kind of a joke?" he shouts. "Have you forgotten I was in Spain, in the Brigades?"

I haven't forgotten; I never knew it. "That's news to me," I tell him.

"But of course!" he exclaims. "I was on Kléber's staff."

"Kléber" was a nom de guerre, naturally.

"That's why Kaminski invited me to his meeting, this winter. . . ."

"Yes," I reply eagerly, "it's precisely because of that meeting that I thought of Malraux!"

Albert looks at me, waiting for the rest.

A few months earlier, in the middle of winter, Kaminski had come looking for me where I worked, in the office of the *Arbeitsstatistik*. It was before the evening roll call. Kaminski was a veteran of the International Brigades in Spain and spoke quite passable Castilian. I was to attend a meeting to be held in two days. An important meeting, he'd added mysteriously.

Two days later, on Sunday.

It was only after roll call, on Sunday afternoon, that we could use our few hours of leisure to hold our meeting. I crossed the camp amid swirling snow. I entered the infirmary compound. In a building off to one side there was a half-basement ward for contagious illnesses: a lazaretto within a lazar house. The SS, whether doctors or guards, avoided this quarantine ward like the plague, to use an apt expression. They were obsessed with hygiene, with cleanliness, with the sleek, hard bodies of the master race. Their horror of contagion made the barracks of the infirmary a highly secure, almost invulnerable area.

Ludwig G. was the head of the Contagious Ward. Although his jacket bore the green triangle of a common-law criminal, he was a German Communist. Some dark deed, some wrongdoing or daring action committed in the thirties for the good of the cause had been judged in a civil court. Common law, green triangle. Impossible to know what life he'd led, before, on the outside. He never spoke about his past. A professional man, probably, judging from the breadth of his knowledge. Physically, he was a small, slight man, given to lively gestures, with astonishingly serene and thoughtful eyes. They were sad eyes, too, like all that is serene and thoughtful. His profile was aquiline. Later on, in ordinary life, I never met Roger Vailland without being reminded of Ludwig G.

I crossed the camp through flurries of snow that Sunday and entered the infirmary compound. At the door to the isolation hut, I tapped the soles of my boots against the iron bar provided for this purpose on the right side of the doorstep. The SS regulation required that only clean shoes be worn inside the huts. On rainy and muddy days, this was quite a challenge, but when there was deep snow outside, all you had to do was tap the bottoms of your boots or galoshes against the metal scraper and the accumulated snow would fall right off.

That day, Kaminski had gathered together a handful of militants of various nationalities. We all knew one another, as we all belonged to the underground Communist organization of Buchenwald.

Jürgen Kaminski had brought us together to listen to a survivor of Auschwitz, a Polish Jew who had arrived in Buchenwald on one of that winter's evacuation convoys. We settled ourselves in the little room that was Ludwig G.'s personal domain, at the end of the basement reserved for infectious cases. Kaminski told us who the man was and where he'd come from. At Auschwitz, Kaminski explained, the man had worked in the *Sonderkommando.* We didn't know what that was, the *Sonderkommando* at Auschwitz. I, at least, had no idea. At Buchenwald, there was no *Sonderkommando,* only a *Sonderbau. Sonder,* as you may know, is a German adjective that means "particular, separate, special, strange"—things like that. The *Sonderbau* at Buchenwald was certainly a special building, and maybe even a strange one: it was the brothel. But the *Sonderkommando,* the special labor squad at Auschwitz, was a mystery to me. I did not ask any questions about it, though, because I assumed I would figure out what it was as the meeting wore on. I was right, as it turned out. Before the meeting ended, I had more than figured it out. It was the special *Kommando* that dragged the victims out of the gas chambers and delivered their corpses to the adjoining crematory ovens to be burned.

Before all this had become clear to me, Kaminski had explained to us that the SS had periodically, systematically, shot each successive labor gang of the *Sonderkommando*. The man before us belonged to a small group of survivors who owed their lives to the confusion reigning in the camp in its last weeks, during the approach of the Soviet Army.

Then he asked the survivor of the *Sonderkommando* to speak to us.

I no longer remember the name of that Polish Jew. I don't even remember if he had a name. By this I mean that I cannot recall if Jürgen Kaminski mentioned his name to us. I do remember his eyes. They were an icy blue, like the cutting edge of a broken pane of glass. I do remember his posture. He sat on a chair, absolutely straight, absolutely rigid, his hands on his knees, motionless. He never once moved his hands during the whole story of his experience on the *Sonderkommando*. I do remember his voice. He spoke in German, fluently, in a rasping, meticulous, insistent voice. Sometimes, for no apparent reason, his voice would grow hoarse, as though suddenly clogged with uncontrollable emotions. Even during these moments of visible agitation, however, he never moved his hands on his knees. He never changed the position of his body on the hard, straight-backed chair. It was only in his voice that his overwhelming emotion broke through, like a groundswell violently stirring the surface of seemingly calm waters. Fear that no one would believe him, probably. Or even that no one would understand what he had to say. But he was perfectly believable. We understood him very well, this survivor of the *Sonderkommando* at Auschwitz.

I could see why he was so anguished, however.

I looked at him, in the half-basement Contagious Ward, and I understood his agony. I thought I understood it, at least.

Because throughout history, there have been survivors of massacres. When armies put their conquered towns to fire and sword, there were survivors. Jews survived even the most savage and murderous of pogroms. There were survivors at Oradour-sur-Glane.* Everywhere, all through the centuries, women whose eyes had been seared and clouded forever by visions of horror survived massacres—to tell the tale: death, just as if you'd been there. They'd been there.

But there hadn't been, and there never would be, any survivors of the Nazi gas chambers. No one would ever be able to say: I was there. You were around, or before, or beside, like those in the *Sonderkommando*.

Which explains the anguish of not being believed, for the very reason that you didn't end up there: you survived. Which explains the feelings of guilt in some people. The malaise, at least. The distress and self-questioning. Why me, alive, instead of a brother, a sister—perhaps an entire family?

I listened to the survivor of the *Sonderkommando* and felt that I could understand the anguish that crept into his voice at times. He spoke for a long while; we listened to him in silence, frozen in the pallid anguish of his story. Suddenly, when Ludwig G. lighted a lamp, we realized that wintry night had fallen, that we had been shrouded in darkness for some time already. We had

---

*The German SS burned this village near Limoges to the ground, killing 642 men, women, and children [translator's note].

sunk body and soul into the night of that story, suffocating, without any sense of time.

"That's it," said Kaminski.

We understood that the man had finished his account, that the return of light signified the end of his testimony. Doubtless a temporary end, even a random one, for clearly his words could have gone on indefinitely, far beyond our ability to listen to them.

"Never forget," added Kaminski in a stern, solemn voice. "Germany! My country is the guilty one—let's never forget that!"

There was silence.

The survivor of the *Sonderkommando* at Auschwitz, this Polish Jew who had no name because he could have been any Polish Jew, even any Jew from anywhere at all, really—the survivor of Auschwitz remained motionless, his hands spread out flat on his knees: a pillar of salt and despairing memory.

We remained motionless, too.

I'd been thinking, for long minutes, about André Malraux's last novel. I was listening to the account of the gas chambers at Auschwitz and remembering Malraux's last novel, *La lutte avec l'ange*. In 1943, a few weeks before my arrest, copies of the Swiss edition had reached Paris. Michel H. had managed to obtain one, which I'd been able to read. We'd talked and argued about it passionately.

At the heart of Malraux's oeuvre is a meditation on death, and consequently a series of reflections and dialogues on the meaning of life. In *La lutte avec l'ange* (an unfinished novel, of which only the first part, *Les noyers de l'Altenburg,* has been published), this meditation reaches one of its most extreme and significant formulations in the description of the gas attack unleashed in 1916 by the Germans on the Russian front of the Vistula River.

At the end of his life, in *Le miroir des limbes,* Malraux revised certain fragments of his unfinished novel, integrating them into his autobiographical texts. I have always found it a fascinating and dashing performance, this way Malraux had of reworking the material of his writings and his life, shedding light on reality through fiction, and illuminating the fiction through the extraordinary destiny of his life, thus drawing attention to the constant elements, the contradictions, the fundamental (and often hidden, enigmatic, or ephemeral) meaning of both life and art.

To succeed in such an undertaking, of course, one must have both an oeuvre and a biography. Professional writers, whose lives are bounded and consumed by writing itself, who have no other biography than that of their texts, would be incapable of bringing it off. The very enterprise itself must seem foolish to them. Indecent, perhaps. But I'm not making a value judgment here. I don't claim to know what is better or worse. I'm simply stating a fact, and an obvious one.

In *Le miroir des limbes,* Malraux explained why, at a time when he was hospitalized and gravely ill, he had felt obliged to return to this particular subject, which he had already dealt with in an earlier novel.

> Since I am working on what may be my last book, I have gone back to *Les noyers de l'Altenburg,* written thirty years ago, for one of those unforeseeable and cataclysmic events that seem like fits of madness in History: the first German gas attack at Bolgako, on the Vistula, in 1916. I don't know why the attack at the Vistula belongs in *Le Miroir des limbes;* I know that it will be a part of this book. Few "topics" withstand the threat of death. This one brings into confrontation fraternity, death, and that part of mankind

which is today seeking to define itself as something far beyond the individual. The spirit of sacrifice is engaged in the most ancient and profound Christian dialogue with Evil: that attack on the Russian front was followed by Verdun, the mustard gas of Flanders, Hitler, the extermination camps . . .

And Malraux concludes:

If I return to this event, it's because I seek the crucial region of the soul where absolute Evil and fraternity hang in the balance.

That Sunday in 1945, however, on a winter's afternoon in the Contagious Ward of the Buchenwald infirmary, I was naturally unfamiliar with André Malraux's reflection on the essential meaning of his own book. I'd simply read *La lutte avec l'ange* a few weeks before my arrest by the Gestapo at Épizy, a suburb of Joigny. I'd discussed the book at length with Michel H. We'd felt that this novel, which seemed different from all Malraux's previous works in both form and substance, still carried on in essence that same meditation that forms the basis of Malraux's existential quest and provides in particular the theme of certain important dialogues in *L'espoir* [*Man's Hope*]—the one between Scali and old Alvear, for example, at the moment of the Battle of Madrid.

And so I thought of Michel H.

Ludwig had just lighted the lamp in his small, glass-walled cubicle in the Contagious Ward. In the bluish twilight, I could see the rows of bunks where the sick lay half-naked. Sometimes they would move about, infinitely slowly, so slowly that they seemed constantly on the verge of collapse.

I thought of Michel H., of *La lutte avec l'ange,* of the autumn of 1943 in the Othe Forest, and of the Tabou, a *maquis* camp to the north of Semur-en-Auxois.

A month after my arrest, when the Gestapo had given up interrogating me, *de guerre lasse,* I was summoned by the *Feldgendarmerie* of Joigny. I found myself back in the parlor of the house in the old part of town where I had been interrogated the first day. The harp was still there, forgotten off in a corner. I think I've already described this place, this first experience of torture. Out in the garden with its sloping lawn, the trees still bore leaves of yellow and russet-gold.

They led me toward a table on which several objects had been laid out. I had a sinking feeling in the pit of my stomach. Or, my heart stopped. Or, my blood ran cold. Any one of these clichés would do.

Because on the table lay Michel H.'s old leather wallet, which I'd seen many times before. A set of keys, which I recognized as well. And a small pile of books. Closing my eyes, I recalled the titles of the books Michel and I had lugged around in our backpacks until recently. We also lugged around plastic explosives, and their heady, tenacious odor had seeped into the pages of those books.

I open my eyes; the warrant officer of the *Feld* is asking me if I know Michel. He says his first name, Michel, and then his last name. He has opened the wallet and put Michel's identification papers on the table. I reach out, pick up Michel's identity card, look at his photograph. The *Feldgendarme* seems surprised, but does not react. I look at Michel's photo.

"No," I say. "Don't know him."

I think, Michel is dead. If he were alive, they'd be confronting me with him, not just his identification papers and personal effects. Michel died in some ambush and the guys in the *Feld* are trying to find out about this dead man.

"No, this stuff doesn't mean anything to me."

I shrug, dropping the papers on the table.

But the officer keeps asking questions that don't fit in with my hypothesis of Michel's death. Questions that make no sense if Michel has been killed and they have his body, which their possession of his identification papers would seem to indicate.

There's something that doesn't jibe with the idea of death, in all these questions. Had they perhaps arrested Michel, and has he managed to escape?

I feel a flicker of hope again.

At Buchenwald, a year and a half later, in the Contagious Ward, I remembered that autumn day. *La lutte avec l'ange* was surely among the books stacked on the table in the *Feldgendarmerie* in Joigny. Perhaps *L'espoir* as well. And the brand-new French translation of an essay by Kant, *La religion dans les limites de la simple raison*. I wasn't able to verify this, but those were the books we'd been carrying around with us at that time, Michel and I, in our backpacks impregnated with the persistent smell of plastique.

It seemed to me then, as we struggled to draw breath in the silence following the Auschwitz survivor's hideous story, that a strange continuity, a mysterious but brilliant coherence was emerging. From those talks about Malraux's novels and Kant's essay—in which he expounds the theory of radical Evil, *das radikal Böse*—to the account given by the Polish Jew of the *Sonderkommando* at Auschwitz (not forgetting those Sunday discussions led by my teacher, Maurice Halbwachs, in Block 56 of the Little Camp), everything was part of the same imperative meditation. A meditation, to use the words André Malraux would write fully thirty years later, on "the crucial region of the soul where absolute Evil and fraternity hang in the balance."

We're sitting in the sun, Albert and I, in the little wood surrounding the infirmary compound, where we have brought to safety the Jew from Budapest. His harsh and somber voice sang the Kaddish from beyond the grave, a grave from which he has been resurrected.

We look out over the plain of Thuringia in the April sunshine.

For the moment, we're both silent. We're chewing on blades of grass. I can't discuss that sentence of Malraux's with Albert, obviously, because it hasn't been written yet. I do tell him about *La lutte avec l'ange.* I relate the episode of the German gas attack in 1916, on the Russian front at the Vistula, which forms the dark heart of the novel. Albert is struck by the startling but telling coincidence, the fantastic premonition that led Malraux to describe an apocalypse of gas warfare at the very moment when the extermination of the Jewish people in the Polish gas chambers was beginning to take shape.

"You have any idea what he's been up to, Malraux?" Albert asks me, after our long silence.

There's a village, a few hundred yards away, on the plain of Thuringia. They must have a matchless view of the camp, the people in this Thuringian village. Of the buildings on top of the Ettersberg, in any case: the kitchen, the control tower, the crematory.

Yes, I know what Malraux's been up to.

At least, I know what Henri Frager, my network chief, the leader of Jean-Marie Action, had told me. After his arrival in Buchenwald in the summer of 1944, Frager informed me, during one of our first Sunday conversations, that Malraux had just taken command of a section of the *maquis* in central France. "He uses the name Colonel Berger," Frager said.

When I burst out laughing, he asked me why. I explained that "Berger" was the name of the hero in Malraux's latest novel. But Frager didn't know about *La lutte avec l'ange.* You couldn't hold it against him. He'd set up and run one of the most active Buckmaster networks in France, so any gaps in his literary education might well be excused.

It was through his active involvement with the British Buckmaster networks, moreover, that Frager had received news of Malraux. The latter's two brothers, Claude and Roland Malraux, Fernand Malraux's sons by his second marriage ("born of the second bed": I'm repeating the very same expression Frager used, one that would not easily be attributable to me), had worked in the Resistance with the Buckmaster organization. Both of them had been arrested a few months earlier, in the spring of 1944.

This particular conversation with Henri Frager took place at the end of that summer, after the liberation of Paris. According to Frager, it was the arrest of his half-brother, Roland, that had prompted Malraux to join the active Resistance.

I don't go into all these details with Albert, however, because it would take too long. And it would just confuse him. I simply say that Malraux has become Colonel Berger. That doesn't surprise Albert; Malraux had already been a colonel, in Spain.

Then we keep quiet.

We keep carefully, even tenderly quiet. After the sound and fury of the last few weeks at Buchenwald, after the croaking chant of the Kaddish a little while ago, we keep with us, in the April sunshine, among the trees growing green again in the little wood beside the infirmary, the precious gift of this fraternal silence. We contemplate the plain of Thuringia, the peaceful villages that dot this plain. Chimney smoke drifts lazily, cozily, into the sky.

It is not smoke from a crematory.

3

THE WHITE LINE

I stopped, looking at the tall trees beyond the barbed wire. The sun was shining on the forest, the wind was sighing in the trees. There was a sudden burst of music, from across the roll-call square. Accordion music, playing somewhere over there. It wasn't café or dance-hall music, but something entirely different: an accordion tune played by a Russian, surely. Only a Russian could entice such music from that instrument: violent, fragile music, a kind of tempestuous waltz, the trembling of birches in the breeze, wheat rippling on the endless steppe.

I advanced a few more paces. The square was empty, vast in the sunlight. I looked at Stalin, who seemed to be waiting for me there.

His portrait was, at least.

On April 12, the day after liberation, when we'd returned to the camp after our night spent under arms in the neighboring forest, we'd found Stalin. His portrait had bloomed in the night, a faithful and gigantic likeness hanging from the main facade of one of the Soviet prisoners' huts, at a corner of the roll-call square over by the canteen.

Impassive, Stalin had observed our return. Not one hair was missing from his mustache. Not one button was missing from his crisp generalissimo's jacket. During the night, the first night of a still-precarious freedom, enthusiastic and anonymous artists had drawn this enormous portrait. It was at least nine by fifteen feet, and strikingly—alarmingly—lifelike.

So: young Russians (all Russians in Buchenwald were young, by the way) had felt the overwhelming need to devote their first hours of liberty to making a huge portrait of Stalin so true to life that its realism even mutated into surrealism. Just as natives erect a totem at the entrance to their village, the Russians had decorated their barracks with the tutelary image of the Supreme Commander.

That morning (now, this was not the morning of April 12, which was the day I met Stalin, but some other morning between April 14 and 19, days for which I have specific points of reference), I'd awakened to the repeated calling of my name. A crackly voice on the loudspeaker was shouting my name in what seemed a rather peremptory manner. Startled awake, I'd believed in those first few seconds of befuddlement that we were still under the control of the SS, subject to SS discipline. For an instant, in spite of my grogginess, I'd had the distinct idea that the SS were summoning me to the front gates of the camp. This was not usually a good sign, being told to report to the gates of Buchenwald. Henri Frager had been summoned like that, a few weeks earlier, and he had never returned.

This time, however, my name was not followed by the usual command: *Sofort zum Tor!* I was not being called to the camp gates, beneath the control tower, but to the library. And instead of my identification number, the voice was calling my real name: not prisoner 44904, *Häftling vierundvierzigtausendneunhun-*

dertvier, but comrade Semprun. I was no longer *Häftling,* but *Genosse,* in the voice on the loudspeaker.

Then I woke up completely.

My body relaxed. I remembered that we were free. My entire soul quivered as a kind of violent happiness came over me. I remembered that I had plans for this new day. Not just the general plan—somewhat absurd, or at least unduly optimistic—to survive yet another day. No, specific projects, more limited, of course, but sensible ones, whereas the other plan was insane.

I intended to leave the camp and walk to the nearest German village, a few hundred yards away on the rich green plain of Thuringia. I'd talked this over with a few pals. It would have a fountain, this German village. We felt like drinking pure, cool water. The water in the camp was disgusting.

I had still more plans for this new day. Lying on my straw pallet in a dormitory in Block 40, I listened idly to the noises of the awakening camp.

Jiri Zak had told me that he and the jazz musicians he'd gotten together over the past two years were going to have a jam session, just for themselves, and just for the fun of it. He'd be on drums. On sax, there was Markovitch, a Serb with real talent. A Norwegian, an outright genius, was on trumpet. When he played "Stardust," we all got goose bumps. The SS, naturally, knew nothing about this jazz combo, whose instruments had been obtained illegally from the main clothing store, the *Effektenkammer.* It must be said that the old German Communists didn't like that barbaric music, either, but nobody had asked their permission about forming this jazz group. They grumbled and put up with it.

I listened to the summons addressed to me over the loudspeaker. The veteran prisoner who had run the camp library was manding, in some annoyance, that I return the three books I still had in my possession. He expected me this morning, without fail. These books, he said, had to be returned to the library that very day.

Actually, I'd been going to keep those books. I didn't much care for souvenirs, but those were books that might come in handy. I meant to use them again. It hadn't occurred to me to return them, to tell the truth. Not simply because I could still use them, but also because the future of the camp library didn't interest me at all, not one little bit. Why should these books be returned to a library destined to disappear?

It seemed I was vastly mistaken. It seemed I had my head in the clouds. With distinct irritation, Anton (that's the name I've decided to give the librarian) explained that I was completely in error. Why would the Buchenwald library disappear?

Because the camp was going to disappear, obviously!

My reply was a model of common sense. It did not appear to convince Anton, who was looking at me and shaking his head.

I was in the waiting room of the library. A tiny, empty room. A side door opened onto the corridor of Block 5. At the two ends of this corridor were the offices of the *Schreibstube,* the secretariat, and the *Arbeitsstatistik,* where I had worked. At the far end of the little room was a door with a window and a counter that allowed the librarian to communicate with the prisoners who had come to borrow books. There we were, the two of us, Anton and I, on either side of the wicket.

On the wooden counter were the three library books he'd wanted me so urgently to return.

"Why?" he asks me.

I suddenly think I see a shifty look in his eye.

"Why, what?" I reply.

"Why would the camp disappear?"

"In a few days, a few weeks at the worst, Hitler will have

been beaten," I tell him. "Once Nazism has gone, the camps will go, too."

His chest and shoulders shake with silent, uncontrollable laughter. He laughs heartily, but without joy.

Stopping abruptly, he lectures me. "The end of Nazism will not mean the end of the class struggle!" he exclaims pedantically, imperiously.

I thank him politely. "Thanks, Anton! Thanks for reminding me of this basic truth!"

He's pleased with himself, not realizing that I'm making fun of him.

"Should we conclude from this that there is no class society without concentration camps?" I ask.

He darts me a look that is wary, even mistrustful. His expression is fixed; he's thinking. He's plainly afraid of some dialectical trap.

"No class society without repression, at least!" he offers cautiously.

I nod my head. "Without violence, rather. This concept is more precise, more universal."

He's probably wondering what I'm getting at.

But I don't want to get anywhere. I'm simply trying to thrust aside the idea his words seem to suggest. The idea that the end of Nazism will not be the end of the world of concentration camps.

"You don't like the word 'repression,'" says Anton. "Yet that's the right word. You don't think we'll have to repress, one way or another, all the former Nazis? Repress, reeducate—"

I can't help laughing.

In the SS system, Buchenwald was also a reeducation camp: *Umschulungslager.*

"We'll need camps like this one for that purpose," he says firmly. He looks at me, smirking just a bit. "You don't like this idea, I can see that! What do you want us to do with Buchenwald? Turn it into a place of pilgrimage, of meditation? A vacation resort?"

"Absolutely not! I'd like the camp to be abandoned to the erosion of time, of nature. . . . I'd like it to be engulfed by the forest."

He stares at me, openmouthed. "Shit, no! What a waste!"

I pick up one of the books I'd placed on the counter. Hegel's *Logic,* in the short version, the one in the *Encyclopedia of Philosophy.*

"Anton, are they going to need books like this one for the reeducation of former Nazis?"

He looks at the title of the volume, then gestures dismissively. "You must admit, you read some strange things! I noticed that yesterday, when I came across the cards of the books you hadn't returned: Hegel, Nietzsche, Schelling . . . nothing but idealistic philosophers!"

I remember the Sunday discussions around Maurice Halbwachs's bunk.

"I've learned a lot from reading Schelling," I tell him.

Surprised at the subdued tone of my voice, he shrugs grouchily. "I still say you made some funny choices!"

He seems dismayed: he's really upset about me.

"I'm not going to leave these books in the catalogue . . . I don't feel *The Will to Power* is indispensable reading," he announces.

I get the impression he's thinking of staying here, in this same camp.

"What?" I exclaim. "You're staying on? You're not going home?"

He gestures vaguely. "No more home, no more family . . . They all died for the Führer! Some volunteered, the others didn't. . . . Died anyway. . . . Here's where I'll be the most useful in a new Germany."

I truly regret having brought back those books. I should have kept them, instead of giving in to this old Communist's mania for order and continuity.

"So," says Anton. He picks up the three volumes on the counter just as I'm about to reach for them myself. "In the meantime," he continues, "I'll put them back where they belong."

As I watch him head for the back of the library and vanish behind the shelves, I wonder if Nietzsche and Hegel really belong there. And Schelling? The single volume of his works in the library at Buchenwald contains his essay on liberty, in which Schelling examines what it means to be human. A problematical foundation, difficult to understand, but "without that initial uncertainty," he writes, "the creature would have no reality: darkness is his inevitable lot."

Sometimes, on a Sunday, as I stood leaning on the bunk where Maurice Halbwachs lay dying, I would feel that darkness was in fact our inevitable lot. The darkness of the mystery of man's humanity, dedicated to the freedom of both Good and Evil, shaped by this freedom.

I watch Anton walk away and I wonder if that idea of Schelling's might be of some use in reeducating the former Nazis of the future camp of Buchenwald.

The roll-call square is deserted when I arrive there after my talk with Anton the librarian. I'm still feeling uneasy after our conversation. But the sun is shining on that vast, silent, and sumptuously empty space, after so many months of noisy haste and the swarming mass of life in a concentration camp.

There's the rustle of an April breeze in the trees beyond the barbed wire. And accordion music: a Russian tune, no doubt about it.

Turning away, I look at the huts, all lined up. I'm face-to-face once more with the giant picture of Stalin.

A few years later, in 1953, at the time of his death, I would remember his Buchenwald portrait.

Pablo Picasso had just earned himself a stinging rebuke from the leaders of the French Communist Party. In honor of the departed, the artist had drawn a young, Georgian Stalin, a conceited man with a swashbuckling air and an evil twinkle in his eye. The portrait was not at all respectful, of course, but it was lively, and full of shrewd irony as well: Stalin looked like a gang leader rather than a supreme commander who had governed the second greatest world power with an iron hand.

In fact, as seen by Picasso, Stalin looked more like Nicolai, my young barbarian of Block 56, than himself as generalissimo.

On April 12, the first day of freedom, after seeing the icon of Stalin hanging on the Soviet prisoner-of-war barracks, I went into the Little Camp. The SS were gone, but life there went on as before. People there went on dying as before. All those who had managed to escape the forced evacuation of the camp went on dying as before. Processions of silent prisoners—talk is tiring—stumbled around the latrine building. Leaning on one another to keep from falling, shivering in the spring sunshine, ghosts in rags would share a *makhorka* cigarette with meticulous and brotherly gestures. The rank, fecal odor of death continued to float over the Little Camp on that day after our liberation.

I find Nicolai outside Block 56. His riding boots gleam, his fatigue jacket looks freshly pressed.

"You saw the Boss's portrait?" he asks me.

I nod.

"We made it during the night," he continues. "In two sections. A different team for each half of the picture. At dawn, we glued both pieces together."

He waves his right hand. *"Prima!"* he exclaims. He flashes me a carnivorous smile. "Now you know what a Russian *Kapo* looks like," he adds.

"But why spend an entire night working instead of celebrating your freedom?" I ask.

"You mean the Great *Kapo*'s portrait?"

"Exactly," I say. "Why?"

He gazes at me with a hint of commiseration. "And why did my mother get out the icons to pray, on some nights back in the village? When things were going really badly, she'd get the icons out of their hiding places and light candles—"

I laughed out loud.

"I thought Communism was soviets plus electricity . . . Not icons plus candles."

"Who's talking about Communism?" asks Nicolai in sincere astonishment.

"If you don't want to talk about Communism, why the portrait of Stalin?"

He lets loose a crushing peal of laughter. Looking straight at me, he taps his right forefinger on his right temple.

"Dourak!" he sneers. "You'll never understand anything, pal!"

It's true that it did take me a long time to understand. But after all, that's no reason to let myself be insulted. Especially since on that April day in 1945, I wasn't the one who'd drawn Stalin's portrait and hung it triumphantly on the front of a hut. I wasn't the one who'd spent my night making that picture—absolutely not. Stalin? He had nothing to do with me, in April 1945. I hadn't yet read a single line of his and hardly knew who he was. At the time, Stalin had no bearing whatsoever on my connection with Marxism. He was never mentioned in our discussions. On those Sundays, certain Sundays in Block 56, for example, when Maurice Halbwachs was still cheerful and lucid, full of intellectual vigor, when he was explaining to us his position on

Marxism. None of us would have thought to bring up Stalin. He was marginal to our preoccupations. Stalin? He didn't come into my life until later. They came later, the years of partial—and partisan—glaciation in my thinking.

But I haven't the time to tell Nicolai he's overdoing it. A sudden change comes over him, and his voice drops almost to a whisper.

"How much you want for your gun?"

He stares greedily at the German submachine gun I'm wearing slung across my chest. Because we've kept our weapons. The American officers had gotten us to return to camp, after our wild night under the stars, after our march on Weimar. But they've left us our weapons. Only on the following day will they ask us to hand them over.

"I don't want anything," I tell him. "I'm keeping it!"

He tries to convince me. He offers me dollars, clothes, real liquor, girls. Girls? I challenge him on that one. He laughs, tells me I'd lose my wager. His guys have made contact with some Ukrainian women who were working in factories around Weimar. He can sneak a whole cartload in for a serious knees-up party, no holds barred, in some discreet part of the camp.

I take his word for it, but tell him I'm not interested. Rather, I'm interested, but not at that price. Not at the price of my brand-new submachine gun.

He mutters curses, in Russian. I know enough to get the point. Especially since Russian curses, at least those of Nicolai and his buddies in Buchenwald, are rather monotonous: you're always sent off to fuck someone's mother, your own or some pal's. But it's always the mothers who get the worst of it, in Russian curses. At least the ones in Buchenwald.

I let him curse long enough to calm down a bit.

"What were you planning on doing with my gun?"

He looks at me, hesitating. Then he decides.

"The Russian *Kapos,* pal—I know their kind!" he tells me in a low voice. "I know what to expect from them. . . ."

He speaks even more softly. Now he's murmuring.

"I'm not going home. I'm staying on this side. I'm taking off in two or three days. Everything's ready. There's a small band of us. Some women are waiting for us—they don't want to wind up in the clink back there, either. We've got some money, a few weapons. We'd need more. . . ."

He eyes my submachine gun lovingly. I back away from him.

"Don't try to take it from me by force, Nicolai. . . . I'll shoot you if I have to."

He nods. "You're just dumb enough to do that!"

He stands up, holds out his hand to me. "So long, then— we'll part as friends!"

But I don't shake hands with him. I'm sure he'd hang on, trying to pull me toward him, so he can grab me and get me off balance. I'd have to use my weapon. Try to use it, anyway.

I move away from him, pointing the submachine gun in his direction.

"So long, Nicolai! You're right, we're still friends!"

His laughter is a little crazy, which isn't at all the same as laughing crazily.

"What was it you said? The soviets plus electricity? Well, you'll find out!"

He turns and walks away toward Block 56.

I'm on the roll-call square of Buchenwald; I look at the giant picture of Stalin. I do not understand how Nicolai can have both hung up the portrait of the Great *Kapo* and prepared his flight far from the latter's protective presence.

It must be said that the behavior of the Russians at Buchenwald was an enigma to us all. Problematical, at any rate. We couldn't fathom how these young hoodlums, full of individualistic and cruel vitality (most of them, anyway) could be the authentic representatives of a new society. We'd had to construct an incredibly elaborate explanation to accommodate the impossibility of changing the premise: Soviet society must of necessity be a new society. That was the point of departure—a compulsory rhetorical figure.

But (we told ourselves) it wasn't the new man of this new society we saw embodied in the young Russian barbarians of Buchenwald. They were only the dregs of this new society: the waste products of a rural archaism that had not yet been caught up in or transformed by the modernizing movement of the revolution. Still, we did sometimes think that the revolution was producing an awful lot of dregs. A real deluge of waste products.

If I had plumbed this mystery of the Russian soul then and there, if I had understood Nicolai's attitude, I would have doubtless spared myself a long detour (not without oases of courage and solidarity) through the deserts of Communism. In 1945, however, it was probably a question not of comprehension, but of desire. It was probably the illusion of a future that prevented me from understanding. Or rather, from having the will to understand, even if I'd had the means to do so. This illusion probably gave me the desire, not to understand, but to desire. And there was nothing more desirable than the future, after so much agony.

But I turn my back on Stalin, or on his portrait, at least. I take a few steps toward the center of the roll-call square.

Up on the platform of the watchtower, an American soldier is leaning on the railing. Perhaps he's listening to the Russian accordion music, as I am. At the top of the tower, a black flag has been furled and craped ever since the liberation of the camp.

Since the death of Franklin D. Roosevelt.

Elle est venue par cette ligne blanche . . .

I murmur the beginning of a poem called "La liberté."

> *Elle est venue par cette ligne blanche pouvant tout aussi bien*
>   *signifier l'issue de l'aube que le bougeoir du crépuscule . . .*
> [It came through this white line that might just as well herald
>   the uprush of dawn as the guttering of twilight . . .]

My voice, of its own accord, grows louder, stronger, fuller, as I
continue my recitation.

> *Elle passa les grèves machinales; elle passa les cimes éventrées.*
> *Prenaient fin la renonciation à visage de lâche, la sainteté du*
>   *mensonge, l'alcool du bourreau . . .*
> [It passed the automatic shores; it passed the gutted heights.
> Renunciation with its coward's face, the sanctity of lies, the
>   executioner's crapulence were coming to an end . . .]

At the top of my lungs, alone on the parade ground, I shout out
the end of the poem by René Char.

Now the American soldier is watching me through his
binoculars.

It was on April 12 that I read the poem "La liberté" for the
first time. It was the right moment: the day after the liberation
of Buchenwald.

On that day, I'd finally had a talk with the young Frenchman
accompanying the two officers of His Gracious Majesty.

The two Britishers had left us alone, sitting out on the front
steps in the sunshine, while they went up to the main SS records
office on the second floor of the building I was guarding. I'd
given them permission to go through the files. Their assignment, in fact, was to trace the fate of those agents of the Allied
action and information networks who had been deported by the
Nazis.

As for the Frenchman, he had been assigned to track down Henri Frager, leader of the Jean-Marie Action network. As it happened, I had belonged to that network, and Frager had been my leader. He was betrayed, as I had been, and arrested a few months after I was. I'd met him again at Buchenwald. I could therefore save the young French officer the trouble of long and useless hours of research. I could tell him that Frager was dead. He had been shot by the Germans. One day, at the hour of the morning roll call, he had been summoned by the *Politische Abteilung,* the camp Gestapo. That evening, he had been reported absent. The next day, the *Politische Abteilung* sent us an official notice. "Release": that was the word chosen to disclose the fate reserved for Henri Frager—his disappearance. *Entlassen:* the usual term used by the Nazi bureaucracy to announce individual executions.

On that day, I was the one who erased the name of Henri Frager from the camp's central card index. That was my work, to erase the names. Or to write them in, just as well. To maintain, at all events, an orderly record of comings and goings, deaths and new arrivals, in the card index. At least in the numerical groups between thirty thousand and sixty thousand. And there was a lot of turnover in those groups, which corresponded especially to the deportees from Western Europe, after the end of 1943.

I'd erased the name of Henri Frager, that day. His identification number became available once again.

I told the young Frenchman all that, to spare him useless research in the records. Then I talked to him about my conversations with Henri Frager, on certain Sundays.

I told him about Sundays in Buchenwald.

Instinctively, to placate the gods of a credible narration, to soften the harshness of a truthful account, I tried to lead the young officer into the universe of death down a dominical path:

a garden path, in a way. A more peaceful approach. I led him into the hell of radical Evil, *das radikal Böse,* through its most banal entrance. The one least removed, in any case, from the normal experience of life.

To initiate the young officer into the mysteries of Sundays in Buchenwald, I evoked the pale and poisonous beauty of Pola Negri in *Mazurka.*

Mazurka? The film?

He stared at me, taken aback. I could tell he was shocked. He didn't necessarily doubt the truth of my testimony, but he was shocked. As though I'd said something improper. As though I'd begun this account at the wrong end, backward. He'd probably been expecting a completely different story. Pola Negri's appearance at Buchenwald disconcerted him. I immediately sensed a certain aloofness in him. I probably wasn't a good witness, the right kind of witness. And yet, I'd been rather pleased with my clever touch. Because anyone could have told him about the crematory, the deaths from exhaustion, the public hangings, the torment of the Jews in the Little Camp, and Ilse Koch's taste for the tattooed skin of deportees. Whereas Pola Negri in *Mazurka*—I was sure no one would have thought to begin an account with that.

Oh, yes, I told him, *Mazurka,* the Austrian film.

Sometimes, I explained, the SS command organized a film show on Sunday afternoons. Sentimental or musical comedies, or both at the same time: they go well together, music and sentiment. I remembered, for example, a film with Martha Eggerth and Jan Kiepura. It was set among mountain lakes on which the two of them warbled in rowboats with alps in the background. I also remembered *Mazurka,* with Pola Negri.

I didn't deserve any particular credit for recalling these films. First of all, because of the exceptional circumstances of such occasions, when they were shown in the main hall in the Little Camp, near the infirmary compound. But especially because they were films I'd already seen during my childhood.

In Madrid, in the thirties, we'd had German governesses. On days when we were allowed to go to the movies, they'd taken my brothers and me to see films in their maternal tongue, German or Austrian films. The film in which Jan Kiepura and Martha Eggerth sang in each other's arms against a background of mountain lakes and pastures was called *Vuelan mis canciones* in Spanish. But its original title (German, of course) escapes me utterly. My memory favors childhood recollections over those of a twenty-year-old youth at Buchenwald.

It might seem at first as though the memory of Buchenwald, of the film shown in the huge wooden hut that served as a *Kino* (as well as an assembly hall for the departure of transports), ought to be more vivid than a childhood recollection of a movie theater on the plaza of the opera house in Madrid. Well, not at all: just one of the mysteries of life and memory.

Anyway, memory had no language problem with the title of the Pola Negri film: it was called *Mazurka* in every language.

So I talked about Sundays in Buchenwald with the young officer who wore the badge with the cross of Lorraine over his heart. I told him of our Sundays in my own way. There was more than Pola Negri, of course. Pola Negri was just a lead-in. I spoke about the Sunday discussions. About the brothel, which was reserved for Germans. About the secret training of the combat troops. About the jazz ensemble of Jiri Zak, the Czech who worked in the *Schreibstube*. And so on.

He listened attentively, but in more and more obvious dismay. What I had to say probably did not correspond with the stereotypical horror story he'd been expecting. He asked me no questions, requested no further details. When I finished, I remained plunged in an embarrassed—and embarrassing—silence. My first account of Sundays in Buchenwald was a complete flop.

So, to get us out of this awkward situation, I began asking him questions. A lot of questions. After all, I had almost a year to catch up on, since the liberation of Paris. Important things had certainly been happening there, things I knew nothing about. Books had been published, plays staged, newspapers launched.

But listening to the young French officer—who probably wanted to redeem himself by replying precisely and at length—gave me the impression that there had not been any exciting new ideas and publications in Paris during my absence.

Albert Camus was the man of the hour, but there was nothing astonishing about that. *L'étranger* was one of the novels that had most intrigued me, in recent years. And *Le mythe de Sisyphe* had provoked passionate discussions within my circle of friends, under the Occupation. Camus, then: business as usual.

André Malraux wasn't writing anymore, it seemed. He had turned to politics. A few months earlier, his speech at the congress of the Mouvement de Libération Nationale had supposedly prevented the Communists from taking control of the unified Resistance. In any case, he had not finished *La lutte avec l'ange*. It did not seem likely that he ever would.

There was Sartre, of course. But Sartre was hardly a newcomer to the scene. In 1943 we'd devoured *L'Être et le Néant,* and we knew pages of *La nausée* by heart. Our gang had gone to see *Les mouches* at the Théâtre Sarah-Bernhardt. While preparing for the entrance exam to the École Normale Supérieure, we'd discussed Sartre in relation to Husserl and Heidegger. Great, an old friend, Jean-Paul Sartre!

Alongside Sartre, the young Frenchman dutifully informed me, there was Maurice Merleau-Ponty. Fine, but that didn't surprise me, as I'd already read *La structure du comportement* [*The Structure of Behavior*].

There was Aragon, with his Elsa by his side. But I wasn't at all interested in the Aragon of that period. His civic-minded and jingoist poetry during the Occupation had left me rather indifferent. (Still, there was *Brocéliande.*) At Buchenwald, that had been the one subject of disagreement with my pal Boris Taslitzky, who was an unconditional Aragonian. I would have to wait until a poem in *Le Nouveau Crève-Coeur,* the "Chanson pour oublier Dachau" ["Song to Forget Dachau"], would revive my interest in Aragon as a poet.

Doubtless irritated to see that none of the news from Paris he was passing on was really news to me, the young Frenchman brought up Raymond Aron. Here's someone special, he seemed to suggest, here's an original talent, a political columnist you must never have heard of before! But I'd interrupted him with peals of laughter. Raymond Aron? You bet I'd heard of him. Not only had I read his work, but I knew him personally. In September 1939, the day Hitler's armies invaded Poland, I'd met Raymond Aron on the Boulevard Saint-Michel. I was fifteen years old. I was with my father and Paul-Louis Landsberg. At the corner of the boulevard and the Rue Soufflot, near the newspaper kiosk that then stood in front of Chez Capoulade, we had run into Raymond Aron. The three men had talked about the war then just beginning, about democracy's chances of survival. Later, Claude-Edmonde Magny had had me read Aron's *Introduction à la philosophie de l'Histoire.*

I was not in the least amazed, in short, that Raymond Aron was playing a stellar role in the intellectual life of Paris during the Liberation.

There were also the missing, the dear departed.

Jean Giraudoux was dead—I hadn't known that. He had died two days after my arrival in Buchenwald. I remembered that at

Épizy, on the outskirts of Joigny, when that damned Gestapo thug had sliced open my scalp with the butt of his automatic pistol, I'd regretted that I wouldn't be able to attend the first public performance of *Sodome et Gomorrhe,* scheduled to take place a few weeks later.

So Giraudoux was dead.

I wondered, as I listened to the young French officer, why there had been no sign to tell me this, in Buchenwald. It was unlikely that the death of Jean Giraudoux would pass unheralded by some natural event—but there had probably been some sign that I had not known how to interpret, that's all. Doubtless, one day that winter, the smoke from the crematory had suddenly grown lighter, more vaporous: the faintest gray wisps over the Ettersberg to tell me of the death of Giraudoux.

I simply hadn't known how to decipher the sign.

There were others missing: Brasillach had been shot; Drieu La Rochelle had killed himself. I'd always preferred Drieu to Brasillach, and I preferred his suicide to the latter's death.

All in all, aside from a few disappearances brought about by the course of nature (or of events), the garden of French literature did not appear to have been trampled or even disturbed. No revelations, no real surprises: the routine of foreseeable, almost organic growth. It seemed amazing, at first, after such a historic cataclysm, but that's how it was. Proving once more that the rhythm of maturation and collapse is not the same in the history of politics as it is in the arts and letters.

Finally, however, as a last resort, the young French officer had told me about the latest collection of poems by René Char.

From his leather satchel he produced a copy of *Seuls demeurent,* published a few weeks earlier. He spoke of it with enthusiasm, particularly when he realized that he had astonished me at last, for I knew nothing about René Char.

It irked me to admit it, but it was true.

On the morning of April 12, 1945, I had not yet heard of him. I'd thought I was familiar with everything—or almost everything—in French poetry, but I did not know who René Char was. I knew hundreds of poems by heart, from Villon to Breton. I could even recite the endless verses of Patrice de La Tour du Pin, which really took some doing! But I didn't know a thing about René Char.

The young Frenchman who carried France in his heart— over the left breast pocket of his tunic, at least—praised the beauty of Char's poems and read me some with delight. In the end, like a good fellow, he gave in to my repeated entreaties: he let me have the copy of *Seuls demeurent* he had carried with him all through the German campaign. On one condition, however. That I return the book to him as soon as I was repatriated.

A young woman had given it to him, and he treasured it.

I promised, writing down the address he gave me. I didn't quibble over the word "repatriated." I could have, though. Because how can you repatriate a stateless person? But I didn't say anything. I didn't want to worry him, make him change his mind. Perhaps he would have been less willing to lend his book to a stateless person.

That is why, a few days later, on the deserted square of Buchenwald, I can shout out the end of René Char's poem, "La liberté."

> *D'un pas à ne se mal guider que derrière l'absence, elle est venue,*
> *cygne sur la blessure, par cette ligne blanche . . .*
> [With a step to stray only in the wake of absence, it came,
> swan upon the wound, through this white line . . .]

I'm finished; I give a big, friendly wave to the American soldier up in the watchtower, staring at me through his binoculars.

4

LIEUTENANT ROSENFELD

Lieutenant Rosenfeld has stopped his jeep on the riverbank, beyond the wooden bridge crossing the Ilm. At the end of the path, amid the bushes just beginning to leaf out, stands the cottage of Goethe.

"Das Gartenhaus," he says.

Lieutenant Rosenfeld gets out of the jeep and beckons me after him.

We walk toward Goethe's little country house, in the Ilm Valley, on the outskirts of Weimar. The sun is shining. The bracing crispness of this April morning hints at the mild spring air so soon to come.

I feel suddenly unwell. It's not uneasiness, still less anxiety. No, on the contrary, it's joy that is upsetting: an excess of joy.

I stop, short of breath.

The American lieutenant turns around, wondering what's wrong.

"The birds!" I exclaim.

We're speaking German. Rosenfeld is an officer in Patton's Third Army, yet we're speaking German. Ever since the day we met, we've spoken to each other in German. I'll translate our remarks for the reader's convenience. To be polite, in short.

"Die Vögel?" he repeats, puzzled.

A few days earlier, some of the inhabitants of Weimar had gathered in the courtyard of the crematory: women, adolescents, old men. No men of an age to bear arms, quite obviously—those who could were doing so still, carrying on the war. These civilians had arrived in buses, escorted by a detachment of black American soldiers. There were many blacks in the shock regiments of Patton's Third Army.

On that day, some of them stood at the entrance to the crematory courtyard, leaning against the high fence that usually prevented access to the area. Their faces were stiff, impassive masks of bronze as they gazed with stern attention on the small crowd of German civilians.

I wondered what they could possibly be thinking and what they might have had to say about this war against Fascism, these black Americans so numerous among the storm troops of the Third Army. In a way, it was the war that had made them full-fledged citizens. Legally, at least, if not always during the day-to-day experience of military life. Yet whatever their social background, no matter how humble their origins, in spite of the overt or veiled humiliation to which they were exposed by the color of their skin, the draft had potentially made them citizens with equal rights. As though the right to kill had finally given them the right to be free.

The only discrimination to which they could now be subject would apply equally to all other soldiers of the American Army, be they white, black, yellow, or of mixed blood: a technical differentiation based on their skill at soldiering. Or else a distinction—impossible to formulate, moreover, yet fraught with moral consequences—with respect to their courage or ardice in battle.

In the crematory yard that day, at any rate, an American lieu-tenant addressed the several dozen women, adolescents of both sexes, and elderly German men from the city of Weimar. The women were wearing spring dresses in bright colors. The offi-cer spoke in a neutral, implacable voice. He explained how the crematory oven worked, gave the mortality figures for Buchen-wald. He reminded the civilians of Weimar that for more than seven years, they had lived, indifferent or complicitous, beneath the smoke from the crematory.

"Your pretty town," he told them, "so clean, so neat, brim-ming with cultural memories, the heart of classical and enlight-ened Germany, seems not to have had the slightest qualm about living in the smoke of Nazi crematoria!"

The women (a good number of them, at least) were unable to restrain their tears and begged for forgiveness with theatrical gestures. Some of them obligingly went so far as to feel quite faint. The adolescents took refuge in despairing silence. The old men looked away, clearly unwilling to listen to any of this.

That is where I'd seen this American lieutenant for the first time. I had followed and watched him for more than two hours, during the entire tour of Buchenwald forced upon the inhabi-tants of Weimar by the American Army.

Shortly afterward, two days later, or perhaps even the very next day, I was sitting facing him in one of the SS command's former offices in the camp, on the Avenue of Eagles that led from the train station to the monumental entrance to Buchen-wald.

On the pocket flap of his olive-drab shirt I could see the metallic badge bearing his name and rank: Lt. Rosenfeld.

As for him, he was looking at the identification number, 44904, and the *S* written on the triangle of red material I was sporting on my jacket of coarse blue cloth.

"Spanish," he said.

Remember, we were speaking German, and the *S* stood for *Spanier.*

"*Rotspanier,*" I replied, to be exact. "Red Spanish."

No doubt I spoke impertinently. Somewhat arrogantly, at least.

Lieutenant Rosenfeld had shrugged. He clearly found this precise detail superfluous.

"I wasn't really expecting to find Falangists here!" he exclaimed.

I said nothing: there was nothing to say.

"Four-four-nine-oh-four," he continued. "That corresponds with the flood of arrivals in January of '44, doesn't it?"

I nodded; it did correspond, and there was still nothing to say.

"Arrested in the French Resistance, right?"

Right.

"Jean-Marie Action network," I added, though. "A Buckmaster network."

I caught a gleam of increased interest in his eye. "Buckmaster" did mean something to him, then.

I knew that the American military administration was preparing a comprehensive report on life and death in Buchenwald. To this end, detainees who had participated in the internal administration of the camp were being interviewed by officers of the intelligence services. Lieutenant Rosenfeld was one of these. And I had been invited to report to him that day because I had worked for the *Arbeitsstatistik,* the department in charge of deportee labor assignments.

"You're a student, I suppose. But of what?" asked Lieutenant Rosenfeld.

That reminded me of something, some distant episode.

"Of philosophy," I replied, as I remembered which distant episode.

"Philosophy makes you smile, does it?" asked Rosenfeld.

I'd smiled, apparently.

But it wasn't philosophy that had made me smile. Not the kind I had studied at the Sorbonne, at any rate. Le Senne's courses would never have elicited the slightest smile, even in retrospect. A discreet yawn, more likely. It was what I'd remembered while I was answering Rosenfeld that had made me smile.

I'd run down the long underground passage. Barefoot, on the rough concrete floor. Stark naked, I might add: naked from head to toe. Stripped to the buff. Like all the other deportees in my convoy, who were running with me.

Before that, there had been the uproar, the dogs, the blows from rifle butts, going through the mud on the double, beneath the harsh glare of the searchlights, the entire length of the Avenue of Eagles. Suddenly we were walking slowly, in chilling silence and darkness.

No more grand Wagnerian lighting. We couldn't really tell where we were, once we'd passed through the huge gate. The SS and the dogs had stayed outside. We'd been taken to a two-story building, then crowded into a vast shower room on the ground floor. We were exhausted by days and nights of this voyage into the unknown. Hours passed. The water from the faucets in the huge room was revolting, lukewarm and fetid. We couldn't slake our thirst. Some of us collapsed into fitful sleep. Others tried immediately to rally and find friends, exchanging bits of food, words of hope, memories we all more or less shared. Later, much later, things got moving again. Doors were opened, orders shouted. In groups of fifteen to twenty men, we were pushed into an adjoining room. We had to undress, leaving all our clothes and personal possessions—those that had survived the many searches during our journey—on a sort of counter. The guys shouting these orders (in a crude, guttural, almost monosyllabic German) were young. They wore wooden clogs and some kind of working clothes of faded grayish fabric. Their heads were shaved. They looked rather muscular. Among themselves, they spoke Russian, a language I had no trouble identifying. Two years earlier, when I'd played on the first team of the Stade Français in the basketball championship, I'd come up against the fellows of the BBCR. I remembered the Fabrikant brothers and their teammates very well. Quite good basketball players, by the way, these sons of White Russian émigrés. I'd overheard them talking among themselves, in the locker rooms or out on the field, and I hadn't the slightest doubt that these young thugs who were bullying us, to hurry us up (the only word of their language mixed in with *Los, Schnell,* and *Scheisse* was *Bistro,* of course), were speaking Russian to one another. Seeing those burly and obviously well-fed Russian youths was a startling initiation to life in the camp, but I didn't really have a chance to think about it. With all that shouting and pushing by the young Russians, things moved right along. We quickly found ourselves, naked as ever, in another of the long line of rooms on the ground floor of the bathhouse. There, armed with electric clippers dangling from the ceiling by their cords, haircutters roughly shaved our heads, then our entire bodies. Stripped to the buff, indeed: the cliché was now quite apposite. But there was no letup—not even time to giggle or sneer at the sight of all those bodies as naked as jaybirds. Or to shiver with fear, imagining what such a prologue might presage. For we had already been pushed *(Los, Schnell, Bistro!)* into a new room almost completely taken up by a bathing pool full of greenish liquid, allegedly a disinfectant. You were better off diving in headfirst of your own accord. Otherwise, the young Russians took open and malicious pleasure in submerging you themselves. So I dived right in, closing my eyes; I had rather unpleasant memories of bathtubs in which the Gestapo shoved your head underwater.

It was after all these ritual purifications that we were sent running through the underground passage linking, as I later learned, the baths and disinfection building with the store for prisoners' belongings, the *Effektenkammer*.

But this wasn't the memory that had made me smile, as you can well imagine. It was the word "philosophy," the idea that I was a philosophy student, as I had just declared to Lieutenant Rosenfeld. Because I'd been asked the same question and I'd given the same reply at the end of that long race down the underground passage in Buchenwald, the day of my arrival in the camp.

There had been stairs to climb, and finally a well-lighted room. On the right, behind a counter that ran the length of the room, some fellows (who were no longer young, whose heads weren't shaved anymore, and who weren't Russian) tossed items of clothing at us as we went by. Underpants and collarless shirts made of coarse cloth, trousers, jackets. A cap as well. And lastly, a pair of wooden-soled clogs.

We'd put on these clothes as they were thrown to us. They were chosen at random, with—at best—a guess at the fit. After a glance at our height or corpulence, these guys tossed us things they picked from different piles lined up in front of them on the counter. The clothing almost never fit, though: it was too big or too small, too long or too short. Mismatched, above all. And so, at the end of the counter, I found myself rigged out in old black-and-gray-striped formal trousers, too long, and a brownish sport coat, too tight. And to top off this ensemble, a dirty fedora. Only the clogs were new, but they were extremely rudimentary: a wooden sole with a simple cloth thong to grip the foot. Running in snow with such shoes was real torture, as I would soon learn.

Wearing these motley rags, haggard, ridiculous, ashamed, twisting that horrible felt hat in my hands, I wound up in front of a table where detainees filled out the identity cards of new arrivals.

At least, I assumed that they were detainees. They weren't SS, anyway. Or soldiers of the *Wehrmacht,* either. They were German civilians, but they wore an identification number and a red triangle sewn on the front of their jackets. So they did seem to be detainees, but—of what sort?

The man I chanced to appear before was about forty years old. Gray hair. Eyes, extraordinarily blue; extraordinarily sad, too. Or devoid, forevermore, of all curiosity. A gaze doubtless turned inward, I felt, upon utter hopelessness. Be that as it may, the man to whom chance had sent me asked for my last name, first name, the place and date of my birth, my nationality. My vital statistics, all things considered. Finally he asked me my profession.

"Philosophiestudent," I replied. "Philosophy student."

A light appeared in the gloomy depths of those extraordinarily blue, extraordinarily embittered blue eyes.

"No," he said, peremptorily. "That's not really a profession. *Das ist doch kein Beruf!"*

I couldn't help making a Germanist's pun for his benefit.

"Kein Beruf aber eine Berufung!"

I was quite pleased with my witticism.

A smile flickered across the stern face of the man filling out my identification card. He probably appreciated my little play on words. Which means that he appreciated my mastery of the German language. In French, my words would have fallen flat, a simple statement. Studying philosophy, I'd said, was not a profession, but a vocation. In German, the phonetic and semantic counterpoint between *Beruf* and *Berufung* was piquant and meaningful. I was satisfied with my impromptu jest.

The detainee with the blue glaze was solemn once more.

"Here," he said, "the study of philosophy is not a proper profession! Here you are better off being an electrician, a pipefitter, a mason . . . What I mean is, a skilled worker!"

He insisted on this last term, repeating *Facharbeiter* several times. He looked me straight in the eye.

"Here, to survive," he added, hammering out the words, "you'd better have that kind of profession!"

I was twenty, I was a second-year university student without much experience of life. I didn't understand at all what that man was trying to tell me.

"I'm a philosophy student, nothing else," I repeated stubbornly.

Then the guy with the blue eyes shrugged impotently—or impatiently. He waved me on and called for the next man in line while he finished filling out my identification card.

"That's why I smiled," I tell Lieutenant Rosenfeld. "Because of that memory."

I've just told him about that distant episode.

He has listened to me with obvious interest.

Then he murmurs, "It's a good beginning."

"Beginning of what?" I ask, surprised by his subdued tone.

He offers me a cigarette. I think I see a hint of concern in his eye, a slight tremor in his hand.

"Beginning of the experience," he says. "And of the account you could give of that experience!"

I'd had less success with the officer with the cross of Lorraine a few days earlier. He'd given me the poems of René Char (loaned, I should say; he'd strongly insisted that I give the book back to him when I returned to Paris), but he hadn't cared for the beginning of my story. It's true that I hadn't begun with this particular opening. I'd chosen to start my account with Sunday: the deep significance of Sundays in Buchenwald. I'd decided to introduce him to these hellish Sundays by heavenly means, with

the images of *Mazurka,* the Pola Negri film. But the French officer had been scandalized by the beginning of my tale. Or at
least astonished, and confused. Pola Negri? He hadn't expected
that at all. He hadn't been able, afterward, to let me take him
into the teeming depth of those Sundays, and all because of Pola
Negri.

What would Lieutenant Rosenfeld have thought of that
other beginning?

"There are all sorts of good beginnings," I tell him. "This one
is anecdotal. One ought to begin with the essential part of this
experience . . . "

"You already know what that is?"

I nod. I take a deep drag on my cigarette. I fill my mouth,
throat, lungs with that delicious, pungent, honeyed smoke. It's
infinitely better than the acrid taste of *makhorka,* the Russian tobacco. I shouldn't even compare the two. But I already know
that for the rest of my life I'll remember with nostalgia those
makhorka butts I smoked with my pals.

The essential part? I think I know, yes. I think I'm beginning
to understand. The essential thing is to go beyond the clear facts
of this horror to get at the root of radical Evil, *das radikal Böse.*

Because the horror itself was not this Evil—not its essence, at
least. The horror was only its raiment, its ornament, its cere-
monial display. Its semblance, in a word. One could have spent
hours testifying to the daily horror of the camp without touching upon the essence of this experience.

Even if one had given evidence with absolute precision, with
perfect objectivity (something by definition beyond the powers
of the individual witness), even in this case one could miss the
essential thing. Because it wasn't the accumulation of horror,
which could be spelled out, endlessly, in detail. One could recount the story of any day at all, from reveille at four-thirty
in the morning to curfew—the fatiguing labor, the constant

hunger, the chronic lack of sleep, the persecution by the *Kapos,* the latrine duty, the floggings from the SS, the assembly-line work in munitions factories, the crematory smoke, the public executions, the endless roll calls in the winter snow, the exhaustion, the death of friends—yet never manage to deal with the essential thing, or reveal the icy mystery of this experience, its dark, shining truth: *la ténèbre qui nous était échue en partage.* The darkness that had fallen to our lot, throughout all eternity. Or rather, throughout all history.

"What's essential," I tell Lieutenant Rosenfeld, "is the experience of Evil. Of course, you can experience that anywhere. . . . You don't need concentration camps to know Evil. But here, this experience will turn out to have been crucial, and massive, invading everywhere, devouring everything. . . . It's the experience of radical Evil."

Startled, he looks at me sharply.

Das radikal Böse! Obviously, he has caught the reference to Kant. Is Lieutenant Rosenfeld a philosophy student, too?

I tell the American lieutenant that I should have begun this account with the stench of Block 56, the invalid's hut. With the stifling and fraternal stink of Sundays spent with Halbwachs and Maspero.

"Evil is not what is inhuman, of course. . . . Or else it's what is inhuman in man. . . . The inhumanity of man, considered as vital possibility, as personal intention. . . . As freedom. . . . So it's ridiculous to oppose Evil, to distance oneself from it, through a simple reference to what is human, to mankind. . . . Evil is one of the possible designs of the freedom essential to the humanity of man—the freedom from which spring both the humanity and inhumanity of man."

I describe the faces of all of us who used to gather around ⎯⎯wachs and Maspero on Sunday.

⎯esides, the essential thing about this experience of Evil is that it will turn out to have been lived as the experience of death. . . . And I do mean 'experience.' . . . Because death is not something that we brushed up against, came close to, only just escaped, as though it were an accident we survived unscathed. We lived it. . . . We are not survivors, but ghosts, revenants. . . . One can only express this abstractly, of course. Or in passing, lightly, offhandedly. . . . Or while laughing with other ghosts. . . . Because it's not believable, it can't be shared, it's barely comprehensible—since death is, for rational thought, the only event that we can never experience individually. . . . That cannot be grasped except in the form of anguish, of foreboding or fatal longing. . . . In the future perfect tense, therefore. . . . And yet, we shall have lived the experience of death as a collective, and even fraternal experience, the foundation of our being-together. . . . Like a *Mit-sein-sum-Tode*—"

Lieutenant Rosenfeld interrupts me.

"Heidegger?" he exclaims. "You've read Martin Heidegger!"

The book was displayed in the window of a German bookstore on the Boulevard Saint-Michel.

In the winter of 1940–41, during the Occupation, when I was in my last year of lycée, the authorities opened a bookstore on the corner of the boulevard and the Place de la Sorbonne, where there had previously been a café called the D'Harcourt. This was the neighborhood where I spent all my time before and after my classes at the Lycée Henri-IV. I often passed this German bookstore, and sometimes I looked to see what books they had in the window, but it never even occurred to me to go inside. Until the day I noticed a copy of Heidegger's *Sein und Zeit*. That day, after long hesitation, I finally went into the shop to purchase the book.

It was because of Emmanuel Levinas. He was the one who had persuaded me to enter that German bookstore. Reading his essays had, at least. During that last year in school, I had discovered the work Levinas had lately published on Husserl and Heidegger in various philosophical journals, essays I had read, reread, and annotated. My curiosity aroused, I'd felt a completely new interest in phenomenology and the philosophy of being.

There were two *classes de philosophie* at Henri-IV. One of them was taught by Maublanc, a Marxist, and the other by Bertrand, a critical rationalist, whose model—whose methodological pattern, at least—was the teaching of Léon Brunschvicg. I was in Bertrand's class. My relations with him were ambiguous. I was his best pupil and the teacher's pet; he liked to hear about my reading and interests outside of class. I valued his good qualities as a teacher, the passion with which he helped his students discover philosophy as a historical process. In the realm of ideas, however, each day I moved farther away from him, from the immaterial barrenness—somewhat steeped in rationalist piety—of his view of the world: an ideal, motionless world, floating above the bloody melee of history.

Bertrand regretted our intellectual differences. He would have liked to see me shine in my philosophy studies, but with the gentle, subtle light of the rational and tempered wisdom that he taught. So when I won second prize in philosophy in the Concours Général, a competition between all the lycées at the baccalaureate level, Bertrand was torn between the joy of having had me as a pupil, of having prepared me so well for that intellectual contest, that fleeting triumph—and the chagrin of knowing that I had discussed the topic ("Intuition According to Husserl") in an objective fashion, without a radical critique of eidetic intentions. Actually, I might add, it was my reading of Emmanuel Levinas, rather than Bertrand's class, that had brought me this academic prize.

Paradoxically (at least at first glance), despite the fact that it was my interest in the real world that made me receptive to the ideas of Husserl and Heidegger I'd discovered through Levinas, this initial approach was completely unconcerned with the historical context of their work. I had no idea, therefore, that Husserl had been driven from the German teaching profession because he was a Jew. I was also unaware that in the editions published before the Nazis came into power, *Sein und Zeit* had been dedicated to Husserl and that this dedication had disappeared when Heidegger's revered teacher had fallen into disgrace, a victim of ethnic cleansing in the German university system. The copy I had bought in the bookstore on the Boulevard Saint-Michel bore no dedication. I could be neither astonished nor indignant at this, since I did not know that Husserl's name should have appeared there. I did not know that Heidegger had deliberately erased it, as one erases a bad memory from one's mind. As one erases a name from a tombstone, perhaps.

Lieutenant Rosenfeld was the first to tell me of Heidegger's connection with Nazism. *Mit-Sein-zum-Tode:* no sooner had I spoken those words (borrowed from Heidegger, but transformed, in their substance) than he began to speak of the philosopher's Nazi involvement.

In any event, my reading of Levinas had led me to overcome my doubts, one distant winter's day: I finally went inside that German bookstore. After more hesitation, I wound up buying the book. An extravagance. The price was ruinous to my modest finances. How many meals must I have sacrificed to possess Martin Heidegger's book?

And so I had spent long, austere evenings that winter, the winter of the 1940–41 school year, studying *Sein und Zeit*. Heidegger (along with Saint Augustine, actually) was the philosopher whose thinking I explored the most systematically, during those months. I will add, to be absolutely explicit, that it was not Emmanuel Levinas who led me to read Saint Augustine's *Con-*

fessions and *The City of God,* but Paul-Louis Landsberg. Above all, there was also my own desire to clarify, once and for all, my neighborly relations with God.

I had not been overly impressed with Heidegger's book. Of course there was a certain fascination—sometimes mixed with irritation—with the philosopher's language. With that abounding obscureness through which one had to hack one's way, cutting clearings, without ever reaching a definitive clarity. A never-ending labor of intellectual decipherment that becomes absorbing through its very incompletion. Were these partial results worth the trouble? Not necessarily. Sometimes, to be sure, I did have the impression of lightning discoveries. An impression soon dissipated, or obscured, or even belied by my progress in mastering the whole, in all its sumptuous emptiness. I had occasionally been driven to outrage or uncontrollable laughter by the unproductive density of the conceptual flow, the esoteric jargon, the purely linguistic hocus-pocus.

Moreover, is the philosophy of Heidegger conceivable in another language besides German? I mean, is the devious work of torsion and distortion performed upon the language by Martin Heidegger thinkable—conceivable—in any language besides German? What other language would bear, without collapsing into dusty shreds, such an instillation of unintelligibility, of tortured and torturing pseudo-etymologies, of purely rhetorical resonance and assonance? But did the German language really withstand all this? Didn't Heidegger deal the language a blow from which it will take a long time to recover, at least in the realm of philosophical inquiry?

Some would say that Heidegger anticipated that question, that he defused it, in a way, by declaring straight out that German (along with ancient Greek, which shuts us up!) is the only conceivable philosophical language. But this is simply a rather primitive—and rather arrogant—ruse that merely obliges us to rephrase the question: Can a philosophical thought be truly profound, truly universal (even when its possible application envisions an extreme singularity), if it can be articulated in only one language, if its essence eludes all translation, which it utterly frustrates in its original expression?

That's not the crux of the matter, however. The main thing is that I find the fundamental inquiry underlying Heidegger's enterprise quite simply unimportant. The question of why is there Being rather than nothing has always seemed meaningless to me. That is, not only bereft of meaning, but bereft as well of all possibility of producing any. Forgetting the question of Being is, in fact, the very condition necessary for the emergence of a consideration of the world, of the historicity of the being-in-the-world of man.

If one absolutely insists on beginning a philosophical meditation with this kind of obtusely radical investigation, then the only meaningful question would be something like this one: Why is man a being who—to exist, to know that he is in the world—feels the vital, compulsive need to ask himself the question of Non-Being, the question of his own finitude? And consequently, the question of transcendence?

"The birds?" asks Lieutenant Rosenfeld as he turns toward me, visibly astonished.

It's a few days later, by the Ilm River, on the outskirts of Weimar. We're walking toward the cottage Goethe used as a country retreat, in the summer months, to enjoy the twin delights of refreshing coolness and solitude.

Yes, the birds. Their murmuring and myriad company, in the foliage of the valley. Their songs, their trills, their warbles suddenly intoxicate me, pierce me to the heart. Their muffled presence, their brilliant invisibility, like a surge of life, a sudden after all those years of glacial silence.

It must be the birds. The abrupt and overwhelming joy of hearing them again has taken my breath away.

Lieutenant Rosenfeld nods, after listening to my explanations.

"What drove the birds away from the Ettersberg?" he asks.

"The smell from the crematory," I tell him. "The smell of burning flesh."

He looks around at the charming countryside along the banks of the Ilm. We can see the castle tower with its baroque pinnacle turret overlooking the fault in the terrain through which the river flows.

"Will they come back to stay?" he murmurs.

We continue our walk.

"Goethe wouldn't be a bad beginning, either," I remark, returning to the conversation we've pursued ever since the first day.

He looks at me with interest—and a flash of irony.

"I'm way ahead of you on that one!" he exclaims. "If Pola Negri confused your French officer, Goethe would have knocked him flat!"

"Not at all! Because I wouldn't have jumped right in with Goethe, just to bowl the guy over! Goethe and Eckermann on the Ettersberg, their refined, learned conversations on the very spot where the camp was built. . . . No, too easy! I'd have started with Léon Blum."

He stops, faces me in obvious surprise. "Blum was evacuated from Buchenwald on April third—I'm the one who interrogated the SS *Obersturmführer* in charge of his departure! He told me Blum was so crippled with rheumatism they had a hard time getting him into the car!"

The villas where the special prisoners were confined were empty on April 11, when the camp was liberated, and we did not know what had happened to the prominent figures of different nationalities who had been held hostage in the SS quarters.

"Where did they take Blum?" I ask.

"South. It seems the first place where they planned to stop was Ratisbonne. The Allied troops haven't found him yet."

"We learned Blum was here in 1944, in August. . . . He was recognized one day by some French and Belgian deportees who were making repairs in the SS villas, after the American bombing raids on the munitions factories of Buchenwald."

We continue walking toward Goethe's cottage.

"But I don't get it," says Lieutenant Rosenfeld, frowning. "Why begin with Blum if you want to talk about Goethe?"

I'm rather pleased at catching him out on this. Ever since I'd met Lieutenant Rosenfeld on April 19 (I can assure you that my frame of reference for this date is indisputable, just as I can be certain of the day the two of us walked in the Ilm Valley on the outskirts of Weimar, April 23, Saint George's Day: "I'm going to give you a present for your name day," Rosenfeld had told me that morning. "I'm taking you to Weimar!"), from that day on, he'd never ceased to amaze and occasionally annoy me with the breadth of his knowledge and culture. No, it doesn't displease me to find him at a loss for once. Because he doesn't seem to get the obvious connection between Blum and Goethe.

"Léon Blum," I tell him, as though this were a well-known fact, "wrote a book a long time ago called *Nouvelles conversations de Goethe avec Eckermann* [*New Conversations Between Goethe and Eckermann*]!"

This is news to him, really exciting news. I tell him a little more about it.

Perhaps the moment has come to talk about Lieutenant Rosenfeld. He stands before me, a few dozen yards from Goethe's summer house. Overjoyed at learning this detail about Blum's oeuvre. Perhaps I will take advantage of this moment to speak of

Walter Rosenfeld, whom I've never seen again, about whom I've never heard anything further, but whose brief appearance in my life was not without effect. Not without significance, no indeed. While I explain to him the subject of Blum's essay, what *Nouvelles conversations de Goethe avec Eckermann* is all about, I will have time to talk to you about Rosenfeld. Because I'm not going to limit myself to succinct bibliographical information about Blum's essay—I'm going to go on at some length. I know myself well enough to be certain that I'm going to talk to Rosenfeld about Lucien Herr, and the Dreyfus affair, and the house on the Boulevard de Port-Royal where Herr lived at the end of his life, where his family still lived when I knew them, in 1942. I'm going to talk about Mme. Lucien Herr—tall, fragile, indefatigable—and the library that opened onto the interior garden where I read *Nouvelles conversations.* The volume was inscribed to Herr by Léon Blum. Getting to the Ettersberg, to the quirk of fate that led Blum as a prisoner of the Gestapo to the very place where the conversations between Goethe and Eckermann occurred, among the oaks and beeches of the Ettersberg forest—that's going to take me some time: just long enough for me to introduce you to Lieutenant Rosenfeld.

At twenty-six, he was five years older than I. In spite of his American nationality and uniform, he was German. I mean that he was born in Germany, in a Jewish family from Berlin that had emigrated to the United States in 1933, when Walter was fourteen years old.

He had become an American to bear arms, to make war on Nazism. To make war on his own country, to put it bluntly. By becoming an American, he had chosen the universality of the democratic cause, an abstraction that could not become reality until his country had been defeated.

I'd listened to his story of this childhood, exile, and return under arms to his homeland, and I'd recalled his stern face and implacable voice when he addressed his compatriots from Weimar in the crematory yard. I also remembered Kaminski, in the Contagious Ward, on a blustery, snowy Sunday a few weeks earlier: he had lighted the lamp after the survivor of the Auschwitz *Sonderkommando* had finished speaking. "Don't forget," he'd said, in the same harsh, somber tone Rosenfeld had used. "Never forget! Germany! My country is the guilty one."

On the day we first met, April 19, the American lieutenant Walter Rosenfeld, a Jew from Berlin, had told me about his childhood, his exile, his return to his native land. Years later, an entire lifetime later, I evoked the memory of Lieutenant Rosenfeld for Axel Corti. He was not a Berliner, but a Viennese. He had written and shot a film trilogy, *Welcome to Vienna*, that told the story of such a homecoming. I evoked for Axel Corti the memory of Lieutenant Rosenfeld: his thin, gangling body, his sad and piercing gaze, his vast erudition. As I described him to Corti, during a discussion we had about collaborating on a film, in my mind's eye I saw the landscape of the Ilm Valley once again, and Goethe's half-timbered cottage at the foot of the hill, across the river, in the April sunshine. Axel Corti is one of the few people to whom I spoke about Lieutenant Rosenfeld, prompted, of course, by this common experience of exile and bitter return to one's native land.

In any case, it was because of Heidegger, because of the intrusion of Martin Heidegger into our conversation, that Lieutenant Rosenfeld had talked to me on that first day about his childhood in Berlin. He had a lot to tell me about the political views and activities of the philosopher of Todtnauberg. Walter Rosenfeld had become familiar with the intellectual milieu of German and Austrian exiles in the United States through his family, first of all, and through his university studies later on. It was because of these people and the many contacts they had maintained with Germany, in spite of the war and censorship, that he was so well informed about Heidegger's pro-Nazi attitude from 1933 until the time of our meeting in April 1945.

During later conversations, Rosenfeld spoke to me about these exiles. He talked about the *Institut für Sozialforschung,* about Adorno, Horkheimer, and Marcuse. He spoke of Hannah Arendt—one of Heidegger's former pupils, by the way—in the most glowing terms. He talked about Bertolt Brecht. And about still others, who had lived and worked in the United States.

Among all those names opening up new horizons for me, arousing my curiosity and appetite for learning, the only ones I recognized were those of Brecht and Broch. As it happened, I had discovered Hermann Broch's *The Sleepwalkers,* as well as Musil's *The Man Without Qualities,* in the library of Édouard-Auguste Frick in Paris, on the Rue Blaise-Desgoffe. Frick was an erudite Genevan, wealthy and generous, a friend to the Esprit movement, who had once offered my brother Alvaro and me the hospitality of his home for several months. He possessed an outstanding library, comprised in large part of German books. I'd devoured them by the dozen.

As for Bertolt Brecht, I discovered him not on the Rue Blaise-Desgoffe, but on the Rue Visconti. In the home of a young woman, a Viennese, who had been my contact, at a certain period during the Occupation, on behalf of the Main d'Oeuvre Immigrée, the underground Communist organization for foreign militants.

> *O Deutschland, bleiche Mutter!*
> *Wie sitzest Du besudelt*
> *Unter den Völkern . . .*

Night had fallen on the Rue Visconti that spring evening in 1943. Curfew had taken us by surprise, making it impossible to
the apartment and risk running into a police checkpoint—

French or German, it would have made no difference. Julia was angry with herself over this violation of the most elementary rules of security, but it was too late to have me leave. It wasn't the future of the world or the fine points of Lukács's legendary *Geschichte und Klassenbewusstsein* [*History and Class Consciousness*] that had made us forget the passage of time. It was literature.

We both had that passion foreigners can experience for the French language when it becomes a spiritual conquest. A passion for its iridescent concision, for its searching clarity. From Jean Giraudoux to Heinrich Heine, one thing led to another, and we had wound up reciting poems to each other. Which is how we lost track of the time and were ensnared by curfew.

Julia had recited some poetry by Brecht for me in that apartment on the Rue Visconti in 1943. She'd talked about the writer for a long time. The next day, when the curfew was lifted, she'd stood on her doorstep and reached out toward my face with anxious affection. "Don't die!" she'd whispered to me.

I'd laughed, a trifle offended that she could have thought I was mortal, or even vulnerable. I could not have imagined what darkness would soon fall to my lot.

So in April 1945, when Lieutenant Rosenfeld talked to me about German writers in exile in the United States, I already knew of Hermann Broch and Bertolt Brecht. Thanks to the library of a rich and cloquent Genevan named Édouard-Auguste Frick and the literary passions of a Viennese who had assumed the name of Julia and who had worked ever since her earliest years within the apparatus of the Comintern.

O Deutschland, bleiche Mutter!

Lieutenant Rosenfeld is now murmuring the end of the poem that opens with this invocation. We're sitting on the soft grass in front of Goethe's rustic cottage, in the meadow that slopes gently down to the waters of the Ilm. And I have just told him the story of my discovery of Brecht's poetry two years before.

> *O Germany, pallid mother!*
> *How have your sons mistreated you*
> *that you sit among other peoples*
> *a scarecrow or a laughingstock!*

The lieutenant recites the end of the poem, his eyes half-closed. A sunbeam catches, incandescent, on the barrel of the automatic pistol lying by his side. *pg/04*

We had not been able to go inside Goethe's country house. The door had been double-locked, padlocked. No one had seemed to know who was in charge, who had the keys. We'd had to settle for taking a stroll around the cottage, but Rosenfeld had told me all about the place. So much, at least, that I could only remember part of it. I must say that he was an omniscient guide, meticulous and full of verve. I'd learned that the cottage was a gift from Duke Karl August in 1776 and that Goethe had stayed there regularly thereafter. The last trace of his passage at the *Gartenhaus* dated from February 20, 1832, Rosenfeld had informed me, with an assurance that seemed somewhat unreal. Even irritating.

That morning, when I'd stepped outside the massive iron gates of Buchenwald to go to my daily meeting with the lieutenant, the American soldier on nonchalant guard duty had called out to me.

"Hey, you—I know you!"

Without even glancing at the pass Rosenfeld had arranged to get me, the sentry pretended to raise a pair of binoculars to his eyes.

"I watched you the other day. . . . You were shouting the top of your head off, all alone out there on the parade ground. . . . What was that?"

"Some poetry," I replied.

His jaw dropped. "Poetry? Well, shit!"

But he hadn't said "shit." In his surprise, he'd sworn in Spanish, saying *"coño."*

"Poetry? *Coño!*" he'd exclaimed.

Then we'd exchanged a few words in Spanish, and I'd decided that I rather liked this American army. Their behavior as well as their uniforms seemed more casual, more relaxed, than in other armies with which I'd had any experience—less military, in a word. And this impression was confirmed by the diversity in background and culture of these citizen-soldiers. The lieutenant with whom I'd been talking for the last four days about life and death in Buchenwald was a German Jew. The noncoms and soldiers who'd come to play jazz with us (I mean, with the secret group organized by Jiri Zak, my Czech Communist pal) were black. And many soldiers from New Mexico spoke a melodious Spanish I found enchanting. And disturbing. That the language of my childhood was not just the language of exile and anguished memory, but also the language of freedom, both thrilled and upset me.

A few days earlier, when Lieutenant Rosenfeld was addressing the German civilians of Weimar in the crematory yard, I'd noticed a very young American soldier. His eyes, wide with horror, were riveted on the corpses piled by the entrance to the building housing the ovens. A heap of fleshless, yellowed, twisted bodies, with jutting bones beneath the dry, taut skin, and staring eyes. I'd seen the appalled, revolted look on the face of the young American soldier, whose lips had begun to quiver. Suddenly, from a few steps away, I'd heard him murmuring. In a low but distinct voice, in Spanish, he had begun to pray. *Padre nuestro que estás en los cielos* . . . I'd been thunderstruck to hear him. Not to hear a prayer—I'd long since denied myself that sad consolation, that desolate refuge. I'd been staggered to realize that my native tongue, sounding suddenly at my side, was the language expressing the somber truth of that moment.

"Poetry? *Coño!*" the other American soldier from New Mexico had exclaimed that morning.

We'd chatted a bit in Spanish. He knew some poetry, too, he'd told me. Which he proceeded to prove, moreover, by reciting with truly Castilian grandiloquence, in spite of his Mexican accent, a poem by Rubén Darío that he concluded by sweeping his arms toward the imaginary horizon of an oceanic shore, along which lumbered troops of elephants in battle harness, marching on parade.

> . . . *y el Rey mandó desfilar*
> *cuatrocientos elefantes por las orillas del mar* . . .

So, as I was saying, Lieutenant Rosenfeld had greeted me that morning by reminding me that it was April 23, the Feast of Saint George. As a present, he'd offered me a trip to Weimar.

The streets of the small city were almost empty when we arrived. I'd been amazed at how close it was: only a few kilometers separated Buchenwald from the first houses of Weimar. Of course, the city wasn't visible from the camp, which had been built on the opposite side of the Ettersberg, overlooking a verdant plain dotted with peaceful villages. But Weimar was very near, and practically deserted in the April sunshine when we arrived. Lieutenant Rosenfeld drove the jeep slowly through the streets and squares. We saw that the entire north side of the marketplace in the center of town had been damaged by Allied bombs. Then Rosenfeld parked the jeep on the *Frauenplan,* in front of Goethe's town house.

The old man who finally opened the door to us was not at all friendly. At first he wanted to deny us admission. Under the circumstances, he told us, we had to have special permission from the authorities. Lieutenant Rosenfeld informed him that actually, under the circumstances, it was he, Lieutenant Rosenfeld, who represented the authorities—indeed, Authority itself, with a capital *A,* in its extreme singularity: all the authority imaginable. This fact clearly vexed the old German, the zealous guardian of Goethe's museum-home, but he could not prevent Lieutenant Rosenfeld from entering this shrine of Germanic culture. So Lieutenant Rosenfeld entered it, with me on his heels. While the old man closed the front door (I'd had time to decipher the Latin inscription above it stating that the house had been built in 1709, for the glory of God and the embellishment of the town, by one Georg Caspar Helmershausen), he shot a glance of pure hatred at Lieutenant Rosenfeld, who was already going off to explore the house, and at the automatic pistol hanging from his shoulder. Then that black, mistrustful eye, brimming with desperate anger, had looked me up and down. Rather, it was my outfit he looked at. I must say it was somewhat unusual, and not very respectable. He had doubtless figured out where I'd come from, which wasn't likely to reassure him.

In reality, we didn't need a guide to visit the house on the *Frauenplan.* Rosenfeld talked about it quite knowledgeably, providing a wealth of pertinent information. The old guardian had followed us anyway. Sometimes we heard him muttering behind us. He was itching to make us understand how much we were intruders, unworthy of profaning such a place. He reeled off the names of the writers and artists from all over Europe whom he had personally ushered through the rooms of this noble house in recent years. Lieutenant Rosenfeld ignored this mumbling, however, continuing to tell me all he knew—and he knew a lot—about Goethe's long life in Weimar. Finally, probably frustrated at not having provoked a reaction, the old Nazi spoke more loudly, describing—to our backs—Hitler's last visit, when he stayed at the Elephant Hotel in Weimar. The voice swelled with admiration in praise of that remarkable man, the Führer. Suddenly unable to stand any more of this, Lieutenant Rosenfeld turned around, grabbed the old man by the collar, dragged him over to a cupboard, and thrust him inside, locking the doors. We were able to complete our visit in peace, out of range of his despairing and malevolent voice.

> *O Deutschland, bleiche Mutter!*
> *Wie haben deine Söhne dich zugerichtet*
> *Dass du unter den Völkern sitzest*
> *Ein Gespött oder eine Furcht!*

Lieutenant Rosenfeld has just murmured the last lines of Brecht's poem. We are sitting on the lawn sloping gently down to the bank of the Ilm. The sun glints on the steel of his automatic pistol, on this Saint George's Day.

Two years have passed since Julia helped me to discover the poetry of Bertolt Brecht. Only two years. Yet I feel as though it has been an eternity since that springtime, that spring night on the Rue Visconti. I realize something, and I smile. An incongruous but serene realization. An eternity, of course: that of death. Two years of mortal eternity separate me from the person I was on the Rue Visconti: the person, that other one, who listened to Julia recite poems by Bertolt Brecht. At dawn, she'd stroked my face with a light, caressing hand. "Don't die," she'd whispered in farewell. I'd started, laughing with astonished pride. Wasn't I immortal, or at least invulnerable?

Two years of frozen eternity, of intolerable death, separate me from myself. Would I ever return to myself, one day? To the innocence—whatever my daily cares—of being transparently present to myself? Would I forever be that other person who had passed through death? Who had fed on it? Who had come apart, evaporated, and been lost in it?

"Time to go back," Lieutenant Rosenfeld has just said, after looking at his watch. He's right, it's time to go back. I look at the April sunshine on the lawn sloping down to the Ilm. I look at Goethe's rustic cottage. I hear the rustling murmur of the birds around me. Renewed life, all in all. An inexplicable feeling comes over me, however: I'm happy to "go back," as Rosenfeld has just said. I want to go back to Buchenwald, to be among my own people, my comrades, the ghosts who have returned after a long, deadly absence.

"Let's go," I reply, standing on the green grass that grows along the Ilm.

5

LOUIS ARMSTRONG'S TRUMPET

"On the Sunny Side of the Street": what a pleasure!

It was Louis Armstrong on trumpet—I could tell even though I was light-headed with exhilaration.

I laughed, delighted.

It was in Eisenach, toward the end of April. In a hotel in Eisenach used by the Allied general staffs as a repatriation center for the prisoners and deportees of the region.

I held the young woman in my arms even more tightly. We'd been up all night, and for the last few minutes we'd been dancing almost without moving. I looked at her: her eyes were wide open. I'd thought it a good omen that she had those blue eyes, the kind that had always had such an effect on me at the parties of my adolescence, two years before.

A century before, rather—it made me laugh. Stupidly, I imagine.

But suddenly she became restless, upset.

"Don't look at me like that," she whispered.

I wasn't looking at her like that. I was just looking at her. The way one looks at a woman, after so many months. With surprise, no doubt, And curiosity, too. So I was looking at her, that's all. But perhaps it was the simplicity of this look, its frankness, that was improper. That was troubling her, precisely.

In any case, her voice wavered, husky with emotion.

"I'd like to be the first woman in your life!" she murmured.

This was going too far, as I remarked to her.

"In my life? Too late! The first one after my death: you can't do better than that!"

The brassy voice of Louis Armstrong opened avenues of infinite desire, of violent, acid nostalgia. The young woman, no longer dancing, now trembled all over. As though seized with a panic longing for the strange past from which I had only just arrived, for the desert revealed, in spite of all my efforts, deep within my eyes.

As though she were attracted by that very panic itself.

In the following weeks, months, that spring, during the summer of my return (strange, hypocritical word; ambiguous, to say the least), I had a chance to confirm the enduring effect of this gaze.

Mine, I mean.

It was no longer so starkly transparent, as it had been two weeks earlier for the three officers in British uniform. For that young woman in Eisenach as well, who went by the name of Martine and belonged to a noncombatant service of the French Army. And my hair was growing back, too. I was dressed like anyone else, like any other twenty-year-old guy, in Paris, in the lovely summer weather. Poorly dressed, of course, like so many others my age at that time of postwar scarcity.

At first glance, there was nothing to indicate where I'd spent the last few years. As for me, I fell silent on that point at once, and for a long while. My silence was neither affected, nor guilty, nor fearful. A silence of survival, rather. Silence humming with an appetite for life. So I didn't become as quiet as the tomb. I kept quiet because I was dazzled by the beauty and riches of the world, eager to live there by erasing all trace of an indelible agony.

But I couldn't manage to quiet my gaze, obviously.

In trains, buses, bistros, at parties, it had an effect on women. I'd turn my head, curious about a face I'd glimpsed, the curve of a hip or shoulder, an intelligent laugh. I'd stare into unknown eyes that would darken, grow disconcerted, glinting with an abrupt, uneasy, perhaps even anxious—but imperious—force: the rough diamond of attraction.

Anyway, the hardest part was over, often through carelessness or inadvertence. The lark was dazzled by a mirror, by what she thought was her own reflection, beautified by the other's interest. Yet there was nothing to see in the mirror, nothing to decipher—but how? through what clever approach?—except the unsilvered surface of a wretched past.

Thus the crazed, ravaged gaze that had so disturbed the three officers of the Allied mission to Buchenwald on April 12, 1945, at the entrance to the administration building of the SS *Totenkopf* Division housing the records they wished to consult— this gaze would lead me to the beauty, the affection, the ardor and languor of women, who made my soul livable once more. At least for a while, now and then. Long enough to store away the memory of a few tiny, wrenching delights.

Having discovered this power, I used it without scruple.

Without scruple, most certainly, but not without some apprehension. Because each of these encounters, each of these adventures, pleasant though they were, revived the pain of memory for me. Each one of them reminded me of what I wanted to forget: death, whose shining darkness was at the source of these pleasures.

All through that summer of my return, through autumn, up to the sunny winter's day in Ascona, in Ticino, when I decided to abandon the book I was trying to write, the two things I had thought would bind me to life—writing, pleasure—were instead what estranged me from it, day after day, constantly returning me to the memory of death, forcing me back into the suffocation of that memory.

After that long absence, I found Louis Armstrong, the coppery sheen of his voice, of his trumpet, and a woman in my arms: everything seemed easy, at the end of that night of revelry, in Eisenach, in the requisitioned deluxe hotel of antiquated charm that reminded me of the seaside resorts once frequented by Valéry Larbaud's A. O. Barnabooth.

I let myself drift along, floating in the frothy dream of the dance, clinging tightly to my partner. A sumptuous dream: desire was in the air. I'd been right not to worry too much about my scrawny, somewhat skeletal body. Blood still flowed through its veins—nothing to worry about. The future was probably full of women with their eyes closed (Martine D. had just closed hers) and their long legs entwined with mine.

Nothing to fear, really.

It did my soul good, that carnal pleasure. My body astounded me, I must admit. At the age of eighteen, I didn't know my own body, so to speak. Rather, I wasn't aware of it or its constraints. I neglected it, at least, or perhaps I didn't value it highly enough. My body had ignored me, too. It wasn't anything objective, anything alive for itself. My body had no *en-soi,* no being-in-itself, with its own demands, joyful or forlorn, requiring my attention. Or a decision on my part, anyway.

My body was only the immediate extension of my wishes, my desires—even my whims. It was nothing other than myself. It obeyed me implicitly, yet without being in any way a separate thing. I would have unhesitatingly concluded the traditional philosophy class essay on the relation between the mind and the body by affirming that they were one and the same. My body was of one substance with me, as were my childhood memories. I was in my body like a fish in water: in my element. I was in it with all my soul, to put it bluntly.

I had rediscovered my body, its reality *pour-soi,* for itself, its opacity, as well as its autonomy in rebellion, at the age of nineteen, in a house in Auxerre used by the Gestapo for interrogations.

Suddenly my body became problematical, detaching itself from me and living through that separation, for itself, against me, in the agony of pain. On the orders of Haas, the local Gestapo chief, I was hung up by my arms, with my wrists handcuffed behind my back. His thugs shoved my head underwater in a bathtub deliberately fouled with garbage and excrement.

My body was suffocating, going crazy, begging shamefully for mercy. My body asserted itself in a visceral revolt intended to deny me as a moral, intelligent being. It asked—demanded—that I give in to torture. To win this contest with my body, I had to subdue it, master it, abandon it to the suffering of pain and humiliation. But it was a victory that had to be won over and over again, minute by minute, and a victory that mutilated me by making me hate an essential part of myself that I had experienced until then in carefree, physical happiness. And yet, each day of silence before the Gestapo—although it alienated me from my body, that panting carcass—brought me closer to myself. To the surprising steadfastness of my self: a disturbing, almost indecent pride at being a man in this inhuman way.

Later, at Buchenwald, my body continued to exist on its own (or disowned), haunted by exhausting hunger and lack of sleep. I was forced to drive my body hard, to treat it with contempt, when necessary.

One day, a few weeks after I arrived in the camp, I'd come down with a high fever from a bout of furunculosis. Instinctively, I'd avoided the *Revier,* the infirmary, the medical attention I might have sought. Patients usually left the infirmary through the crematory chimney: I knew that already from listening to the veterans of Buchenwald. So I'd had the boils that were invading my armpit lanced by a French pal, a doctor in the *Revier,* and I'd continued working at my job. Everything had gone back to normal.

Sometimes I'd wondered, however, if my body would be marked forever by the torments of hunger, sleep deprivation, and chronic exhaustion.

But no, not at all.

That night, at Eisenach, my body astonished me. A few days of freedom, of more substantial nourishment, of sleeping whenever I wanted, had put new life into it, as well as an arrogance that made it forget all about recent panicky fears. A real dinner served at a real table, a few glasses of Moselle wine, and there my body was: tipsy, all right, but feeling sprightly and in top form. Enough to make one laugh with joy.

So then I leaned closer to the young woman in the becoming blue uniform and whispered in her ear.

J'ai pesé de tout mon désir
sur ta beauté matinale . . .
[I weighed with all my desire
upon your early-morning beauty . . .]

Fireworks went off in her eyes.

"Well, aren't you poetic!"

It wasn't I who was poetic, of course. Only vicariously, in any case. But Martine knew nothing of René Char. I couldn't hold that against her, as I hadn't known a thing about him, either, until just a few days before. Until April 12, to be exact.

Martine D. was not the first woman of my life, however. Not even the first one after my death. That one, the first woman after the snow and death and hunger and smoke, was named Odile. And I didn't dance with her in Eisenach, in the fancy hotel requisitioned by the Americans. It was at the Petit Schubert, Boulevard du Montparnasse, that I would dance with Odile for the first time, a few days after my return. After my white night at Eisenach.

There was Armstrong's trumpet, again—all the trumpets of paradise. There was the late night, the alcohol, the crazy confidence of a life begun anew. There was Odile M., the cousin of a friend from my adolescence. After dinner—some conversation, some laughter, a confused discussion about Albert Camus in the home of people I didn't know, on the Avenue de Saxe— a gang of us had wound up after midnight at the Petit Schubert.

Odile danced only with me. I held her in my arms, time passed, love at dawn seemed a likely possibility.

Then I murmured the words of René Char in the young woman's ear. Just because it hadn't worked in Eisenach didn't mean I was going to pass up this rhetorical resource, this poetic gambit with the indecent and delicious language of intimacy.

*J'ai pesé de tout mon désir
sur ta beauté matinale . . .*

Odile stopped dancing, looked at me, and we left the Petit Schubert.

A few days later, on May 8, 1945, I crossed the courtyard of the Hospice du Kremlin-Bicêtre in radiant sunshine.

It was the day of the victory over the Nazi armies, as you probably remember. And even if you don't, you may have learned this date by heart. Remembering and memorizing dates—it's not the same thing. French schoolchildren don't remember the battle of Marignan, either, yet it's a date they learn by heart.

As for me, I really remember May 8, 1945. It's not a simple date from a school textbook. I remember the dazzling sky, the blondness of the girls, the enthusiasm of the crowds. I remember the anguish of the grieving clusters of families at the entrance of the Hôtel Lutétia, waiting for relatives who had not yet returned from the camps. I remember a woman with graying hair, her face still smooth and youthful, who got on the metro at the Raspail station. I remember that a shifting movement among the passengers pushed her closer to me. I remember that she suddenly noticed my clothes, my short hair, that she looked into my eyes. I remember that her lips began to tremble, and her eyes filled with tears. I remember that we stayed face-to-face for a long time, without a word, close to one another in an unimaginable proximity. I remember that I will remember that woman's face my whole life long. I will remember her beauty, her compassion, her sorrow, the nearness of her soul.

And I also remember having crossed the courtyard of the Hospice du Kremlin-Bicêtre beneath a bright sky, amid the ringing of bells proclaiming victory.

I was to meet Odile M. again that day, in the austere room used by the intern on duty at the hospital. She'd asked me to come at lunchtime, when she'd have her break. "An hour or two—it'll depend on the emergencies that come in. I'd rather see you than go eat in that disgusting cafeteria," she'd said. "Besides," she'd added with a giggle, "she who sleeps forgets her hunger, if you get what sleeping means!"

When Odile began to undress, amid the muffled hubbub of bells, horns, and rejoicing that reached us from outside, in that spare little room of the Hospice du Kremlin-Bicêtre (she hadn't known the etymology of the second part of this compound name, but she wasn't even grateful to me for explaining it to her—she couldn't have cared less), she accidentally knocked over the German officer's leather satchel I'd brought back from

Buchenwald. At the time, I carried everything I owned around in it.

Odile knelt to gather up my scattered things. That was when I saw her pick up the volume of René Char, *Seuls demeurent*.

I remembered that I'd promised the French officer to give this book back to him as soon as I returned to Paris. He'd given me an address, Rue de Varenne. Actually, he hadn't spoken of my return, but of my repatriation.

I thought about all that could be said regarding these two words: return, repatriation. The second one made no sense when applied to me, of course. First of all, I hadn't returned to my homeland, in coming back to France. And then, if you thought about it, it was clear that I would never again be able to return to any homeland. I had no native country anymore. I would never have one again. Or else I'd have several, which would amount to the same thing. Can you die—think about it—for several countries at once? It's unthinkable. Yet dying for your country is the best ontological proof of its existence. The only one, perhaps. So all these possible deaths would cancel themselves out. When the need arises, you die only once and for one country only. You mustn't fool around here: no pluralism when it comes to your homeland, which is one and indivisible, unique.

As for me, I'd never thought about dying for my country. The idea of the homeland had never crossed my mind. (This verb is probably too lightweight to use in talking about such an idea, however; if it exists, that idea, I don't think it crosses your mind: instead it must strike you, bowl you over, crush you, I suppose.) So this idea had never entered my mind whenever I had occasion—rather frequently, those past few years—to think about my chances of dying. About risking my life, in other words. It was never a "homeland" that was at stake.

So: no repatriation.

But the word "return" wouldn't have been completely appropriate, either, in spite of its apparent neutrality. One could certainly say, in a purely descriptive way, that I had returned to my point of departure. This point was a casual, incidental thing, however: I had not returned home. I could have been arrested anywhere, and returned anywhere. Which brings us immediately back to our previous discussion of repatriation, of its improbability. I'll go even further: had I really returned somewhere, here or elsewhere, home or anyplace at all? Sometimes I felt certain that there hadn't really been any return, that I hadn't really come back, that an essential part of me would never come back, and this certainty upset my connection with the world, with my own life.

A few hours later, on the Rue de Varenne, when the door finally opened, it had taken so long for someone to answer the bell that I was on the verge of leaving.

A young woman appeared in the doorway just as I was about to turn away in discouragement.

I was holding the book I intended to return to its owner. The French officer had told me it was very precious to him because it had been a gift from a woman. Was this she? In any case, I thought of a poem by Char.

> *Beauté, je me porte à ta rencontre dans la solitude du froid. Ta*
> *lampe est rose, le vent brille. Le seuil du soir se creuse . . .*
> [Beauty, I go to meet you through wintry loneliness.
>   Your lamp is pink, the wind glistens. The threshold of
>   evening deepens . . .]

I recited these words to myself in silence when I saw Laurence appear in the doorway on the Rue de Varennes. A young unknown woman, rather, whose first name would turn out to be that one. Who was still nameless but not unnamable. I thought of all sorts of given names (in several languages) with which to address her, to encompass that vision. In the end, the one I murmured to myself was the most universal name, the one containing all the rest: *Beauté* . . .

But she started at the sight of me, raising her right hand before her face to hide her eyes. To hide me from her eyes, rather.

"So it's you . . ."

She said these words in a low and plaintive voice. I couldn't quite tell if they were a question or a statement of despair.

"Marc died the day before yesterday," she added.

And she tore the volume of René Char from my hands, clasping it to her heart.

Later, night had fallen, lamps were lighted: everything had been said. Marc was the name of the officer at Buchenwald; he'd never told me. He'd been mortally wounded during some of the last fighting of the war, three days before the German surrender. The day after our meeting at the entrance to the *Totenkopf* barracks, however, he had written a long letter to Laurence, in which he spoke of our encounter, our conversations. The young woman read it to me at one point, in a rare moment of openness. For she'd been mostly aloof, almost hostile, sometimes angry. And then suddenly, melting, she'd seek refuge in my arms, overcome.

Offering herself, in fact, letting go, but pulling herself together almost immediately.

Now, after a long silence and bitter tears, with a supple movement of her entire body, graceful despite her feverish haste, Laurence stood up. She walked to the far end of the room.

I'd closed my eyes: there was something dazzling about her beauty.

Yet it wasn't desire that made me tremble. My mouth wasn't dry, no warmth was rising from my groin toward a pounding heart. Desire wasn't improbable, of course, but it lay in the future. Something piercing and tender, later on. For the moment,

I was shaken with astonishment: that so much loveliness should be possible.

Beauté, je me porte à ta rencontre . . .

At that instant, I heard the first bars of the record Laurence had placed on the record player. Then, the voice of Louis Armstrong: "In the shade of the old apple tree . . ." For a fraction of a second, a fragment of eternity, I felt as though I'd really returned. Really come back. Home.

But I've gotten ahead of myself.

I'm still with Martine D., in Eisenach, under the chandeliers of a luxury hotel with old-fashioned charm. I've just recited two verses of *Seuls demeurent* to Martine, who has just announced that she finds me poetic, but that's as far as it will go. A tall guy has suddenly popped up next to us. A French officer in battle dress, a black beret on his buzz cut.

"Evening, old boy!" says the officer, taking Martine's arm and drawing her toward him.

He looks as though he owns her.

I understand that there's nothing left for me but to go find my pals from Buchenwald, who are leaving for Paris with me on the convoy of the repatriation mission.

"Evening, young man," I reply, quite dignified.

Stewed to the gills, I realize that. Quite dignified, nevertheless.

The officer's left eyebrow shoots up—that's his only reaction.

"You're from the camp?" he asks.

"As you can see. . . ."

It must be obvious, actually. I'm wearing Russian boots, trousers of coarse cloth with my identification number—44904—sewn on the left leg. I have on a kind of gray sweater with KL BU painted in green on the back. Hard not to see that I've just come from Buchenwald, no question.

"It was rough, huh?" asks the officer in the commando beret, looking suitably grave.

"Not at all," I reply. "It was a health spa, that camp!"

That's what the veteran inmates of Buchenwald would throw in our faces when they compared their terrible years—from 1937 to 1942, more or less—to the ones we'd known.

But the officer wearing the beribboned black beret knows nothing of this coded language. Taken aback, he looks at me, probably thinking that I'm drunk or have fallen on my head. In any event, he shrugs and is gone.

Taking Martine with him, naturally.

Is it dismay at her departure? Or the lucid distress that ordinarily follows sleepless nights? I'm suddenly unhappy, standing motionless amid the French and American soldiers dancing with girls of all kinds, watched by the restless, wild-eyed camp survivors, by the stuffy German headwaiters. Unhappy with the answer I've given him, which could be amusing only to me. Unhappy that he left before I could really answer his question. Which was a stupid one, I have to say. Stupidly put, at least. "It was rough, huh?" was a question that went nowhere, that even precluded any further questioning, through an answer that was inevitable, affirmative, but led to nothing. Yes, it was rough: what of it?

I should have expected it, I should have been prepared to answer such a badly framed question. For two weeks, whenever I'd had to deal with people from the outside, I'd heard only the wrong questions. But in order to ask the right ones, perhaps you had to know the answers already.

hy did you drop her, that girl, when you seemed to be getting along?" Yves Darriet asks me a little later.

I'd just rejoined my pals in a corner of the room. We were going to continue getting politely plastered until the departure of the convoy, scheduled for early that morning.

"I don't know," I say. "There was this big jerk of an officer, with a beret full of ribbons, who came and got her. She seemed to be his."

She wouldn't be mine, in any case.

A few days earlier, I'd heard women's voices, close by. I was on the deserted roll-call square at the time. I'd just returned my books to Anton, the librarian. I was contemplating the portrait of Stalin. The Russian accordion was playing a fiery *gopak*.

There were these women's voices, laughter—a real aviary. I turned around.

The young women of La Mission France had tightly fitting blue uniforms. They wanted to visit the camp; they'd been told it was fascinating. They asked me to come with them.

I noticed one woman's blue eyes. I looked into those eyes. Martine D. lifted her hand, as though to protect herself. Then she let it fall. Her gaze held steady in mine. We were alone in the world, for an instant, face-to-face. Alone on the square of Buchenwald, among the age-old beeches. There was sunshine, wind in the trees, and we were alone. For a few long seconds, anyway.

Then another young woman exclaimed, "But it doesn't seem so bad!"

She was looking at the bright green barracks on the edge of the square. She looked at the flower bed in front of the canteen building. Then she looked across the square and saw the squat chimney of the crematory.

"Is that the kitchen?" she asked.

For a fraction of a second, I wished I were dead. If I had been dead, I wouldn't have been able to hear that question. I was suddenly horrified at myself for being able to listen to that question. For being alive, in short. An understandable reaction, even if it was absurd. Excessive, at least. Since this question about the kitchen infuriated me precisely because I wasn't really alive. If I hadn't been a small fragment of the collective memory of our death, this question wouldn't have left me so angry. Fundamentally, I was nothing other than a conscious residue of all that death. An individual patch in the impalpable material of that shroud. A dust mote in the ashy cloud of that agony. A still-flickering light from the extinguished star of our dead years.

And doubtless I knew, with the most ancient, visceral knowledge, that I would begin to live again, taking up the thread of a life once more within my grasp. I even felt a desire, a violent longing for that future: the music, the sunshine, the books, the "white" nights, the women, the solitude. I knew that it was necessary and right to live again, to return to life, that nothing would prevent me from doing so. But this avid, impatient knowledge, this wisdom of the body, did not obscure the fundamental certainty of my experience. Of my bonds with the memory of death: bonds that would last forever.

"Come," I told the young women of La Mission France. "I'll show you."

I took them to the crematory that one of them had taken for a kitchen.

Show them? Perhaps the only possible way to make people understand is, indeed, to show them. The young women in blue uniforms, in any case, have seen. I don't know if they understood, but as far as seeing goes, they saw.

I let them in through the small door that led to the crematory cellar. Abruptly, they became quiet: it had dawned on them that this building was not a kitchen. I pointed out the hooks where deportees were suspended, for the crematory cellar also served as a torture chamber. I showed them the clubs and blackjacks. I showed them the elevator that hoisted the corpses up to the ground floor, directly in front of the row of ovens. They had nothing more to say. No more laughter, no more conversation, no more aviary twittering. Silence. Deep and heavy enough to betray their presence behind me. They followed me, like a mass of abruptly anguished silence. I could feel the weight of it at my back.

I showed them the row of ovens, the half-charred corpses they still contained. I barely spoke to them. I simply told them the names of things, without comment. They had to see, to try to imagine. Then I led them out of the crematory, into the interior courtyard surrounded by a high fence. There, I didn't say anything more, not one thing. I let them look. In the middle of the courtyard, there was a pile of corpses a good nine feet high. A heap of yellowed, twisted skeletons with terror-stricken faces. We could hear the Russian accordion on the other side of the fence, still playing the frenzied *gopak,* its cheery strains swirling about that mound of cadavers: the dance of the last day's dead, left there by the fleeing SS, who had let the crematory go out.

I thought about the huts of the Little Camp, where the elderly, the sick, the Jews were still dying. The end of the camps, for them, was not the end of death. It wasn't the end of the class struggle, either, as Anton the librarian had just reminded me. I reflected, as I looked at those wasted bodies with their protruding bones and sunken chests, heaped up nine feet high in the center of the crematory courtyard, that I was looking at my comrades. I decided that one had to have experienced their death, as we had done, we who had survived their death (but who did not yet know if we had survived our own), to look upon them with a pure and fraternal eye.

I heard the joyful rhythm of the *gopak* in the distance and told myself that these young women had no business here. It was ridiculous to try to explain things to them. Later on, in a month, in fifteen years, in another life, doubtless I'd be able to explain all this to anyone. But today, in the April sunshine, among the rustling beeches, these dreadful and fraternal dead needed no explanation. They needed us to live, quite simply, to live with all our strength in the memory of their death: any other kind of life would uproot us from this exile of ashes.

I had to take them out of here, those young women of La Mission France.

I turned around: they were gone. They'd fled from the sight. And I could understand why. It couldn't have been much fun to come to Buchenwald as a tourist and be brutally presented with a small mountain of such unpresentable corpses.

I emerged onto the square, smoking a cigarette. One of the young women was waiting for me, the one with the blue eyes: Martine Dupuy. I learned her name a few days later, in Eisenach.

She had just gone off with her commando captain, however, and Yves Darriet is asking me why I left her. I've known Yves since the first days of our quarantine in Block 62 of the Little Camp. He'd arrived from Compiègne in the huge convoys of January 1944, as I had. André Verdet, Serge Miller, Maurice Hewitt, Claude Bourdet, and Maurice Halbwachs were among the many others who also arrived at that time. After quarantine was over, Yves and I had shared days and nights in the same wing of block 40: *Flügel C.* A musician in outside life, he was the one who'd provided the arrangements for Jiri Zak's jazz ensemble and found a saxophonist for the orchestra. Sometimes, before the evening curfew or on Sunday afternoons, we'd trade poems. He'd recite Victor Hugo, Lamartine, Toulet, Francis Jammes to me. I'd reel off some Rimbaud, Mallarmé, Apollinaire, André Breton. As for Ronsard and Louise Labé, we'd recite them together. In unison, I mean.

It was Darriet who put me on the list for the convoy leaving tomorrow, or rather, in a little while. A few trucks of the Abbé

Rodhain's repatriation mission are leaving at dawn for Paris. Yves is one of those being repatriated. He came looking for me in Buchenwald, and since he's a true pal, with a sense of humor, I made the same comments to him that I've already made to you about this supposed repatriation. He didn't take them the wrong way at all. He didn't take them lightly, either, which didn't surprise me.

"Anyway, you're just in time," Yves tells me when I rejoin the group of future repatriates. "We were trying to figure out how we should talk about all this, so that people would understand us."

I nod: it's a good question. One of the right questions.

"That's not the problem," someone else exclaims immediately. "The real problem isn't talking about it, whatever the difficulties might be. It's hearing about it. . . . Will people want to hear our stories, even if they're well told?"

So I'm not the only one wondering about this. The question is self-evident, I admit.

But the discussion becomes confused. Everyone has something to say. I won't be able to transcribe the conversation properly, identifying the speakers.

"What does that mean, 'well told'?" asks someone indignantly. "You have to tell things the way they are, with no fancy stuff!"

This blunt affirmation seems to have the support of most of the future repatriates present. Most of the potential future narrators. Then I stick my nose in, pointing out something that seems obvious to me.

"Telling a story well, that means: so as to be understood. You can't manage it without a bit of artifice. Enough artifice to make it art!"

But this patent fact doesn't seem convincing, judging fr the protests I hear. I probably went too far with my play words. Only Darriet gives me a smile of approval. He knows me better than the others.

I try to be more explicit.

"Listen, guys! The truth we have to tell—that is, if we've got the stomach for it, because many won't even have that—isn't easily believable. . . . It's even unimaginable—"

A voice interrupts, goes me one better.

"That's right!" says a fellow who's been drinking gloomily and with determination. "It's so unbelievable that I myself plan to stop believing it, as soon as possible!"

Nervous laughter. I press on.

"How do you tell such an unlikely truth, how do you foster the imagination of the unimaginable, if not by elaborating, by reworking reality, by putting it in perspective? With a bit of artifice, then!"

They talk all at once. In the end, one voice stands out, dominates the uproar. There are always voices that take charge of noisy conversations like these, I can tell you.

"You talk about understanding . . . but what kind of understanding are you talking about?"

I look at the speaker. I don't know his name, but I know him by sight. I've noticed him before, on certain Sunday afternoons, strolling in front of the French hut, Block 34, with Julien Cain, the director of the Bibliothèque Nationale, or with Jean Baillou, the head of the École Normale Supérieure. He must be an academic.

"I imagine there'll be a flood of accounts," he continues. "Their value will depend on the worth of the witness, his insight, his judgment. . . . And then there will be documents. . . . Later, historians will collect, classify, analyze this material, drawing on it for scholarly works. . . . Everything will be said, put on record. . . . Everything in these books will be true . . . except that they won't contain the essential truth, which no historical reconstruction will ever be able to grasp, no matter how thorough and all-inclusive it may be."

The others look at him, nodding, apparently reassured to see that one of us can formulate the problems so clearly.

"The other kind of understanding, the essential truth of the experience, cannot be imparted. . . . Or should I say, it can be imparted only through literary writing."

He turns toward me, smiling. "Through the artifice of a work of art, of course!"

I think I recognize him now. He's a professor from the Université de Strasbourg.

Last summer, shortly after the liberation of Paris, I'd given a talk on Rimbaud one Sunday afternoon in a room in the *Revier*. It was the clandestine Committee of French Interests, overseeing all the resistance organizations, that had proposed these cultural gatherings. Which were sometimes musical, featuring Maurice Hewitt, and sometimes literary, presenting some sort of extemporaneous lecture. It seemed that these Sunday events were good for troop morale.

Be that as it may, Boris Taslitzky and Lucien Chapelain had asked me to give a talk on Rimbaud before the usual audience at these diversions organized by the underground solidarity apparatus. So I gave my talk, in a room in the *Revier* that was packed for the occasion. It was summer, so I was wearing the blue cloth jacket that the *Effektenkammer,* the clothing store, had issued to me for that season. At the entrance to the room, before the Rimbaldian lecture could begin, Chapelain, quite ill at ease, had asked me to take off my jacket. He didn't want anyone to see the *S* on the red cloth patch I wore on my chest and which identified me as a Spaniard. Certain chauvinists on the French committee—it takes all kinds to make a national resistance—

were of the opinion that these leisure activities were usually too international in flavor, too cosmopolitan. They wanted to see things take on a more typically French tone. Chapelain, who was a Communist, and who was speaking to me in the name of the underground committee of the *Parti Communiste Français,* which was anxious to avoid minor conflicts with the nationalist resistance groups, therefore asked me to remove my jacket. "You understand," he told me, "to hear you speak, no one would suspect you're Spanish. These old farts won't find a thing to complain about!" I was a bit bewildered, actually. Chapelain's request seemed to me truly Ubuesque. But after all, I liked him and the other comrades I'd dealt with in the PCF. So I took off my jacket, to keep the sight of that *S* from upsetting those thoroughbred Frenchmen and their sanctimonious convictions about national purity.

At the end of the talk, four or five deportees came up to me, mature men of around forty. They were all professors at the Université de Strasbourg. Intrigued by some of the things I'd said about Rimbaud, they wanted to know what field of study I was in, whether I intended to become a teacher.

The man speaking to us at Eisenach, at the end of that sleepless night, was one of those professors from the Université de Strasbourg.

"Through the artifice of a work of art, of course!"

After these words, he thinks for a moment. No one says anything, waiting for him to finish. Because he's not finished, that's obvious.

"The cinema would seem to be the most appropriate art form," he adds. "But there certainly won't be many film documents. And the most significant events of camp life have surely never been filmed. . . . In any case, the documentary has its limitations, insuperable ones. . . . A work of fiction, then—but who would dare? The best thing would be to produce a film right now, in the still visible truth of Buchenwald . . . with death still clearly present. Not a documentary, a work of fiction—I really mean that. It's unthinkable. . . ."

Silently, we think about this unthinkable project. We sip slowly at our drinks, at our return to life.

"If I understand you correctly," says Yves, "they'll never know, those who haven't been there!"

"They'll never really know. . . . That leaves books. Novels, preferably. Literary narratives, at least, that will go beyond simple eyewitness accounts, that will let you imagine, even if they can't let you see. . . . Perhaps there will be a literature of the camps. . . . And I do mean literature, not just reportage."

"Perhaps," I add, "but what's problematical is not the description of this horror. Not just that, anyway—not even mostly that. What's at stake here is the exploration of the human soul in the horror of Evil. . . . We'll need a Dostoyevsky!"

This plunges the survivors who don't yet know just what it is they've survived into deep thought.

Suddenly a trumpet begins to play.

Some black Americans from a shock battalion in Patton's army have gathered at the far end of the room. They begin a little jam session, just for fun. The white tablecloths and empty glass decanters gleam with the hesitant light of sunrise.

With a shiver of pleasure, I recognize the first phrase of "Big Butter and Egg Man." I raise my glass to the musicians. They can't see me, true. But I drink to them, to the glory of that music, which had so often made life bearable to me.

About two years earlier, in September 1943—two weeks before my arrest by the Gestapo, in Joigny—I was at a party on the Rue Washington in the home of a charming friend, a medical student. Her mother had one of those double-barreled names, handed down by a long line of country squires, and her opinions were of a piece with her social background. She adored her daughter, however, and put up with the girl's friends with a kind of benign inattention. Hyacinthe organized extravagant parties in the huge apartment on the Rue Washington. There were all the records imaginable, a record player with an automatic changer, and a lavish country-style buffet.

On the day of the party, I had a morning appointment with Henri Frager, the leader of Jean-Marie Action. Avenue Niel, on the sidewalk, between numbers 1 and 7. There was a serious reason for this meeting, an urgent reason. For some time, there had been signs that the network had been penetrated by a Gestapo agent. Perhaps an infiltrator, perhaps someone in the network who'd been arrested by the Gestapo, unbeknown to us, and turned. Whatever the case, something was going on, going wrong somewhere. Arms caches were being discovered; a parachute operation had been interrupted by the German police (luckily, they'd bungled it, so the English plane had been able to get away without dropping its cargo). Still other disturbing signs pointed to the presence of an enemy agent in the network. And even worse, at a high level, given the kind of operations with which he seemed to be familiar.

Michel H. and I had our suspicions. We thought we'd identified the traitor. So that day, I was bringing Frager all the arguments, all the indications—there's rarely irrefutable proof, in matters of this kind—that had led us to suspect "Alain" (that was his cover name).

Frager was indeed impressed by the array of facts, incongruous details, and striking coincidences that had persuaded us of Alain's treachery. He authorized me to cut all direct links with him for the time being, to ignore all demands for contact he might make. A year later, in Buchenwald, when I'd met up again with Henri Frager there, the first news he passed on to me was the confirmation of our suspicions. Alain must have been executed, Frager told me.

But that's another story.

I did not want to start telling you now about the adventures of Jean-Marie Action. I wanted to recount what happened at a party on the Rue Washington, in the home of my friend Hyacinthe. I was reminded of it by a musical theme of Armstrong's, played by some black soldiers, in Eisenach, at the end of a long night.

The apartment where Hyacinthe lived had one peculiarity. You could get to it both through the main door on the Rue Washington and through another entrance on the Avenue des Champs-Élysées. It was this possibility of double access that had occurred to me during my rendezvous with Koba.

The sun was shining on the lawn of the Parc Montsouris.

I saw Koba arrive, at the appointed time. But Koba always arrived on time, whatever the hour, the place, the weather. Moreover, he didn't arrive, properly speaking. He'd be there, abruptly, without anyone having seen him arrive. He "took shape," like the characters in certain biblical stories. Perhaps it was because he was a Jew that he possessed this biblical virtue of sudden incarnation.

The sun was shining on the Parc Montsouris, and Koba appeared at the end of a path, at the appointed time. I called him Koba because that was his nom de guerre, but I did so in all innocence. I wasn't aware, in 1943, that Koba had been a pseudonym used by Stalin during the time when, sporting a beard and the scarf of a romantic revolutionary, he was a leader of the armed expropriation groups—bank robbers, in other words—of the Bolshevik apparatus in Georgia. In 1943, I knew nothing of Stalin, almost nothing. I knew only that this young man who'd just appeared at the end of a tree-lined walk in the Parc Montsouris was a Communist. I knew he was a Jew. I knew he was called Koba, but I didn't know the legendary origin of this name. I knew he was my contact with the MOI, the Communist organization for foreigners (Julia had introduced me to him). I also knew that he belonged to a shock group.

That day, Koba was concerned with only one thing: I had to come up with an apartment for him in the Champs-Élysées neighborhood, near the Hôtel Claridge. An apartment where he could hide out for a few hours.

"One night, in fact," he explained. "Only one night. I'd get there right before curfew!"

I told him immediately I had just the apartment he needed. His jaw dropped, while his opinion of me soared.

"On condition," I added, "that you can carry out your plan on a specific date, which has already been decided!"

This confused him, so I explained. In a few days, there was going to be a party in an apartment that was ideal for him. I particularly mentioned the two possible methods of access.

"You go in from the Champs-Élysées; I'll give you the name of one of the tenants. You call out his name to the concierge, you go up the stairs making a lot of noise, and as soon as the automatic timer light switches off, you come back down quietly in the dark. By crossing the courtyard you'll get to the service stairs of the building on the Rue Washington. The apartment's on the third floor, I'll let you in. You'll be a friend of mine, no one will ask you anything. You'll spend the night with us. There'll be stuff to eat, pretty girls." (He drank all this in, more than a touch surprised.) "You know how to dance, right? I don't mean the polka, of course. Real dancing? You like pretty girls?"

He started. "You trying to make a fool of me?" he muttered.

"No, it's not that at all! But we'll have to fool everyone else. First off, we've got to change what you're wearing."

Koba looked at his clothes, fury in his eye. "What, you're saying I'm not well dressed?"

"Too well dressed," I told him. "Too spiffy. You're obviously gotten up as the spoiled son of some well-to-do grocers. Disguise yourself as a student—much more casual!" (Koba considered me, then his ready-made suit, uncertain whether to laugh or scowl.)

"You'll still have your piece on you when you get to the Rue Washington? If so, we'll have to figure out where to ditch it!"

He whistled through his teeth. "Say, pal, you think of everything! Where'd you learn that—with the Gaullists?"

I replied curtly that Jean-Marie Action wasn't the BCRA, but the Brits, the Buckmaster networks.

"Besides," I added, "I think of everything because I'm a novelist in civilian life!"

He looked me up and down, as if to say that was better than nothing, but only just. I was undaunted.

"The German you're going to liquidate at the Claridge—he's a big shot?"

He had a fit, shouting that it was none of my business.

"Oh, yes, it is," I argued. "If he's a big shot, the Krauts might start rounding people up. You have to plan for everything, including a police raid on the Rue Washington!"

In the end, after studying the location, checking certain details, Koba made his hit the evening of the party at Hyacinthe's place. He arrived afterward at the apartment, at the appointed hour: calm, as though nothing were wrong. Calm on the surface, at least. He'd gotten rid of his weapon along the way, in the purse of a young woman who was a militant in the MOI.

He fooled everyone, Koba. He danced, he even picked up one of the prettiest girls there. He did almost drink too much, though. He talked a bit too much as well. Luckily, I was the one to whom he was talking too much. I did the same, by the way, I talked too much. He told me about the Claridge, I told him about the young soldier who sang "La Paloma." His German was an important guy in the *Abwehr*, no problem. Everything had gone just fine, but when Koba had entered his room, he'd found the guy wasn't alone. With him was a gorgeous woman, undoubtedly a prostitute. Koba didn't say "prostitute," he said, "fallen woman." Hearing him use that expression really astounded me—I wondered where he could possibly have read it. In any case, the high-ranking officer of the *Abwehr* was in his apartment at the Claridge with a fallen woman.

"I had the piece you'd given me," said Koba.

I had in fact gotten him a Smith and Wesson 11.43 picked out from some stuff from a parachute drop. No better weapon for operations of this kind.

"But I'd rigged up a silencer for it," he continued, "given the location. I don't like silencers, ordinarily, they're like rubbers. . . . You miss out on the noise and the flash. Anyway, I needed a silencer."

Koba was pensive, telling his story slowly. The fallen woman had turned toward him as soon as he appeared, pointing his weapon. She had a strange look on her face, explained Koba. Panic, yes. But at the same time, a kind of understanding, as though she approved of what he was going to do. As though she accepted her death.

"Because I had to take them both out. I couldn't run the risk of leaving her behind," said Koba furiously. "Never again, never again," he murmured, after a long silence and a few glasses of cognac.

We talked a lot, drank a lot, too.

He was haunted by that look from the fallen woman. Me, I talked about the young German soldier singing "La Paloma."

About his blue eyes stricken with astonishment. But that will re-main our secret, that conversation.

Koba disappeared: I never found a trace of him. As for me, there are days when I feel the same way.

At Buchenwald, an old Czech member of the Comintern told me that "Koba" had been Stalin's alias. When the camp was liberated, it did occur to me that Koba must have been more like Nicolai, my young barbarian of Block 56, than like the Gener-alissimo whose portrait the Russians had hung up on their hut like a totem.

I remembered Koba, at the end of an April night in 1945 in Eisenach, because the black American soldiers had just lit into a famous piece by Armstrong, "Big Butter and Egg Man," the very same piece that was playing at Hyacinthe's party on the Rue Washington when Koba came out of the night like a death-dealing archangel.

A young woman came into the kitchen, where I was getting him a big glass of cold water. One of the loveliest girls at the party.

"Say," she asked me, laughing, "where'd your friend come from? Will you lend him to me?"

I pushed Koba toward her.

"I got him from nowhere, I just invented him. But I'm not lending him—I'm giving him to you!"

She laughed even louder, provocatively. She dragged my buddy from the MOI combat group off to the living room, where the dancing was.

But it wasn't Koba I invented. I invented another Jewish buddy, Hans Freiberg. I put him at my side, the day we shot down the young German soldier who was singing "La Paloma."

Kommt eine weisse Taube zu Dir geflogen . . .

Hans had stood in for Julien Bon, my Burgundian pal. I invented him so that he could take the place, in my novels, that Koba and other Jewish friends have held in my life.

A flurry of snow, all of a sudden, on the May Day flags.

I'd arrived in Paris two days earlier. The night of my return, I'd slept in the home of Pierre-Aimé Touchard (known as Pat) on the Rue du Dragon. We'd talked until dawn. At first, I was the one asking him questions. I was a year behind and I wanted to know everything, understandably. Speaking very softly, Touchard answered my questions in his slow, deep voice. His replies confirmed, with a few added details, what I'd already been told by the René Char officer. What I mean is, the officer who'd told me about René Char.

Pat was gracious enough to answer my questions patiently, without asking me a single one himself. He must have sensed that I wasn't yet able to reply.

Unhappily—or at least unluckily—for me, I encountered only two kinds of reactions from people on the outside. Some avoided questioning you, treated you as though you'd returned from a banal trip abroad. Oh, so you're back! The thing is, though, they were afraid of what you might say, terrified of the moral discomfort your replies might cause them. Other people asked heaps of superficial, stupid questions (of the It-was-rough-huh? type), but if you answered them, even succinctly, addressing the truest and deepest part, the opaque, unspeakable heart of the experience—they became quiet, agitated, wrung their hands, hoping to heaven they could just leave it at that. And then they'd fall silent, the way you fall into a void, a black hole, a dream.

Neither group asked questions because they wanted to know the answers. They asked questions to show good manners, be polite, observe social conventions. Because they had to make do or make believe. As soon as death turned up among the answers, they didn't want to hear any more. They became incapable of listening any further.

The silence of Pierre-Aimé Touchard was different. It was friendly, open to whatever I might say, whatever impulse I might follow. It wasn't to avoid my answers that he didn't question me, it was to allow me the choice of speaking or being silent.

That's how things were when a young woman entered the room where I was talking with Pat. I recognized her: it was his stepdaughter, Jeanine.

She saw me and stood rooted to the spot. As though she'd seen a ghost, one might say in a cheap novel. Well, she really was seeing a ghost. And life is often like a cheap novel.

"You see, Jeanine," said Pierre-Aimé Touchard, "you see that people do return from there?"

I'd returned from there, in fact. I was a revenant, which suited me fine.

Then the young woman began to weep silently, her two hands crossed over her face.

"I met Yann," I told her. "This winter, in the beginning of the winter. We spent some time together in Buchenwald!"

Yann Dessau was Jeanine's fiancé. He still hadn't come back. He wasn't a revenant yet.

One day, late in 1944, in front of one of the French blocks in the camp, I'd run into him. We'd stood there, face-to-face, certain we'd met before, not recognizing one another. Not identifying one another, at least. Yet just a year—a little more than a year—had passed since our last encounter, at a party given by Claude-Edmonde Magny in her studio on the Rue Schoelcher. A farewell party, in more than one way: farewell to our beloved studies, farewell to Paris, farewell to the *jeunes filles en fleurs*.

I'd gone there with Catherine D., who was more or less accompanying me through life at the time.

> *Jeune fille aride et sans sourire*
> *ô solitude et tes yeux gris . . .*
> [Arid girl without a smile
> O solitude and your gray eyes . . .]

I used to submit the poems I was writing at the time to Claude-Edmonde Magny, for her opinion. She'd thought the portrait of Catherine D. a good likeness, or rather, an accurate one.

It was that evening that Claude-Edmonde told me she'd just written me a long letter, about my poems, in fact. "If I publish it one day," she said, "I'll entitle it, *Lettre sur le pouvoir d'écrire* [*Letter on the Power to Write*]." And so she did, in fact, much later.

It was a lovely farewell party. Yann Dessau and all his friends were there. Brilliant students at the École Normale Supérieure, at Sciences Politiques: at the top of their class. All in all, it was a farewell to adolescence. We were abandoning our studies, going off into the *maquis,* going underground.

There were the girls, too, the transient or lasting companions we had when we were twenty: Jeanine and Sonia, Annette and Catherine. And there were others, lost to memory.

A year later, hardly more than a year, I met Yann Dessau in front of Block 34 in Buchenwald. I had trouble recognizing him. And he had the same trouble with me. Shadows of ourselves, no doubt, the both of us, difficult to identify using the memories we had of each other. The voyage of initiation was drawing to a close: we had been transformed by this voyage. Soon, we would be completely different.

But when the Americans liberated Buchenwald, Dessau was no longer in the camp. A few weeks before, he had been sent off in a transport to Neuengamme, in northern Germany. And there had been no news regarding the survivors of that camp. The end of Neuengamme was said to have been chaotic.

Yann Dessau had not come back yet; Jeanine wept in silence.

Then, without thinking about it beforehand, without, as it were, deciding to do so (if there was any decision on my part, it was rather to keep silent), I began to speak. Perhaps because no one was asking me anything, plying me with questions, pressing me for information. Perhaps because Yann Dessau would not come back and someone had to speak in his name, in the name of his silence, of all the silences: thousands of stifled cries. Perhaps because the returning ghosts must sometimes speak for those who have disappeared, the survivors taking the place of those who have gone under.

On the Rue du Dragon that night, in the home of Pierre-Aimé Touchard, a member of the Esprit movement and the friend who had acted *in loco parentis* for me when I was a boarder at the Lycée Henri-IV in 1939, my first year in exile, I spoke for a long time, interminably, pouring out a spiraling, seemingly endless story to the fiancée of Yann Dessau, who had not yet returned, who was perhaps among the castaways in the wreckage of Neuengamme.

Jeanine had sunk to her knees on the carpet. Pierre-Aimé Touchard was huddled in his armchair.

I was not to speak of such things again for sixteen years, at least not in such excruciating detail. I talked until dawn, until my voice faltered and grew hoarse, until I lost my voice completely. I told of sweeping despair, of death in its slightest twists and turns.

I did not speak in vain, apparently.

Yann Dessau finally did return from Neuengamme. Clearly, we must sometimes speak in the name of the missing. Speak in their name, in their silence, to give them back their power of speech.

And the day after that dawn, a brief whirlwind of snow swept down upon the flags of May Day.

I was on the corner of the Avenue Bel-Air and the Place de la Nation. I was alone, I was watching the parade of demonstrations surge by, signs and red flags waving overhead. I could hear the distant sound of the old songs.

I had come back, I was alive.

Yet sadness gripped my heart—a poignant, aching distress. It wasn't a feeling of guilt, not at all. I've never understood why one should feel guilty for having survived. Anyway, I hadn't really survived. I wasn't sure of being a true survivor. I'd crossed through death, which had been an experience of my life. There are languages that have a word for this sort of experience. In German, the word is *Erlebnis*. In Spanish, *vivencia*. But there is no single French or English word that means life as the experience of itself. You have to find periphrases. Or use the word *"vécu,"* which is only approximate. And questionable. A bland, flabby word. First of all, and above all, it's passive, this word for what is "lived through" or "experienced." And it's in the past, as well. But the experience of life, which life makes of itself, of oneself in the midst of living it—is active. And in the present, inevitably. In other words, this experience draws on the past to project itself into the future.

At all events, it wasn't guilt that was preying on me. That feeling is only secondary, vicarious. The naked anguish of living comes first: the anguish of being born, born of the chaotic void by irremediable chance. One doesn't need to have known the concentration camps to experience the anguish of living.

So, I was alive, standing stock-still on the corner of the Avenue Bel-Air and the Place de la Nation.

The unhappiness I felt did not arise from any feeling of culpability. Of course, there was no merit in having survived. Unscathed, at least to all appearances. There was no difference in worth between the living and the dead. None of us deserved to live. Or to die, either. There was no merit in being alive. Nor would there have been any in being dead. I might have felt guilty if I'd thought that others had been more deserving of survival than I was. But surviving wasn't a question of worthiness, it was a question of chance. Or mischance, depending on how you looked at it. Living depended on a throw of the dice and nothing else. Which is what the word "chance" means, anyway. I'd lucked out, that's all.

Suddenly, just as a procession of deportees in striped clothing marched out of the Rue du Faubourg-Saint-Antoine into the Place de la Nation, amid the respectful silence that fell as they passed by—suddenly the sky darkened. A snowstorm, brief but violent, descended on the May Day flags.

The world around me vanished into a kind of dizzying whirlwind. Buildings, the crowd, Paris, the spring, flags, songs, the chanted cries—everything faded away. I realized why I was weighed down with sadness, despite the illusion I had of being there, alive, on the Place de la Nation, on that May Day. It was precisely because I wasn't truly sure of being there, of having really returned.

I was swept away by a staggering memory of snow on the Ettersberg. Snow and smoke on the Ettersberg. A perfectly calm giddiness, heartbreakingly lucid. I felt myself floating in the future of this memory. There would always be this memory, this loneliness: this snow in all the sunshine, this smoke in every springtime.

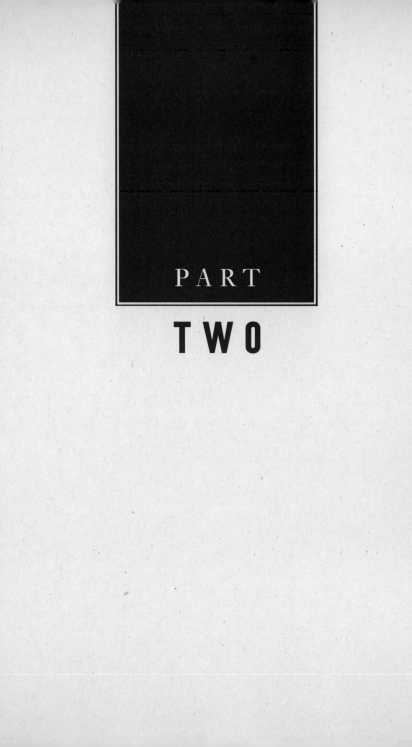

PART

TWO

6

THE POWER TO WRITE

"You wondered what was missing from those extraordinary little pastiches of Mallarmé (a Mallarmé who had read Proust and adopted the prosody of Aragon) you used to compose in three hours last year and that dazzled me every time. What they were missing was simply to have been written by you. . . ."

She stopped reading, looked up at me.

I felt vaguely like telling her that Mallarmé would probably never have read Proust: it couldn't have interested him. Or me, by the way. In the summer of 1939, between the two wars of my adolescence, I'd read *Du côté de chez Swann*. It hadn't really interested me. I didn't read any more of the *Recherche*. It was too familiar, and almost too familial. What I mean is, it was like the chronicle of a family that might have been mine. Besides, I was too accustomed to the Proustian phrase, to the meandering sentence that lost the occasional subject or predicate along the way. It was so easy for me to see in Proust the sinuous rhythm and prolixity of my maternal tongue: I felt right at home there.

That summer when I was fifteen, in 1939, what really impressed me, opened new horizons for me, was the prose of Gide.

Paludes, to be precise. There was writing that had nothing to do with the raucous and baroque complexity of Castilian.

But I said nothing to Claude-Edmonde Magny.

She looked at me and I looked at the sky over the Cimetière Montparnasse. The blue of an August sky over the grave of César Vallejo.

In sum, I possess nothing to express my life, except my death . . .

Looking up at the blueness of the sky, I was remembering this poem by Vallejo in Spanish, naturally. Because little of the work of the Peruvian Vallejo had been translated. And he was not bilingual, as were the Chilean Vicente Huidobro and the Spaniard Juan Larrea. In spite of a few French words slipped into his *Poemas humanos* for ironic effect, César Vallejo wasn't truly bilingual like the two others.

En suma, no poseo para expresar mi vida, sino mi muerte . . .

So I was remembering the beginning of this poem by Vallejo in Spanish, while I studied the blue sky over his tomb in the Cimetière Montparnasse.

I'd rung the bell at Claude-Edmonde Magny's door, on the Rue Schoelcher, at six in the morning. I knew that she sat down at her worktable at dawn. She was going over the proofs of a book of critical essays that was to appear a few weeks later: *Les sandales d'Empédocle.* We had often talked about the book since my return from Buchenwald three months earlier. Of course, we didn't necessarily discuss it at six in the morning, or at her home on the Rue Schoelcher. Because we'd picked up our old habit of strolling around the neighborhood of Montparnasse. But we no longer encountered Sartre's double, who in 1942 used to haunt the bistros: Patrick's, Le Dôme, Le Select, La Coupole. After the third mistake, this man (whose real identity and profession we never learned) used to wave us away whenever we ran into him in one of those places. Sitting at his table, he would shout at us, "I'm not Jean-Paul Sartre!" Just to confuse Claude-Edmonde, I'd pretend that Sartre was a rather perverse old faker, and a clever one, to boot, disguising himself as a Sartre look-alike so that people would leave him alone.

I'd rung Claude-Edmonde Magny's doorbell at six in the morning. I was certain I wasn't awakening her. She hadn't asked me anything, seeing me turn up like that, worn out after a sleepless night. She'd offered me some real coffee.

It wasn't the first time I'd appeared at her door at such an untimely hour, since my return. She could probably guess what unreasonable reasons I had—or else she considered that it was up to me to broach the subject, if necessary. In any case, I hadn't talked about Buchenwald with her at all. Not really, anyway. Of course, I wasn't talking about it to anyone.

However that may be, Claude-Edmonde Magny opened her door to me, offered me some real coffee, and we talked. We picked up where we had left off, a conversation interrupted by my absence.

I'd met her in 1939, at a conference organized by Esprit. Before the summer, but after the defeat of the Spanish Republic. It was at Jouy-en-Josas, as I recall. My father, who had been the general correspondent in Spain for the personalist movement founded by Mounier, was attending this congress, and I was accompanying him. I was fifteen, a boarding student at Henri-IV since the fall of Madrid to Franco's troops. The conference must have taken place during some school vacation. Perhaps the Easter holidays, it would be easy to check. Or maybe over a weekend. But the date isn't at all important. The Spanish Civil War was lost, we were in exile, the world war would soon begin: that's the vital point. I remember that the shadow of this looming conflict lay over all the proceedings of the Esprit congress. I clearly remember how impressed I was by the speeches of Luccioni, Landsberg, Soutou. I remember that Paul-Louis Landsberg's wife was blond and beautiful and that she drove a convertible.

It was there, if I remember correctly, that I met Claude-Edmonde Magny for the first time. At that event, around that date. That was when she began to use that name, which was a nom de plume, to sign her essays of literary criticism. Ten years older than I was, she had passed the competitive *agrégation* examination in philosophy and was teaching in provincial lycées. In Rennes, during the phony war of 1939–40. She only came back to Paris in about 1941, after which we saw one another regularly.

But on the day in question, early in August, three months after my return from Buchenwald, Claude-Edmonde Magny had decided to read me a long letter she'd written two years earlier, in 1943, especially for me. I knew this letter existed, but was unfamiliar with its contents in detail. In 1947, this text would be published by Pierre Seghers in a limited edition dedicated to me, under the title *Lettre sur le pouvoir d'écrire*.

She looked up at me, having interrupted her reading after the passage on the pastiches of Mallarmé.

So I felt vaguely inclined to make a small correction with regard to Marcel Proust. I hadn't really read Proust, although you wouldn't have known it to listen to me. Because I was capable of talking about Proust quite pertinently, even peremptorily, for as long as you liked. I hadn't read the *Recherche,* but I'd read just about everything written about it. Actually, I'd started this novel in 1939, during summer vacation—*adieu, vive clarté de nos étés trop courts . . .* [adieu, bright clarity of our too short summers]—but I hadn't kept on reading it. I was not to finish the *Recherche* until forty years later: a lifelong reading. It was in Washington, in 1982, that I would read *Le temps retrouvé*. Yves Montand was singing at the Kennedy Center. The Potomac was wreathed in morning mist; there was an exhibition of Dutch paintings at the National Gallery; Vermeer's *View of Delft* was not among them, to my intense regret. In its absence, I stood for a long time before the portrait of the young woman wearing a turban. An entire lifetime between the first and last volumes of Proust. An entire lifetime between my escapades at the Mauritshuis, in The Hague, where my father was chargé d'affaires for the Spanish Republic—visits interrupted by the end of the civil war, our departure for France, my arrival at the Lycée Henri-IV—and the exhibition at the National Gallery in Washington.

But I certainly could not have told Claude-Edmonde Magny all this. In August 1945, when I was having this conversation with her, I did not yet know where or when I would finish reading Marcel Proust. On the other hand, I could have told her that I'd never puzzled over the shortcomings of my little poems: I knew perfectly well what was wrong with them.

I didn't say anything, though.

The strain of living was so great, that morning. The anguish of that awakening in the middle of the night, of the headlong flight that followed, still wrung my heart.

Why did Odile and I sleep in a deserted apartment near the Duroc metro station? Was it empty because of the holidays? Or had its occupants not yet returned from some country retreat, where they had gone for the duration of hostilities that were still dragging on, off in the Far East? The deserted apartment belonged to one of Odile M.'s aunts or female cousins. Odile had a large and generous family. They were quite willing to lend her their keys, which worked out well for us.

On the evening when we met at Le Petit Schubert, a few days

after my return from Buchenwald, we left the nightclub, our pals, the snug, brassy world of jazz. In the brisk May dawn, we realized that we didn't have enough money left to pay for a hotel room. She was quite unable to put me up that night. In the end, after running through all kinds of far-fetched possibilities that had us laughing helplessly, in each other's arms, standing there on the sidewalk in front of La Closerie des Lilas, I took Odile to a house not far away, the home of the Herr family, on the Boulevard de Port-Royal.

When I'd arrived in Paris a few days before, Mme. Lucien Herr had placed at my disposal the attic room where I had sometimes found refuge during the Occupation.

A nightingale burst into song, welcoming the dawn just breaking with a slanting golden light as we crossed the vast garden hidden (Is it still there? I feel abruptly, cruelly uneasy, as I write these lines, at the idea that this garden might have disappeared) behind the bourgeois facade—Haussmannian, in a word—of No. 39 on the Boulevard de Port-Royal.

The song of the nightingale to salute our arrival.

We slipped quietly into the Herr family's house. Everyone was asleep. Odile had taken off her shoes to climb the stairs. In passing, I glanced into the library on the ground floor, evoking the spirits of all those who had gathered there around Lucien Herr.

In the case of Léon Blum, however, an old friend of the family, it wasn't his spirit I called to mind. He was alive, had even been liberated not long before by Italian partisans and American soldiers, in the village in the Dolomites where he had arrived after his long journey from Buchenwald. It was that very day, May 4, if I have calculated correctly, that the press announced this news.

But I didn't say anything to Odile about either Léon Blum or the other regular frequenters of this venerable house. We were still shaking with repressed giggles when we flung ourselves onto the bed, in the first light of dawn.

Three months later, early in August, we went to the apartment on a dead-end street off the Boulevard des Invalides, not far from the Duroc metro station.

It was a vast, richly furnished apartment. Looking beyond the wall at the end of the street, we could see branches swaying in the distance, filling the transparent night air with their lush rustling. We chose a marriage bed. The fine sheets found in the impeccably tidy linen cupboard had the fresh, lavender scent of an old-fashioned trousseau.

Everything seemed to be going well, and the evening promised to be another celebration.

But I should probably have paid attention to a few barely perceptible signs. Such as the vague, fleeting malaise I'd felt while walking through the empty apartment with Odile, looking for a bed in which to spend that night. True, it was nothing definite, nothing heart-stopping, no sudden pounding in the temples. More like a passing misgiving, a close, lukewarm feeling just barely touching my soul. I should have paid all the more attention in that I know perfectly well, after three months' experience, how fragile my happiness in life had become. How steadfastly I had to cling to it. I already knew that my appetite for life, the eagerness that pushed me to burn each day's candle at both ends, to make of that summer of my return a season of nights without end—I knew that this vitality would not keep me from being vulnerable.

In that apartment near Duroc, the sight of those chairs and settees in their white dustcovers had filled me with a secret distress, reminding me insidiously of my childhood, of the apartment on the Calle Alfonso-XI, in Madrid, after our long summer vacations at the ocean shore.

At the end of our last summer, the summer of the civil war,

we had not returned to Madrid, for events had flung us into exile and loss. I did not—and never would—see again those large rooms with their ghostly furniture, draped in sheets as white as shrouds. In previous years, though, the apartment to which we came home at summer's end had echoed with our cries, our racing footsteps. There was something upsetting in that excitement. For strangely, returning home provoked a feeling of dismay. It was precisely this return to the familial hearth that aroused uneasiness.

In 1953, when I returned to Madrid for the first time to work there in the underground Communist organization, I ran all the way to the Calle Alfonso-XI. Right after dropping my suitcase off at the hotel where I'd registered with my false passport, I dashed across Madrid to the Calle Alfonso-XI.

The city of my childhood had not yet become the sprawling industrial metropolis, so savagely magnificent and dilapidated, that it is today. There one still breathed the dry, pure air of the neighboring hills, the sky was still a deep blue, the water was still deliciously cool and clear, like the snows and springs from which it flowed. But above all, the neighborhood around El Retiro, remembered from my childhood, had not changed at all. My loving and attentive eye could superimpose these images upon my memories: they melted into one another, the colors matching down to the faintest nuance.

And yet, on that June evening in 1953, in spite of the perfect coincidence between those past and present images, I felt a vague pang in my heart, something I couldn't really put a name to, as soon as I arrived on the Calle Alfonso-XI, as soon as I looked up at the balconies on the top floor of the house, the balconies of the apartment where I had spent my childhood.

Never, during those years lived abroad, had I ever experienced such a poignant feeling of exile, of strangeness, as in the privileged moment of my return to my native land.

But I'm getting ahead of myself.

I'm with Odile, in the seventh arrondissement of Paris, going through an elegant apartment where the white dustcovers protecting the armchairs and settees abruptly remind me of the uncertainty, the vague distress I used to feel coming home after vacation. The covers were a sign of deracination. Suddenly, not only did it become clear that I was not at home, but also that I was nowhere. Or anywhere at all, which amounts to the same thing. From that moment on, my roots would always be nowhere, or anywhere: in this very uprooting itself, at all events.

But this confused feeling lasted only a moment—all the briefer in that Odile had immediately begun whipping the white covers off the chairs in the room where we were. She moved through the camphor-scented air, graceful, vigorous, alive. The whiteness of the cloth covers formed a swirling halo around her.

She was trumpeting a tune from *Carmen,* as she waltzed across the room.

Even today, a lifetime later, it takes only a moment of daydreaming—anytime, anywhere—or of deliberate inattention to an idle conversation, a clumsily told story, a mediocre play, for my memory to unfold (suddenly, in slow motion, with no apparent connection to my preoccupations or wishes of the moment) a flight of images of blinding whiteness. The wings of gulls, at dawn, seen through the bay windows of a hotel room in Brittany? The jibs of sailboats gleaming in the silvery light of the Bay of Formentor? Milky mists, tattered by whirling winds in the Strait of Eggemogging?

There are times when I cannot identify these images. Then I remain on the threshold of their intelligibility, stirred by an indefinable emotion: something strong and true remains hidden, slips away from me. Something disintegrates as soon as it appears, like an unsatisfied desire. But at times these images come sharply into focus instead of dwindling away and swindling me.

I recognize the long hall of the apartment on the Calle Alfonso-XI in Madrid, echoing with the sound of our running footsteps and flung-open doors. In the dim light of a late-summer evening, I recognize the fine furniture swathed in white dustcovers. And then, summoned by—and strangely governed by—this childhood memory, all the others reappear: a flight of pigeons, Place de la Cybèle; the seagulls of Brittany; the sails of Formentor; the mists of Little Deer Isle. And the memory of Odile, flitting through a Parisian drawing room, warbling Bizet's "Toreador Song" at the top of her lungs, joyfully snatching from the armchairs and sofas the snowy shrouds she transformed into banners celebrating the pleasure to come.

At Le Petit Schubert, Boulevard du Montparnasse, a few days after my arrival in Paris, I'd held Odile M. in my arms. In Eisenach, in the old hotel where the Americans had set up a repatriation center, the French commando officer had whisked Martine away from me. But at Le Petit Schubert, as it happened, nothing happened. Nothing except the light kindled in Odile's eyes, my enhanced awareness of her body. She was still in my arms. She seemed to belong to no one. Nobody appeared to have any rights of preemption or *cuissage* over her. She was going to be mine.

Days passed, and weeks: she was mine.

But this relationship of belonging ought probably to be reversed. It was I who belonged to her, rather, since she was life and I wanted to belong to life, completely. She reinvented for me, with me, the behavior of life. She reinvented my body, or at least a use of my body that reflected not the strict economy of survival, but the extravagant largess of love.

Yet in spite of her, in spite of me, in spite of the exuberance of that summer of my return, sometimes the memory of death caught up with me, enveloping me in its cunning shadow.

In the middle of the night, as a rule.

I'd awakened with a start, at two in the morning.

"Awakened" isn't the most appropriate word, by the way, even if it is correct. Because I truly had been startled out of the reality of dreams, but only to plunge into a dream—no, a nightmare—of reality.

A moment before, I had been wandering through a troubled, restless, and unfathomable world. Suddenly a voice had blared through all this confusion, bringing order out of chaos. A German voice, resonant with the all too recent truth of Buchenwald.

"*Krematorium, ausmachen!*" said the German voice. "Crematory, shut down!" As this hollow, peevish, imperious voice rang through my dream, instead of making me understand that I was dreaming (which is what usually happens in such cases), it made me believe, strangely enough, that I had finally awakened again— or still, or for always—in the reality of Buchenwald, which I had never left, in spite of all appearances, and which I would never leave, despite the masquerades and make-believe of life.

For a few seconds—an endless time, the eternity of memory—I'd found myself back in the reality of the camp during a night air-raid alert. I heard the German voice giving the order to shut down the crematory, but I felt no anguish at all. Quite on the contrary: at first I was filled with a kind of serenity, a kind of peace, as though I were recovering an identity, a familiarity with myself in some perfectly habitable place. As though— and I understand that this statement might seem unacceptable, or at least outrageous, but it's true—as though the night on the Ettersberg, the unquiet sleep of my companions in the crowded bunks, the feeble, raspy breathing of the dying, the flames of the crematory, were a sort of homeland. A place of plenitude, of vital coherence, in spite of the voice of authority angrily repeating, "*Krematorium, ausmachen! Krematorium, ausmachen!*"

This voice swelled, soon grew deafening, then jolted me awake. My heart was pounding; I had the impression I'd cried out.

But no, Odile was sleeping peacefully at my side.

I sat up in bed, damp with sweat. I could hear Odile breathing evenly. I turned on a bedside lamp. I threw off the sheet, looked at her naked body. A ghastly fear gripped me, despite the piercing certainty of her beauty. All this life was only a dream. An illusion. Even though I might lightly caress Odile's body, the curve of her hip, her delicate nape—it was only a dream. Life, the trees in the night, the music at Le Petit Schubert: only a dream. It had all been a dream ever since I'd left Buchenwald, the beech wood on the Ettersberg, the ultimate reality.

I bit my clenched fists to keep from screaming. I huddled in the bed, trying to catch my breath.

I should have been more wary, that night. I shouldn't have ignored the portents of *le malheur de vivre*. The sorrow of living.

First there had been, briefly, the malaise provoked by the furniture neatly wrapped in white winding sheets, in the apartment where Odile had taken me to spend the night. Later, we'd gone out again. We'd strolled along to Saint-Germain-des-Prés. We'd had dinner with friends, on the Rue Saint-Benoît. After dinner and a drink at Le Montana, we'd walked some more, down to Montparnasse.

We lived from day to day, that summer. Our pockets were always empty. Me, in any case—I lived by my wits, but quite cheerfully, of no fixed abode: a razor, a toothbrush, a few books, some old clothes in a suitcase were my viaticum.

At Le Petit Schubert, in the staircase leading down to the basement room, I'd received a second warning. The club's little jazz ensemble had been playing "Stardust." I tripped, had to lean on Odile to keep my balance. Thinking I'd wanted to feel the proffered warmth of her body against mine once more, she took for a gesture of physical tenderness what was only a sign of distress. I didn't see the point of enlightening her. I didn't tell her about Jiri Zak's jazz orchestra in the camp, about the Norwegian trumpeter who played such marvelous solos in "Stardust" on Sunday afternoons in Buchenwald.

She leaned on me, her hip pressing against mine. We went down the last few steps together, close together, into the sound of that stunning trumpet solo. But there were snowflakes falling in my memory. Unless they were wisps of gray smoke.

I'd woken up with a start.

Awakening had not brought comfort, however, had not swept away the anguish—on the contrary. It deepened the distress while transforming it. Because the return to wakefulness, to the sleep of life, was terrifying in itself. That life was a dream—after the radiant reality of the camp—is what was terrifying.

I'd turned on a bedside lamp, thrown off the sheet.

Odile's body offered itself to my gaze in the languid fullness of repose, but the soothing assurance of her loveliness had not distracted me from my pain. Nothing would distract me from my pain. Nothing except death, of course. Not the memory of death, of my experience of it: the experience of moving toward death with the others, my companions, of sharing it with them, fraternally. Of being *for* death with the others—pals, strangers, *mes semblables, mes frères:* the Other, my fellow man. Of grounding our common freedom on death. Not this memory of death, therefore, but personal death, the one you cannot experience, of course, but which you can determine.

Only voluntary, deliberate death could distract me, free me from my pain.

I moved away from Odile, chilled by this realization. With her charming and unpredictable irresponsibility, she was for me the incarnation of life in all its carefree innocence. She was the present moment, constantly renewed, intent only on persevering in this way of being in the world: a light and abundant presence, a kind of state of grace, of complicitous and affectionate liberty.

But nothing erased the deadly knowledge from which our libertine companionship had sprung. She confessed that the reason she had chosen me, on the first evening we met, from among all the young men attracted to her freshness, her carefree flirtatiousness, her lovely body, and the candid gaze that seemed to promise a wealth of tenderness—was precisely because she knew where I had been, because my eyes, she later admitted to me, had seemed to brim with a strange darkness, an icy, almost insane need.

Odile nursed me with the inventive gestures of physical love, with her bubbling, spontaneous laughter, her insatiable vivacity. But she was helpless before the storms that broke out in my life, and powerless to avert disaster. As soon as the darkness overtook me—dimming the light in my eyes, trapping me in the stubborn silence—and the voice of the SS *Sturmführer* demanding the shutdown of the crematory rang out in the middle of the night, awakening me from the dream that was my life, Odile was defeated. She stroked my face, the way one caresses a frightened child; she talked to me, to fill the silence, that absence, that void, with comforting chatter.

It was intolerable.

Odile was clearly meant to bring joy and liveliness to the world: the milk of human kindness. She was not made to listen to the voices of death, still less to take them on, to take responsibility for these insistent murmurs herself, thereby risking her own equilibrium, her own peace of mind.

But who around us, so soon after our return, would have been ready to listen endlessly to the fatal voices of death?

I'd turned off the lamp, slipped out of bed, fumbled into my clothes. I'd fled into the night, back to Le Petit Schubert. The jazz group was still playing for a half-dozen night owls. Sitting at the bar, I was offered a drink. I was flat broke, but they knew me. They'd seen me with Odile a few hours earlier. They'd often seen me with her, with friends, over the past few weeks. Since my return. It's true they had no idea I'd returned, from Buchenwald or anywhere else. My hair was growing back quite quickly. And besides, there were all sorts of former servicemen around, with more or less short hair, in that summer of 1945. No one asked anyone about his or her past. That was a summer when only the present mattered.

So I was offered a drink. And the bartender wasn't surprised to see me come back without Odile. The bouncer nodded at me in recognition.

I listened to the music—it was the only thing to do. Almost all the customers had left, at least those who'd come to dance, anyway. Six or so patrons were still listening to the club's jazz combo, which was rather good. The musicians were really going at it, now that they were playing for themselves.

I left the bar, went to sit with the other customers. We were clustered around the musicians, who were improvising on some classic themes, by Louis Armstrong in particular. That suited me—I knew Armstrong's repertoire well. We sat there; time passed. Nothing bound us together, nothing except the music. That was enough, it seemed. Perhaps the only thing we had in common was the same love for that music. The same respect for that music of freedom: violent, tender, rigorously inventive. It was enough, apparently.

At dawn, the club closed. It was still too early to go knocking on Claude-Edmonde Magny's door, on the Rue Schoelcher. I walked around rather aimlessly, in the bleak chill of early morning.

Finally, I climbed over the gate of a little park at the end of the Rue Froidevaux, where I stretched out on a bench.

During that jazz session in Eisenach a few months earlier, in the light of another dawn, I'd had an intuition that I'd been mulling over ever since. That music—those glittering or sorrowful sax and trumpet solos, the muffled or pounding drums throbbing like a lively pulse—was inexplicably at the heart of the universe I wanted to describe, the book I wanted to write.

Music would be its formative material, its matrix, its formal imaginative structure. I'd pattern the text—why not?—after a piece of music. It would be steeped in the atmosphere of all the music that had been a part of this experience, not just the jazz. The songs of Zarah Leander that the SS were constantly playing over the camp loudspeakers. The stirring martial music the orchestra played every morning and evening on the roll-call square at Buchenwald, during the departure and return of the work *Kommandos.* And then the clandestine music through which our world was linked to that of freedom: classical music performed on certain evenings in a basement of the *Effektenkammer,* the main store, by a string quartet gathered around Maurice Hewitt, and the jazz played by Jiri Zak's group.

Music, the different kinds of music, would punctuate the progress of the narrative. A Sunday, why not? The story of one Sunday, hour by hour.

Thus, ever since that April dawn in Eisenach, after the discussion with the repatriates about the best way to tell our story, I'd been thinking about this idea, letting it work its way through my imagination. It didn't strike me as outlandish, this idea of structuring a narrative around a few pieces by Mozart and Louis Armstrong in order to point out the truth of our experience.

But my project turned out to be unrealizable as a systematic whole, at least for the moment. The memory of Buchenwald was too dense, too pitiless, for me to master immediately such a spare, abstract literary form. Whenever I awoke at two in the morning, with the voice of the SS officer in my ear, blinded by the orange flame of the crematory, the subtle and sophisticated harmony of my project shattered in brutal dissonance. Only a cry from the depths of the soul, only a deathly silence could have expressed that suffering.

"What they were missing was simply to have been written by you. To have revealed you, even in the most superficial way. . . ."

Claude-Edmonde Magny has returned to her reading of the letter she had written to me, two years earlier. Here we are, back with my little poems. With those extraordinary little pastiches of Mallarmé that always dazzled her. Those are her own words, I'm just repeating them here. I'm not speaking for myself. Nothing would induce me to offer an opinion of those early poems of mine—that would be presumptuous of me. Besides, I've kept no trace of them. Those works have vanished into the turmoil of those years, along with almost all my memory of them. We'll have to take Claude-Edmonde Magny at her word.

Some time has passed, since she interrupted the reading to which she has just returned. Two hours during which she has made coffee, several times. I've told her about my awakening in the middle of the night: the sense of it, the insanity of it.

Now she has gone back to her letter.

"What they were missing was simply to have been written by you. To have revealed you, even in the most superficial way. To have been connected somehow with what is essential in you, with what you want more than anything—but without yet knowing what that is."

Claude-Edmonde breaks off again. She looks at me.

"Do you know, now?"

What I want more than anything else is rest. Not only physical rest, after a sleepless night. I feel like an indestructible ghost, an everlasting survivor. I already know how easily I regain my strength. Bodily repose is secondary, all things considered. What I want more than anything is the repose of the soul.

In other words, I want to forget.

"I think I know. . . ."

She waits for the rest, which doesn't come.

I want only to forget, nothing else. I find it unjust, almost indecent, to have made it through eighteen months of Buchenwald without a single minute of anguish, without a single nightmare, carried along by constantly renewed curiosity, sustained by an insatiable appetite for life (whatever the certainty of death, whatever the precious and unspeakable daily experience of it may have been), having survived all that—only to find myself from then on the occasional prey of the most naked, the most intense despair, a despair nourished almost as much by life itself, by its serenity and joys, as by the memory of death.

And so, that night, what drove me from my bed, what tore me from the arms of Odile, was not only the dream haunted by the voice of an SS *Sturmführer* ordering the shutdown of the crematory, it was also, and even more importantly, finding myself alive once again, forced to accept that absurd (or at least improbable) situation of having to project myself into a future unbearable to imagine, even as a happy one.

I had gazed at Odile's body, at her beauty, languid in sleep, its promises so close at hand: happiness, a kind of happiness, I knew that. But this was useless knowledge that gave me no security, no way out.

Everything would begin all over again, after that sort of happiness, the happiness of a thousand little heart-rending pleasures. Everything would begin all over again as long as I was alive, or rather, as long as I was a revenant. As long as I was tempted to write. The joy of writing, I was beginning to realize, would never dispel the sorrow of memory. Quite on the contrary: writing sharpened it, deepened it, revived it. Made it unbearable.

Only forgetting could save me.

Claude-Edmonde is watching me, probably hoping that I'll explain myself more clearly. Tired of waiting, she goes back to her letter.

"For a time I believed that this anonymity of your poems was due to the fact that they were pastiches (by intention, but no matter), or else that it reflected a deeper cause: the strangeness words in the French language still possessed for you, whatever their grammatical familiarity—these words that know nothing of your childhood, your ancestors, words in which your soul was not profoundly rooted. . . . You have not yet escaped the limbo of literary creation: nothing you can do has any *gravity,* in the almost physical sense of the term."

She stops abruptly, looks at me.

"I wrote that two years ago! Today it would be rather the contrary. . . . Everything you might write risks having *too much* gravity!"

She's perfectly right; I gesture in agreement.

She looks for another passage in her letter, flipping through the typed pages.

"Listen," she says. "Sometimes it seems as though I'd written to you in preparation for our conversation today, which we could hardly have anticipated!"

She reads the passage.

"What I wanted to say is this: literature is possible only at the end of a first period of rigorous self-discipline and as a result of that exercise through which the individual transforms and as-similates his painful memories, at the same time constructing a personality for himself. . . ."

I sink deeper into silence, into the exhaustion of the desire to live.

"You returned three months ago," she continues. "You have never spoken one word to me about Buchenwald. Not directly, at least. That's peculiar, even bizarre. . . . I know others in the Resistance who have come back from deportation. . . . They're all possessed by a true frenzy of communication . . . of attempts at communication, anyway. . . . You, you maintain the most perfect silence. . . . We've picked up our conversations from be-fore exactly where we left off. . . . But you've shown up here three times, at the crack of dawn . . . without explanation. . . . Mind you, you're welcome to do so, it's one of the privileges of friendship: getting something without giving anything in ex-change. . . . The first time you turned up at six in the morning, you remember what you talked about to me?"

I nod. I remember quite well.

"Schelling!" she exclaims. "His inquiries into the nature of freedom. . . . I was astonished that this book should be in the camp library, happy that Schelling had interested you. . . . Be-cause after all, for a while before your arrest, you seemed to me enthralled by Marx, by your reading of Lukács, of his *Geschichte und Klassenbewusstsein*. . . . I felt you were falling, like so many others have, for the most pernicious of all illusions, the one Marx advances in one of his theses on Feuerbach: philosophers have merely interpreted the world, when what is important is to change it . . . which is incredible foolishness, a piece of bombast fraught with consequences. . . . With a few words, Marx liqui-dates philosophy as a specific autonomous activity. . . . He places it at the service of power, preferably absolute, because power must be absolute—whatever its source, popular or divine—to transform the world, or at least claim to, with some historical legitimacy. . . . But anyway, you spoke to me of Schelling, of his essay on the essential meaning of freedom. . . . And while on this subject you briefly described those Sundays spent with Maurice Halbwachs."

She breaks off, tries to wring a few more drops from a coffeepot that remains stubbornly empty.

"Those beautiful Sundays!" I exclaim. "In the afternoon, after roll call, when we'd devoured our Sunday noodle soup, I'd go off to the Little Camp. . . . Those too sick to work were in Hut 56. . . . We'd gather there around the bunk assigned to Halbwachs and Maspero. . . . The loudspeakers were playing songs sung by Zarah Leander. . . . That's where Schelling came up, a *Bibelforscher*—a Jehovah's Witness—talked to me about him."

She listens with such keen attention that deep lines appear in her face. But I'm worn out, and pause to rest.

"Telling about a single Sunday, hour by hour, that's one possibility. . . ."

I look up at the blue sky over the tomb of César Vallejo, in the Cimetière Montparnasse. He was right, Vallejo. I possess nothing more than my death, my experience of death, to recount my life, to express it, to carry it on. I must make life with all that death. And the best way to do this is through writing. Yet that brings me back to death, to the suffocating embrace of death. That's where I am: I can live only by assuming that death through writing, but writing literally prohibits me from living.

I make an effort, forcing the words out, one by one.

"It's rich material, a Sunday, hour by hour. . . . It's dense, astonishing, abominable. . . . There's abjection, cruelty, grandeur. . . . Everything is human: nothing of what is called inhuman in our superficial moral language, which renders everything commonplace, is beyond man. . . . You know what the last book I r was, before my arrest in Joigny? It was Michel who brought it to me . . . the French translation of Kant's *Religion Within the Boundary of Pure Reason* . . . 1793, you remember? The theory of radical Evil, *das radikal Böse*. . . . Thus my interest in Schelling and his writings, which got all bogged down in the conceptual hysteria of romantic idealism, of course, but where he builds on Kant and the critique of theodicies to elaborate on the very strong and significant idea of an original foundation from which springs human freedom, capable of producing Good and Evil, ontological equivalents. . . . Hence the impossibility of decreeing the inhumanity of Evil. . . . In Buchenwald, the SS, the *Kapos,* the informers, the sadistic torturers all belonged to the human race just as much as the best and purest among us, among the victims. . . . The frontier of Evil is not that of inhumanity, it's something else altogether. Hence the necessity for a moral philosophy that transcends this original foundation from which spring both the freedom of Good and the freedom of Evil. . . . An ethics, therefore, that has broken free forever of theodicies and theologies, since God, by definition, as the Thomists have said often enough, is innocent of Evil. An ethics of the Law and its transcendence, of the conditions of its sovereignty, and thus of the violence it in fact necessitates. . . ."

But I've gone off on a tangent—that's not at all what I wanted to tell her.

"The complexity of those Sundays! There's the brothel, for those few allowed to frequent it. There's traffic in all sorts of things. There's homosexual love, often involving mercenary motives or an abuse of power, but not always . . . sometime resulting from pure and simple passion. There are the songs of Zarah Leander, the clandestine orchestras, the improvised theatrical productions. . . . There are political meetings, the training of the international resistance's combat groups. There are the arrivals and departures of the convoys. There's death from exhaustion, in the hideous solitude of the *Revier*."

I fall silent again; she waits for me to continue.

"There are so many obstacles in the way of writing. Strictly literary, some of them. Because I don't want to do a plain eyewitness account. Right from the start I mean to avoid, to spare myself, any recital of suffering and horror. Anyway, others will try that approach. . . . There's also the fact that I'm not able, at this point, to conceive of a novelistic structure in the third person. I don't even want to consider tackling things from that direction. So I need a narrative 'I' that draws on my experience but goes beyond it, capable of opening the narrative up to fiction, to imagination. . . . Fiction that would be as illuminating as the truth, of course. That would help reality to seem true-to-life, truth to seem convincing. That's a difficulty I'll manage to overcome, sooner or later. In one of my drafts, I'll suddenly find the right tone, a suitable distance, I'm sure of it. But there's a fundamental obstacle, a spiritual one. . . . Do you remember what I spoke to you about, that second time I came over here so early?"

She nods. She remembers. "You talked about Faulkner, *Absalom, Absalom!* That novel was also in the library at Buchenwald. . . . You read it in German."

"That's it," I reply. "Faulkner, you know how much I like him. *Sartoris* is one of the novels that has influenced me the most. But *Absalom, Alsalom!* carries the intricacy of the Faulknerian narrative to obsessive extremes, a narrative that's always constructed in reverse, toward the past, in a dizzying spiral. It's memory that counts, that controls the rich mystery of the story, impels it along. . . . You probably recall our conversations two years ago. . . . Hemingway builds the eternity of the present moment through a narrative that's almost cinematographic . /

whereas Faulkner endlessly tracks the haphazard reconstruction of the past: its inherent density, opacity, ambiguity. . . . My stumbling block—but it's not a technical problem, it's a moral one—is that I can't manage, through writing, to get into the present, to talk about the camp in the present. . . . So all my drafts begin before, or after, or around, but never *in* the camp. . . . And when I finally get inside, I'm blocked, and cannot write. Overwhelmed with anguish, I fall back into nothingness: I give up . . . only to begin again elsewhere, some other way. . . . And the same thing repeats itself."

"That's understandable," she says softly.

"It's understandable, but it's killing me!"

She stirs a useless spoon around in her empty coffee cup.

"It must be the path you'll have to take as a writer," she murmurs. "An ascetic path: to put an end to all that death through writing."

She's probably right.

"Unless it puts an end to me!"

That's not just a play on words, and she knows it.

"You remember Wittgenstein?" she asks, after a long silence.

I was looking out at the blue sky of August over the Cimetière Montparnasse. Yes, with a bit of effort I could have remembered Wittgenstein, our conversation about him. But I was utterly worn out, didn't feel like remembering Wittgenstein, making that effort.

I was thinking about César Vallejo.

I've always been lucky with poets. I mean that my encounters with their creations have always been well timed: at the opportune moment, I inevitably find a poetic work that can help me to live, to sharpen my consciousness of the world. That's what happened with César Vallejo. And later, with René Char and Paul Celan.

In 1942, it was the poetry of César Vallejo that I discovered. It hadn't been a pleasant year, that one. I'd been forced to abandon my preparation at the Lycée Henri-IV for the competitive entrance exam for the École Normale Supérieure: I'd had to earn a living. A "survival" was more like it—just enough to scrape by. I barely managed that much, by giving Spanish lessons to pupils of all ages, and teaching Latin to young dunces (some of them odious) from well-to-do families. I had a decent meal only about once every two days or so. Often, I lived on little buckwheat rolls purchased without ration vouchers at a bakery that used to be on the Boulevard Saint-Michel, at the spot where the Rue Racine and the Rue de l'École-de-Médecine converge.

But I'd discovered the poetry of César Vallejo.

> *Me gusta la vida enormemente*
> *pero, desde luego,*
> *con mi muerte querida y mi café*
> *y viendo los castaños frondosos de París . . .*

Claude-Edmonde Magny had just mentioned Wittgenstein; I kept to myself the poem by César Vallejo that came into my head. I did not translate it for her, nor will I translate it here. It will remain a kind of secret, a sign of complicity with any Spanish-speaking reader.

She'd asked if I remembered our conversations about the *Tractatus,* three years earlier.

I'd come across this book while browsing in the bookstore of Édouard-Auguste Frick, on the Rue Blaise-Desgoffe. That's also where I'd discovered Musil and Broch. I'd been attracted immediately by Wittgenstein's title, by its insolence. By its megalomaniac aspect, as well. *Tractatus logico-philosophicus:* talk about daring! It was a bilingual edition, German-English, published by a British university. That winter, the winter of 1940–41, I was in the *classe de philosophie,* the final year of studies before the baccalaureate exam. In addition to the classic works on the syllabus, I was reading Heidegger and Saint Augustine, as I've already noted.

It was Levinas who'd led me to take up Martin Heidegger. As for Saint Augustine, that was because of Paul-Louis Landsberg, who had appeared in my adolescent life in 1938. It was a flesh-and-blood appearance, moreover: I knew him as a real person before I read and thought about his writings, in particular his essay *L'expérience de la mort.*

It was at The Hague, in the Netherlands, where my father was the chargé d'affaires of the Spanish Republic. He and Landsberg shared the same world of Christian values: they belonged to the personalist movement espoused by the journal *Esprit.* That year, when the civil war began to go badly in Spain—in other words, to put it bluntly: when the war began to go in the direction of History, which is not necessarily all to the Good, since History, throughout the thirties, took rather a bad turn, favoring totalitarian reactions to the crises of democratic and capitalist modernity—anyway, when the war began heading toward defeat for the Spanish republicans, Landsberg had come to the Netherlands for some conference or symposium. On the philosophy of Saint Augustine, as it happened.

One evening, Landsberg had dined at the legation with his wife. Just before dinner, I'd received permission to remain in the drawing room with them. I was almost fifteen years old: I had now joined the grown-ups. For my brothers and sisters and I were numerous enough to fall into very distinct age groups, each with its own norms of behavior.

I'd been allowed to stay and listen while the adults talked, that evening, before going in to dinner with the Landsbergs. The conversation focused mainly on the European situation. On the civil war in Spain and the congenital weakness of democracies in the face of Fascism. It was in this context that Saint Augustine made his sudden appearance, through a reference to the political implications of his thinking and to an incident that had occurred at the conference Paul-Louis Landsberg had come to the Netherlands to attend. I'm unable to dredge up from my memory all the details of that incident, or its import, obviously. I remember only Landsberg's wife, exclaiming in protest in the drawing room, where bay windows looked out over a garden planted with magnolias, and beyond them, 1813 Square. But surely it was not the season when the magnolias were in bloom, because I remember logs burning in the large fireplace. Paul-Louis Landsberg's wife had stood up abruptly in the drawing room (Rex, a playful young Irish setter lying next to me, had leaped nervously to his feet) to comment on the incident at the Augustinian symposium.

"A scholastic, can you imagine that!" she cried, with deliberate exaggeration. "Calling Paul-Louis Landsberg a scholastic!"

I hadn't really understood what she meant. I'd also found it strange that she would speak of her husband in the third person. But I found her alluring: blond and beautiful, drawn up to her full height, she was a touching and passionate picture of womanhood, an unforgettable image, for my dreamy adolescence, of the mysteries of femininity.

"You remember Wittgenstein?" Claude-Edmonde Magny had asked me.

She might just as well have asked if I remembered Heidegger. Because the conversation in question, which had taken place three years earlier, had concerned both a long-winded chapter dealing with the *Sein-zum-Tode* in Heidegger's book—a chapter stuffed with hollow banalities, blustering obfuscation, and his usual linguistic mannerisms—and a trenchant, limpid sentence (the ultimate meaning of which, however, was uncertain) from the *Tractatus* of Ludwig Wittgenstein.

Her eyes glittered behind her severe glasses.

"The imitation-leather notebook, you remember? *'Der Tod ist kein Ereignis des Lebens. Den Tod erlebt man nicht . . .'*"

She quoted the proposition, from Wittgenstein's treatise, on which I'd written a long commentary three years before, in a big imitation-leather notebook I used as a kind of private diary. That was the only time in my life, when I was eighteen, that I kept a diary. Later on, after I'd given up the idea of writing and begun long years of underground activity, I lost the habit of keeping such a record. Then, when I began publishing books during my forties (one of the reasons behind this one is to explain why I started so late in life), I systematically destroyed the log books, the notebooks of all kinds that go into a written work, as well as all the drafts left unfinished when a project turned out to be infeasible, or when the desire to complete it had melted away. I shouldn't like to leave behind the shameless traces of a tentative search for form—it would be almost indecent. Only the finished work counts, whatever its real value, of which the author is doubtless the most expert connoisseur, albeit not the best judge.

And so, if one were inclined to draw a conclusion from this attitude (improperly, no doubt: each of us has the right to react differently in this case), one would have to say that testaments are not betrayed by the legatees, but by the testators themselves. It's Franz Kafka who is responsible for the publication of his unfinished works, and not Max Brod. The author had only to destroy them himself, if he was truly unsatisfied with them!

Well, anyway, when I was eighteen I kept a sort of diary, more philosophical and literary, actually, than of a really private nature. I've always been careful about my privacy. In the big, black, imitation-leather notebook I'd written down my thoughts on the sentence from Wittgenstein's *Tractatus* and Martin Heidegger's pages on being-for-death in *Sein und Zeit*.

"La mort n'est pas un événement de la vie. La mort ne peut être vécue" ["Death is not an event in life. Death cannot be lived"]: this is the traditional translation, by Pierre Klossowski, of Wittgenstein's proposition. I'd slightly changed the translation of the last part (the beginning poses no problem: everyone translates it the same way) in my long, youthful lucubration. *"On ne peut vivre la mort"* ["One cannot live death"], I'd written. Later, years later, in a short novel called *L'évanouissement* (which I sometimes mention in this narrative because the novel happens to concern the same period I'm covering here, my return, my repatriation into exile), I translated that second part of Wittgenstein's proposition in yet another way: *"La mort n'est pas une expérience vécue"* ["Death is not a lived experience"]. But these variations arise from the difficulty of translating into French the verb *erleben* [to experience] and its noun *Erlebnis* [experience], a difficulty I would not have encountered had I been translating these words into Spanish.

No doubt, I'd written three years earlier, in the black imitation-leather notebook, no doubt death cannot be a lived experience (*vivencia,* in Spanish): we've known this ever since Epicurus, at least. Nor can it be an experience of pure consciousness, of the *cogito.* It will always be a mediated, conceptual experience, the experience of a social, practical occurrence. Such evidence, however, is spiritually quite meager. In fact, to be rigorous, Wittgenstein's pronouncement ought to be phrased like this: *"Mein Tod ist kein Ereignis meines Lebens. Meinen Tod erlebe ich nicht."* In other words: *my* death is not an event in *my* life. I will not live *my* death.

That's it, and it's not much.

"By the way," I asked, "where's the notebook? You never gave it back to me."

Claude-Edmonde blushed slightly, making a gesture of regret. Or helplessness.

"Lost!" she exclaimed. "I thought your text was interesting and loaned the notebook to Jean, so that he might read it."

Years later, when I wrote *Le grand voyage,* in Madrid, in a clandestine apartment on the Calle Concepción-Bahamonde, I remembered this detail. I remembered this conversation with Claude-Edmonde Magny. In a way, my book was a reply to her *Lettre.* It was impossible that I should not remember this conversation in August 1945, the letter she had read to me. When the power to write was at last restored to me, it was unthinkable that I should not recall the *Lettre* she had once written to me. As I was carrying through to a successful conclusion—or to an unsuccessful one, but in any case, to a conclusion—the project that had earlier failed, I thought of the imitation-leather notebook, and her reply when I'd asked about it.

In Madrid, on the Calle Concepción-Bahamonde, I wondered who Jean was. Or rather: to which one was she referring, Jean Gosset or Jean Cavaillès? I knew that she'd known both of them, at the time. She probably saw Gosset more often than she saw Cavaillès. She'd had me read a few of the latter's works. Difficult texts, at least for me; logic and the philosophy of mathematics were not my favorite fields. But impressive writing: rigorously coherent and methodical. Once I'd seen the two of them, Cavaillès and Gosset, leaving a restaurant. I knew they were deeply involved in the underground world of the Resistance. The real one, I mean, the only one, in my opinion: armed resistance.

Jean Gosset died after being deported; Jean Cavaillès was shot.

I knew what had happened to them, of course, when

Claude-Edmonde Magny mentioned the disappearance of my notebook. I understood that my text had been lost with them, with one of them. The loss didn't bother me too much—the loss of my notebook, obviously. I didn't ask which of the two men she meant that morning. But in Madrid, fifteen years later, while writing *Le grand voyage,* I regretted my lack of curiosity, which had probably been due to the fatigue of a sleepless night. I found myself hoping that Jean Cavaillès had been the one to whom Claude-Edmonde had loaned my private diary. Naturally, Cavaillès could only have smiled, kindly at best, at reading such an impetuous, juvenile text as the one I still vaguely remember. Nevertheless, I would have liked that clumsy and feverish essay on the experience of death to have had as its final reader, before vanishing deservedly into oblivion, Jean Cavaillès.

On the last day, I'd also remembered Wittgenstein.

It hadn't seemed like a last day, actually, my last day at Buchenwald. Nothing had led me to suppose that it would be. It had begun like all the other days since April 12, the day after the liberation of the camp, and could have finished up like all the others. On the morning of that particular day—which would turn out to be the last—there was nothing of the solemnity or the emotion mixed with anxiety that usually marks the last hours of a crucial period in your life. Nothing, in fact, would have allowed me to guess that Yves Darriet would decide to include me in a convoy of the Rodhain mission that was leaving Eisenach for Paris the next day.

The problem posed by the Spanish detainees in Buchenwald had not yet been entirely resolved. We knew that since we'd been arrested in the Resistance, sooner or later we'd be taken back to France. I'm not saying repatriated—I've already explained myself on that point, and at some length. Speaking only for myself, by the way. Most of the Spaniards in Buchenwald (survivors of the *maquis,* shock groups of the MOI, or guerrilla fighters from the southeast of France) would probably have accepted the term "repatriated." By which I mean that their homeland was the war against Fascism, and had been since 1936. France was the second arena of that struggle, that homeland, and they would not have balked at the word "repatriation." In any case, they would have been less inclined than I am to analyze the concrete significance of the word, weighing the pros and cons, the positive and negative aspects, the "yes, but" and the "no, however" sides of the question. Most of the Spanish deportees would not have split as many hairs as I have on this point.

So we knew that the Allied military authorities had decided to send us back to France, but we didn't know when that would be. Sooner or later, basically. We were living in that uncertainty.

My last day in Buchenwald—the one when I again thought of Wittgenstein—had begun like any other uncertain day. One more day in the confused period between death and life, reality and dream, that had begun with the liberation of the camp. I don't even remember the date of this last day, I have to figure it out. And to do that, I can't begin on the day the camp was liberated, April 11, because I'd soon wind up lost on the tortuous path of memory. A foggy path, too. Out of all those long days, only a few moments remain effortlessly in the light of memory, as I think I've already said. Moments often impossible for me to date, even to situate in chronological order. Other moments, though, fit themselves easily into the proper sequence.

Yet in spite of my hazy memory, I know that the traces left by those days haven't vanished irretrievably. They don't come naturally, spontaneously to mind, of course. I have to go looking for them, systematically flushing them out. The recollection exists somewhere, however, beyond my seeming forgetfulness. I must make an effort, brush aside all present preoccupations, deliberately cut myself off from my surroundings, shine the inner light of patient, concentrated attention on those far-off days. Then, faces emerge, episodes and encounters float back to the surface of life. Words blown away by the whirlwind of time past can be heard once again. As though, somehow, the film taken long ago by an attentive camera had never been developed: no one will ever have seen these images, but they exist. Thus I keep in reserve a hoard of pristine memories I might use should the need ever arise, should that day ever come.

Be that as it may, if I want to establish the date of my last day in Buchenwald—the one on which I again happened to recall Wittgenstein and that hollow, abrupt sentence from the *Tractatus*—it would be better if I began at the end of the story, to work backward in time, guided by a few indisputable markers. And the end occurred on May 1.

I was in Paris, that day, on the Place de la Nation, on the corner of the Avenue Bel-Air, when a sudden snow flurry swept over the red flags of the traditional parade.

I'd spent the day before, which had to be April 30, at Saint-Prix, in the house where my family had lived during the Occupation, on the hill that joins Montlignon to Saint-Leu and which Victor Hugo describes in a famous poem. The day before that, April 29, I'd arrived in Paris. I'd spent the night in the home of Pierre-Aimé Touchard, on the Rue du Dragon. And on the preceding day, April 28, the convoy of trucks belonging to the Rodhain mission had reached the repatriation camp at Longuyon. It was there that I was able to understand how right I was, how unrepatriated I had been: it was at Longuyon that I recovered my identity as a stateless person, which I never again questioned, in spite of all administrative appearances and official appointments. And so, gradually, I concluded that April 27—the day before my return to France through Longuyon and the confirmation of my fundamental inability to be considered a repatriate—is the day spent covering the distance between Eisenach, the convoy's point of departure, and Frankfurt, where we spent the night in a hut in a displaced persons camp. So, the conclusion of this brief itinerary: it's on April 26 that Yves Darriet came to get me to take me to Eisenach, on my last day at Buchenwald.

That day, around midmorning, I went to Block 34 to see Boris Taslitzky.

Since April 12, I'd been carrying René Char's *Seuls demeurent* around with me everywhere. Once again, a poet had entered my life at the perfect moment. I read snatches of his work to my pals. Soon I was able to recite the poems by heart—with all my heart.

Yves Darriet liked them as much as I did, and André Verdet did, too. I often saw Verdet, who was putting together an anthology of works by the poets of Buchenwald. I'd given him something I still vaguely remembered from my distant youth. But Verdet was familiar with Char, which irritated me a bit. He remembered *Ralentir travaux,* a collection written in collaboration with Breton and Éluard. I didn't resent too much the fact that he was ahead of me on this; the main thing was that his enthusiasm was boundless.

Boris Taslitzky, for his part, was more reserved. This reticence was not entirely sincere, however, and was probably a response to my having challenged him by waggling the volume of Char under his nose: "Now here's a real poet, better than your Aragon!" Which was a mite provocative. Somewhat brusque, too, I must admit. But I used to tease him with an intentionally exaggerated contempt for Aragon's poetry; it was a game we played.

That day, we sat down in the mess hall of Wing B, in Block

34 (a one-story wooden hut), and put the poems of Char and Aragon to the test.

I read to Boris from *Seuls demeurent,* he recited verses by Aragon. From *Crève-Coeur*—I remembered them quite well. I felt they displayed virtuosity, but no real depth. Then, determined to convince me or lure me over to his side, Boris recited occasional verse and some Resistance poetry, but also earlier works, mostly from *Hourra l'Oural!* I was impressed by the semantic and moral violence of these older poems, by their atmosphere of social apocalypse.

These last few years, I've occasionally thought about analyzing Aragon's poems from that period by comparing them with contemporaneous works by the German Bertolt Brecht and the Spaniard Rafael Alberti, studying the textual and political violence they have in common, however specific—and obvious—their other culturally distinctive characteristics may be.

These are certainly not the only literary works to be tinged with violence, during that period of crisis in the late twenties and early thirties. In protest against the hypocritical or cynical morality of bourgeois society, violence swept like a tidal wave through literature, the arts, and all fields of thought in the wake of the catastrophe of 1914–18. As far as I am aware, no comprehensive study has yet drawn up the inventory of spiritual disasters brought about by that war. To say nothing of the political ones.

But on top of the expressionist, surrealist, Dadaist, and libertarian violence, in the end Communism has added—especially after the crash of 1929, which shook not only the capitalist world but the USSR as well, causing various and often (at least seemingly) contradictory upheavals that all converged nevertheless on one essential point: an increase in the role of the state, as welfare dispenser or prison warden—Communism, as I was saying, has added the cold, enlightened, rational, and in a word, to-talitarian violence of an *Esprit-de-Parti* convinced it was follow-ing the course of History, like the Hegelian *Weltgeist*. And these three poets will prove to have been the most gifted spokesmen of this Communist violence.

I was familiar with the poetry of Rafael Alberti, his political poems of the thirties, of the Civil War. But their violence had not shocked me, at the time, no more than Aragon's had. I was still living in the same universe of truths and values as trenchant as the sword of the exterminating angels. Incidentally, these works displayed the full maturity of Rafael Alberti's talent, in the rigorous form and rich prosody of an oeuvre that has since then too often tied itself in knots in obedience to the shifting imperatives of Communist political strategy.

As for Bertolt Brecht (whom I'd discovered thanks to a young Viennese woman whose nom de guerre was Julia), he is un-questionably the greatest of the three, the one who mastered the widest range of voices, from the epic to the elegiac. He is also—paradoxically, as the only one of the three who was not a militant of the Communist Party—a paradigm of the fake opti-mism, guile, and base behavior that marked every Marxist intel-lectual in the bygone days of perverse revolutionary Virtue.

In April 1945, in the mess hall of a French hut in Buchen-wald, Block 34, we recited Char and Aragon, my pal Taslitzky and I.

Boris was in the middle of a full-throated rendition of a poem by Aragon in praise of the Ogpu when he was inter-rupted by a sudden shout.

We looked around.

An elderly French deportee was sitting at the end of the table. Caught up in our recitations, we had paid no attention to him. He was eating. He had carefully arranged his provisions in front of him. He was eating seriously: meticulously.

For the past few days, the American Army had been in charge of revictualling the camp. Work in the kitchens had been reorganized. There was now ample food for the deportees, food that was even too rich, often too copious for debilitated digestive systems long unused to such fare. This abundance had lately claimed as many victims as had the aftereffects of the earlier famine.

The old Frenchman must have been mistrustful, however, unable to believe in all this bounty. He must have thought it was too good to last. So he had punctiliously laid all his food reserves out on the table and he was eating with fastidious care. You can never tell; he was building up his strength in case things went wrong again. He was taking nourishment, just on the off chance, even if he wasn't really hungry anymore. He spread margarine thickly on slices of black bread, cut them into tiny squares, chewed them slowly, with some sausage. He'd probably been eating like that for quite a while. He probably had no intention of stopping before he'd eaten everything, swallowed it all down. He chewed slowly, making the pleasure last. But this word is clearly inappropriate: there's something gratuitous in the word "pleasure." It contains the notion of lightness, of unpredictability. It's much too casual a word to apply to the solemnity with which the old Frenchman carried out, rather obsessively, this ritual feeding.

So: he had shouted to get our attention. And he'd gotten it.

"Too obscure, your poets!" he yelled. "Bluffers, language-manglers!"

But he did not wish to let himself be distracted from the business at hand by righteous indignation. He put another morsel of black bread into his mouth, chewed it slowly.

We waited for the rest, moved to pity by his great age and the angry distress in his pale, washed-out eyes. All of a sudden, the rest arrived. Raising his voice so that it echoed through the empty mess hall, he recited for us Victor Hugo's *La légende des siècles*. Specifically, the passage about the dismal plain of Waterloo. As a finale, he drew himself up and acted out the arrival of Blücher on the battlefield, instead of the expected forces of Grouchy. With a sweep of his arm, he evoked the final advance of the Imperial Guard, *"tous ceux de Friedland et ceux de Rivoli portant le noir colback ou le casque poli"* ["the veterans of Friedland and those of Rivoli, in black calpac or polished helmet"], hurled into the inferno of Waterloo.

We listened to him, trying to keep a straight face. It wasn't bad, actually; I'm rather fond of *La légende des siècles*.

In spite of Boris Taslitzky's persuasive diction, it wasn't that day, April 26, in the mess hall of Block 34, that Louis Aragon managed to win me over. It was a few weeks later that I was captivated by Aragon. By himself, in person, by the indisputable charm of his conversation, however affected (in a slightly devious way) it may sometimes have been.

The summer of my return—I use this word, despite any possible reservations, for the sake of convenience—I used to visit Boris often in his studio on the Rue Campagne-Première. (Or was it the Rue Boissonnade? I'm not sure.) Even though I was avoiding all my former comrades in Buchenwald, and had already begun the cure of silence and studied amnesia that would become radical a few months later, in Ascona, in the canton of Ticino in Switzerland, when I abandoned the book I was trying to write (thus abandoning as well all attempts at writing anything, for an indefinite period), I continued to see Boris Taslitzky.

At the time, I didn't wonder why I made an exception for him. I'd visit him on impulse, suddenly feeling like walking to Montparnasse, turning up unexpectedly at his studio to watch him paint or draw. To compare notes with him: the marvels, ironies, miseries of our return to life.

Today, mulling this over, trying to understand my instinctive avoidance of everyone I knew from Buchenwald—unless I just happened to run into them—except Taslitzky, I think I know why. He possessed two qualities that made me feel extraordinarily close to him. Firstly, a tonic and insatiable appetite for life, ready for whatever surprises might come his way. And then, as a kind of dark counterweight to this blazing vitality, a keen sense of what we had lived through: death experienced right up to its blinding limit.

I would arrive at his place on the Rue Boissonnade or Campagne-Première, whichever; Boris would be working on one of those appallingly realistic pictures through which he was undoubtedly trying to exorcise the images that haunted him. But the reality of the camp that had created those images was too close, and too unbelievable, brutally lacking in any referential tradition of myths or allegories that would have made it easier to represent this reality. What's more, color—and Boris's palette was an extremely rich one—color has no place in the reproduction of such a reality. In short, realism betrays this reality, which is fundamentally hostile to it.

Sometimes, when I visited Boris in his studio, I would see Louis Aragon there. I recall his easy flow of words, his need to shine, to fascinate, the way his hands were constantly in motion, his unbearable habit of walking endlessly up and down in the studio while he held forth, observing his reflection in every shining surface, admiring himself in all the mirrors. But I also recall his attentive silence, his ability to listen and ask questions on those rare occasions when Taslitzky would speak about Buchenwald, trying to define what was at the heart of that experience.

On one such occasion, Aragon suddenly turned and startled me by exclaiming, "Our hero's being very quiet!" An agitated Boris begged him with looks and gestures to say nothing further, but Aragon calmly carried on.

"Come now, it's true! Boris claims that you were positively heroic. . . . At times I've been quite jealous of the friendship he feels for you! But how is it that you never say anything, when the conversation turns to the camp?"

Taslitzky vanished, embarrassed at having thus been put on the spot and in the spotlight. We could hear him rattling around in the kitchen.

I tried to tell Aragon why I kept quiet about Buchenwald. I explained that I was trying to write, that I preferred not to talk about it too much, to keep the writing fresh, avoiding the routines and tricks of stories repeated too many times.

This wasn't completely true, of course. At least it was only part of the truth. A very small part, even. But it did allow us for the first time to have a real conversation, an unforgettable discussion about literary truthfulness, or, which amounts to the same thing, about fiction and the true lies of literature.

Twenty years later, after I had published *Le grand voyage* and had just gotten myself expelled from the Spanish Communist Party, someone rang my doorbell. Louis Aragon was out on the landing. He had brought me a copy of his novel *La mise à mort* [*The Execution*]. There was a dedication, *"Contre vents et marées"*: "Against winds and tides."

But it wasn't because of this inscription—at least not solely because of it—that I would have forgiven Louis Aragon for many things. Not simply because of his pathetic image in his last months, either: a hoary phantom, a puppet from the great circus of stooges, in whose eyes there yet gleamed, however, a deep and long-repressed truth. No, it was above all because of a poem in which I detect a trace of those conversations in the studio on the Rue Campagne-Première (or Boissonnade—who cares!) and which was published in *Nouveau Crève-Coeur* in 1948.

It's a compilation of occasional poems, of "almanac verse," as the title of one of them puts it (another title needs no commentary: "Un revirement de la politique est possible en France" ["A Change of Political Path Is Possible in France"]), poetic works of rather paltry staying power. But suddenly, you turn a page and find "Chanson pour oublier Dachau" ["Song to Forget Dachau"].

Ne réveillez pas cette nuit les dormeurs . . .
[Tonight do not awaken those who sleep . . .]

I murmured the end of Aragon's poem, years later. It was in a nightclub on the Rue Saint-Benoît. A young German woman was sitting at the same table I was and I thought her beautiful: sleek, blond, innocent. But that particular night, I'd had the feeling of awakening from a dream. It still happened to me, sometimes, in spite of a deliberate and fairly successful decision to forget. That night, though—or was it perhaps the presence of that young German beauty?—I'd felt once again that life had been nothing but a dream since my return from Buchenwald a few years before. Perhaps I'd had too much to drink, that night, having awakened from this dream that was life. Perhaps I hadn't had enough to drink yet, when I noticed the young German woman sitting at the same table—although I was probably going to drink too much. But maybe drink had nothing to do with this story, and there was no need to look for some extraneous, accidental reason for the anguish I'd thought I'd mastered and forgotten for good, and which abruptly welled up again.

The young German woman was sleek, blond, innocent. I couldn't bear innocence, that night.

Nul ne réveillera cette nuit les dormeurs
Il n'y aura pas à courir les pieds nus dans la neige . . .
[No one will awaken those who sleep, tonight
No one will have to run barefoot in the snow . . .]

I recited Aragon's poem silently to myself, while looking at the young German woman I found so beautiful. Desirable as well, I'm sure. I don't remember the desire, but it's not improbable. The main thing was that I couldn't bear her supposed innocence. Especially since I myself felt guilty, that night: the exception that proves the rule. Awakening from this dream that was life, for once I felt guilty for having deliberately forgotten death. For having wanted to forget it, for having succeeded. Did I have the right to live in forgetfulness? To live, thanks to this oblivion, at its expense? The blue-eyed innocence of the young German woman made that oblivion unbearable to me. Not only my personal oblivion: the general, massive, historical forgetting of all that past death.

Ton corps n'est plus cette dérive aux eaux d'Europe
Ton corps n'est plus cette stagnation cette rancoeur
Ton corps n'est plus la promiscuité des autres
N'est plus sa propre paunteur . . .
[Your body is no longer adrift on the waters of Europe
Your body is no longer that stagnation that rancor
Your body is no longer crowded in with others
Is no longer its own fetor . . .]

There are in this text, no doubt, rhetorical scoriae, prosodic flourishes, that Aragon found himself unable to resist. No doubt his poem would benefit from a good polishing, a rigorous purification that would reveal the very structure of the language, eliminating all excess verbiage—the kind of work that always characterizes the poetry of Paul Celan. Of René Char, often.

Still, several diamonds of the first water can be found in "Chanson pour oublier Dachau," several surprisingly accurate forays into the experience of deportation, so difficult to understand from the outside.

> *Quand tes yeux sont fermés revois-tu revoit-on*
> *Mourir aurait été si doux à l'instant même*
> *Dans l'épouvante où l'équilibre est stratagème*
> *Le cadavre debout dans l'ombre du wagon . . .*
> [When your eyes are closed do you see does one see
> At that moment dying would have been so sweet
> In the terror of struggling to keep your balance
> In the dark boxcar the corpse on its feet . . .]

I recited Aragon's poem to myself, choosing the verses that most profoundly stirred my memory. I recited it silently, impassively, that night, in a nightclub on the Rue Saint-Benoît. I looked at the innocent young German woman, who remembered nothing, of course, and I recited to myself this poem of remembrance. But I have also recited this poem to myself out loud. In the streets of great cities, at times, despite knowing I would draw pitying looks from passersby. I've shouted it out before the ocean's roar on the Spanish beach of Oyambre. Before the shifting mists of the shores of Little Deer Isle, in Maine.

I will have recited this poem by Aragon throughout my life. It will have been my lifelong companion.

I recited the end of this poem not so very long ago, on March 8, 1992, on the roll-call square of Buchenwald.

I had gone back there for the first time in forty-seven

Until then, I had always refused such a return, for which I'd felt neither the need nor the desire, for all sorts of reasons. But this narrative was almost finished—at least that was my erroneous impression—and the idea of verifying its coherence, its internal truth, had suddenly appealed to me. Besides, historical circumstances had changed with the democratic reunification of Germany. I decided to take advantage of an opportunity to go back there: a German television station had invited me to participate in a program on Weimar, a cultural landmark with its own concentration camp.

On the square of Buchenwald, one day in March 1992, I recited Aragon's poem to myself in a low voice. I had just discovered that I would have to rewrite a large part of my story. That I would have to reimmerse myself once more in that long mourning process of memory. Endless, once again. But I didn't feel sad about it, curiously enough.

I was accompanied by Thomas and Mathieu Landman, my grandsons through bonds of affection, which are as strong as any other. I had chosen them to accompany me to Germany, and they truly did keep me company. Throughout our journey I felt their fond presence—young, laughing, deeply moved—warming my old memories, the ashes of my past. And they stood by me, on the square of Buchenwald. Mathieu took photographs, Thomas gazed at the horizon that met my twenty-year-old eyes, at the foot of the Ettersberg. There was the squat chimney of the crematory on our right. There was the sighing of the wind that blows for all eternity on the Ettersberg. There was the noisy chirping of the birds: they had returned, and I thought of Lieutenant Rosenfeld. A forest without birds, once upon a time, a forest of beeches whose birds had been driven away by the nauseous stench of the crematory oven.

Then I recited to myself the end of this poem.

Il y a dans ce monde nouveau tant de gens
Pour qui plus jamais ne sera naturelle la douceur
Il y a dans ce monde ancien tant et tant de gens
Pour qui toute douceur est désormais étrange
Il y a dans ce monde ancien et nouveau tant de gens
Que leurs propres enfants ne pourront pas comprendre

Oh vous qui passez
Ne réveillez pas cette nuit les dormeurs . . .

[There are in this new world so many people
For whom tenderness will nevermore be natural
There are in this old world so very many people
For whom all tenderness will now be strange
There are in this old and new world so many people
Whom their own children can never understand

Oh you who pass by
Do not awaken those who sleep, tonight . . .]

"No hay derecho . . ." murmurs Morales, his face turned toward me.

On the bed where he is lying in the *Revier,* the white sheet covers his body like a shroud. His face is wasted, its pallor heightened by several days' growth of bristly, bluish-black beard.

I'd left Boris Taslitzky a little while before. After the recitations of René Char, Louis Aragon, and *La légende des siècles,* I'd gone back to my block, number 40, to wait for the midday meal. Because we were now allowed two meals, at noon and at suppertime. I still did not know that April 26 was to be my last day in Buchenwald. I had not yet had any reason to remember Ludwig Wittgenstein.

Years later, when I published *L'évanouissement*, in which figure both Wittgenstein and his *Tractatus*, one esteemed critic
thought that I'd made up the character. He thought this philosopher was a lovely novelistic invention. I must say that at the time,
around the mid-sixties, Wittgenstein was hardly known at all in
France. Reading the review, I was torn between a somewhat
rueful astonishment at the critic's ignorance, and a sense of literary satisfaction. Believing me capable of inventing a character as
fascinating and unbearable as Wittgenstein was fine praise indeed.

But at Buchenwald, on April 26, 1945, at that hour of the
day, I had not yet invented Wittgenstein. I hadn't even thought
of him. I hadn't remembered the peremptory sentence from his
Tractatus about which I'd written at such length, three years earlier, in the notebook of black imitation leather that Claude-
Edmonde Magny had loaned to one of her two Jeans, Gosset or
Cavaillès. I was in front of the door of Block 40, in the sunshine:
idle, daydreaming, awaiting the distribution of the midday meal.
I was wondering what I was going to do that afternoon.

I saw Bolados arrive, on the double.

He was the head of the underground Spanish Communist
organization in Buchenwald. Number one, in short, of the rul-
ing troika. Next to him were Palazón, in charge of the military
apparatus, and Falcó, secretary of the organization. All these
names were pseudonyms, by the way, under which the men had
been arrested in France, in the Resistance, and they had kept
them. It wasn't until after April 12, after the camp was liberated,
that I learned their real names. Palazón was called Lacalle, Falcó's
name was Lucas. And Bolados was Nieto, Jaime Nieto.

One week earlier, on April 19, the delegates of all the Communist parties in Buchenwald had met to draw up a political
declaration. Eleven parties were represented at that meeting:
those of France, the USSR, Italy, Poland, Belgium, Yugoslavia,
the Netherlands, Czechoslovakia, Spain, Austria, and Germany.

The Spanish delegate had signed both his names, adding his pseudonym of Bolados—by which he was known in Buchenwald—in parentheses after his real name, Jaime Nieto.

He raced up to me.

"Good, you're here! Morales is dying, he wants to see you!"

We dashed off to the infirmary, which was at the other end of the barbed-wire enclosure.

"No hay derecho," Morales has just murmured to me.

He's right. It isn't fair.

Diego Morales arrived in the camp toward the end of the summer of 1944, after a brief time in Auschwitz. Time enough, however, for him to have figured out the principles behind the selection process specific to the massive extermination complex of Auschwitz-Birkenau. Even before the decisive testimony of the survivor of the *Sonderkommando,* Morales had given me my first idea of the absolute horror that was life at Auschwitz.

In our camp, Morales had immediately been assigned to skilled work in the Gustloff factory, where he was a truly outstanding fitter (or a milling machine operator—I'm not up on my metalworking terminology). He was so meticulous and capable that the underground organization finally gave him a vital job at the end of the automatic rifle assembly line, where he had to cleverly sabotage a key piece of the mechanism to render the weapon useless.

Assigned to my dormitory in Block 40 after his quarantine period, Morales had amazed me with his abilities as a storyteller. I never tired of listening to him. Admittedly, his tale was a storyteller's dream.

He used to say that a book was responsible for the adventurous nature of his life. "A fucking little book," he'd say, laughing. *Un jodido librito* . . . Reading this book had turned his life upside down, plunging him headfirst—no mistake about that—into the whirlwind of political turmoil. At the age of sixteen, in fact, he had read the *Communist Manifesto,* and his life had been changed. He still talked about it, at Buchenwald, with deep emotion. The way others speak of Lautréamont's *Les Chants de Maldoror* or Rimbaud's *Une saison en enfer.*

At nineteen, Morales had fought in the Spanish Civil War in a guerrilla unit operating beyond the front lines, in enemy territory. It was after the fall of the Spanish Republic, at Prades, that he received his second literary shock. He had been taken in and hidden by a French family after his escape from the refugee camp at Argelès. It was in their home that he had read *Le Rouge et le Noir.* Of course, the fact that this book had been recommended to him by a young woman, whose memory he still cherished (with a devotion both sensual and sublimated), may well have had something to do with the novel's seductive hold on him.

Whatever part may have been played by his former flame, however, Morales credited Stendhal's book with effects comparable to those caused by Marx's pamphlet, albeit in a different domain. If the *Manifesto* had helped him comprehend the great and inexorable workings of history, *The Red and the Black* had initiated him into the mysteries of the human soul, about which he spoke with heartfelt and subtle precision. He was unstoppable once launched upon this subject, and I did not deprive myself of that pleasure.

"It's not fair," Morales has just murmured to me, moments after I've sat down next to his cot, moments after I've taken his hand in mine.

He's right, it's not fair that he should die now.

Morales survived the war in Spain, the fighting on the Glières plateau; that was his worst memory, he told me: the long trek through deep snow, under machine-gun crossfire, to break free of the encircling German troops and detachments of the French *gendarmerie* and militia. He survived Auschwitz. And Buchenwald, despite the daily risk of being caught red-handed by a civilian *Meister* or an SS *Sturmführer* while engaged in sabotage on the Gustloff assembly line, which would have led him directly to the gallows. He had survived a thousand other dangers only to end up, stupidly, like this.

"Morirse así, de cagalera, no hay derecho," he whispers in my ear.

I've knelt down by his cot so that he needn't strain to speak to me.

He's right: it's not fair to die idiotically of the runs after so many chances to die weapons in hand. And after the liberation of the camp, on top of that, just when the most important battle had been won, and liberty restored. Just when opportunities of dying under arms, in the anti-Franco guerrilla struggle in Spain, were beckoning to him once again as a token of freedom—it was stupid to die of galloping dysentery brought on by food that had suddenly become too rich for his weakened digestive system.

I don't tell him that death is stupid, by definition. As stupid as birth, at least. And just as stupefying. This would not be any consolation. Besides, there's no reason for him to appreciate such enlightened metaphysical considerations at this moment.

I shake his hand in silence. I remember having already held the dying body of Maurice Halbwachs in my arms. It was the same decomposition, the same stench, the same visceral shipwreck setting adrift a tearful soul that yet remained lucid until the last moment, a tiny, flickering flame no longer nourished by the body's vital oxygen.

Ô mort, vieux capitaine, il est temps, levons l'ancre . . .

I had murmured a few verses of Baudelaire to Halbwachs, as a prayer for the dying. He had heard me, he had understood me: his eyes had shone with a terrible pride.

But what can I say to Diego Morales? What words can I murmur in consolation? Can I console him at all? Wouldn't it be better to speak of compassion?

I can't very well recite Marx's *Manifesto* to him! No, only one text comes to mind. A poem by César Vallejo. One of the most beautiful in the Spanish language. A poem from his book on the Civil War, *España, aparta de mi este cáliz* [*Spain, Take This Cup from Me*].

> *Al fin de la batalla,*
> *y muerto el combatiente, vino hacia él un hombre*
> *y le dijo: "No mueras, te amo tanto!"*
> *Pero el cadáver ¡ay! siguió muriendo . . .*
> [When the battle was over,
> and the soldier was dead, a man came to him
> and said, "Do not die, I love you so!"
> But the corpse, alas! continued dying . . .]

Before I can murmur the beginning of this heartbreaking poem, a convulsion runs through Morales, a kind of pestilential explosion. He empties out, literally, soiling the sheet that covers him. He clings to my hand, with all his strength gathered into this last effort. In his eyes I see the most dreadful distress. Tears course down the dying soldier's cheeks.

"*Que vergüenza,*" he says with his last sigh.

Do I hear this whisper? Do I sense upon his lips the words that express his shame?

His eyes roll back: he is dead.

I feel like crying, *No mueras, te amo tanto*, like the man in Vallejo's poem. "Do not die, I love you so! But the corpse, alas! continued dying . . ."

He continues dying, he continues entering the eternity of

death. That's when I remember Ludwig Wittgenstein. "Death is not an event in life. Death cannot be lived," this idiot Wittgenstein had written. Yet I have lived the death of Morales, I am living it now. The way I had lived the death of Halbwachs a year earlier. And hadn't I likewise lived the death of the young German soldier who sang "La Paloma"? The death that I had given him? Hadn't I lived the horror, the compassion, of all those deaths? Of all death? And the fraternal kinship of men before death?

I close Morales's eyes.

It's a gesture I've never seen performed before, that no one has taught me. A natural gesture, like those of love. Such gestures come to you naturally, from the depths of the most ancient wisdom. Of the most primal knowledge.

I stand up, I turn around. They're all here: Nieto, Lucas, Lacalle, Palomares . . . They, too, have lived the death of Morales.

"I think that readers often overlook all the *terror* there is in Keats, in the beginning of 'Hyperion,' for example:

There was a listening fear in her regard
As if calamity had but begun . . ."

Claude-Edmonde Magny has returned to the reading of her *Lettre sur le pouvoir d'écrire*.

"Keats saw the worm at the core of every fruit, the flaw at the heart of all existence, he knows there is no salvation for man in this world and he is terrified. But this terror is now cosmic, and no longer psychological. It manages to be the serene transportation of an experience that was atrocious, true, but that has now been left behind. . . ."

She pauses. She looks at me.

But I don't want to speak. I'm exhausted, emptied of all possible words.

Two years after that August morning on the Rue Schoelcher, I received a copy of *Lettre sur le pouvoir d'écrire*. Seghers brought out a first edition of three hundred copies on Lafuma wove paper; mine was No. 130.

In 1947, when her essay was published, I was no longer seeing Claude-Edmonde Magny as often as I once had. I would even say that by then I met her only by chance, on the occasion—most infrequent—of an exhibition opening, an evening at the theater. Things of that sort. Things as casual, as futile as that.

I'm certain, in any case, that I never returned to her studio on the Rue Schoelcher. Neither at six in the morning nor at any other, more suitable, hour. The last time I rang her doorbell must have been that morning, at the dawn of an August day in 1945, on the eve of Hiroshima.

It's true that in 1947 I had already abandoned my plan to write. I had become someone else, to stay alive.

In Ascona, in Ticino, on a sunny winter's day in December 1945, I had to choose between literature or life. I'm the one who forced myself to make this decision, of course. I was the one who had to choose, I alone.

Like a luminous cancer, the account I was wresting from my memory, bit by bit, sentence by sentence, was devouring my life. My taste for life, at least, my desire to go on with that miserable joy. I was convinced I would reach some ultimate point at which, solemnly, I would have to acknowledge my failure. Not because I couldn't manage to survive the writing. Only a suicide could put a signature, a voluntary end to this unfinished—this unfinishable—process of mourning. Or else this very incomple-
would put an end to mourning, arbitrarily, through the
donment of the work in progress.

A young woman, without realizing it, without having planned it, helped me keep hold of life. Her name was Lorène, she'll appear in due course, soon: her time is coming. Because of her, I was saved, or lost—it's not for me to say: I reject in advance any judgment on this matter. In any case, she kept me alive.

I was living in Solduno, that winter, near Locarno. My sister Maribel had rented a house in the Maggia Valley, in sunny Ticino, so that I might rest. So that I might write, as well. I'd spent the autumn of my return, then the winter, with her and a three-year-old nephew. Jean-Marie Soutou, my brother-in-law, was off with Jean Payart in Belgrade, opening the French embassy there. Sometimes my sister and I were joined by another brother, Gonzalo, who lived in Geneva. Peaceful times, full of laughter, stories, memories: a happiness woven of shared understanding. Everyone fussed over me, the ghost, the revenant. I let myself be cherished and I tried to write. Rather: I tried to survive the writing that was tearing at my soul.

I used to meet Lorène in Ascona, a neighboring village on the lake. Lorène knew nothing about me, nothing important: where I came from, who I really was. She hardly knew what I was doing there. She had no other reason to be interested in me than myself: that's what was so overwhelming. Myself, in the present, during a seemingly carefree winter in Ascona, where we were both taking it easy, recovering. She, from a grimly unsuccessful venture into marriage. I was—I don't remember anymore. I'd invented some reason for my being there, with my family, but I've forgotten the details.

Thanks to Lorène, who had no idea of this, who never knew anything about it, I came back to life. In other words, to oblivion: that was the price of life. A deliberate, systematic forgetting of the experience of the camp. Of writing, as well. There was no question, in fact, of writing anything else. It would have been absurd, perhaps even ignoble, to write anything at all that would pass over that experience in silence.

I had to choose between literature and life; I chose life. I chose a long cure of aphasia, of voluntary amnesia, in order to survive. And during this work of returning to life, this period of mourning for writing, I grew apart from Claude-Edmonde Magny. Her *Lettre sur le pouvoir d'écrire,* which had accompanied me everywhere since 1947, even on my clandestine journeys, was the only link, an enigmatic, fragile bond with the person I would have liked to be: a writer. A bond with myself, then, with the most authentic—albeit frustrated—part of me.

But I know nothing of all that on this August morning of blue sky over the Cimetière Montparnasse, over the tomb of César Vallejo.

"What poets did we read together?" asks Claude-Edmonde Magny. "Keats, of course. . . . And Coleridge, Rainer Maria Rilke, I remember."

"César Vallejo," I reply. "I translated a few of his poems for you."

"Vallejo, that's right!" she says softly. "I put flowers on his tomb, faithfully, while you were gone!"

Have I really come back?

7

BAKUNIN'S UMBRELLA

Time had passed, it was now December, and Lorène was waiting for me outside a movie theater in Locarno.

I'd been to see the matinee showing of an American film based on a play by Eugene O'Neill. A rather brutal story about sailors on a long ocean voyage.

"Do you want me to show you Mikhail Alexandrovitch Bakunin's umbrella?" she asked gaily.

Lorène was at the wheel of a Mercedes cabriolet convertible, a rather old model, but still magnificent. The car was parked in front of the movie theater, in the sunshine. In spite of traditional Swiss discretion (perhaps less widespread in Ticino, so close to Italy), I was the object of envious glances.

My pulse quickened immediately.

Bakunin wasn't the cause of my excitement, not really. Neither he nor his umbrella. She could have said anything at all, it would have had the same effect on me. It was her presence that was disturbing, the fact that she was there, waiting for me.

I'd gone over to stand next to her, leaning with both hands on the edge of the door. She looked up at me, with laughing, golden light in her eyes.

"Yes," I replied, "show me this famous umbrella!"

I'd have used any excuse whatsoever to stay with her, to take refuge in the likely comfort of her arms.

I'd watched the O'Neill film—I mean: the film version of one of his plays—almost in a daze. The images went by in a staccato rhythm, without much internal cohesion, despite their undeniable power. I wasn't able to fit them into the continuity of a story, the flow of a temporal narrative. Sometimes their meaning escaped me, and I could see only their aggressive formal beauty.

It was as if I'd been struck with amazement, put into a trance. One devoid of all anxiety, however: plunged into the serenity of the softest and most flawless despair.

It wasn't the film itself (was John Ford the director?) that had put me in this stupor, of course. It was what had come first, the newsreel they had shown before the feature.

Suddenly, after reports on a sports event and some international conference in New York, I'd had to close my eyes, blinded for a moment. When I opened them again, I hadn't been dreaming, the images were still there, on the screen, inescapable.

I've forgotten what the pretext or the occasion was, but the subject of the newsreel that day in the movie theater of Locarno was the discovery of the Nazi concentration camps by the Allied armies a few months earlier.

The camera's eye explored the interior of a hut: skeletal deportees at the end of their strength lay collapsed in bunks, staring fixedly at the intruders who were bringing—too late for many of them—their freedom. The camera's eye watched the American Army's bulldozers pushing hundreds of wasted corpses into common graves. The camera's eye noticed the gestures of three young deportees with close-cropped hair, wearing striped clothing, as they shared a single cigarette butt at the entrance to a hut. . . . The camera's eye followed the slow progress of a group of deportees hobbling across the open space of a parade ground, in the sunshine, toward a place where food was being distributed. . . .

These scenes had been filmed in different camps liberated by the Allied advance a few months before. In Bergen-Belsen, in Mauthausen, in Dachau. There were also some images of Buchenwald, which I recognized.

Or rather: which I knew for certain came from Buchenwald, without being certain of recognizing them. Or rather: without being certain of having seen them myself. And yet I had seen them. Or rather: I had experienced them. It was the difference between the seen and the experienced that was disturbing.

Because it was the first time I'd seen such images. Until that winter's day—somewhat by chance, much more through a spontaneous strategy of self-defense—I'd managed to avoid filmed images of the Nazi camps. I had the ones in my memory, images that sometimes burst cruelly into my consciousness. Images I could also summon deliberately, even giving them a more or less structured form, organizing them into a course of anamnesis, a kind of narrative or intimate exorcism. That's exactly what they were: intimate images. Memories that to me were as consubstantial, as natural (despite their unbearable element) as those of my childhood. Or those of happy adolescent initiations of all kinds: into friendship, reading, the beauty of women.

All of a sudden, though, in the quiet of that movie theater in Locarno, where whispers and murmurs died away into a rigid silence of horror and compassion (and disgust, probably), these intimate images became foreign to me, objectified up on the screen. They also broke free of my personal procedures of memory and censorship. They ceased being my property and my torment, the deadly riches of my life. They were, finally, nothing more than the externalized, radical reality of Evil: its chilling yet searing reflection.

The gray, sometimes hazy images, filmed with the jerky motions of a handheld camera, acquired an inordinate and overwhelming dimension of reality that my memories themselves could not attain.

Seeing clusters of deportees appear on the movie screen, roaming the roll-call square at Buchenwald in the confusion of their regained freedom, beneath an April sun that was so close and so distant, I saw myself returned to reality, reinstated in the truth of an indisputable experience. Everything had been true, so, it was all still true. Nothing had been a dream.

In becoming, thanks to the film corps of the Allied armies, a spectator of my own life, a voyeur of my own experience, I felt as if I were escaping the wrenching uncertainties of memory. As if—although this might seem strange at first—the dimension of unreality, the context of fiction inherent in any cinematic image, even the most strictly documentary one, gave the weight of incontestable reality to my inmost memories. On the one hand, of course, they had been taken from me; on the other, their reality was confirmed: I had not imagined Buchenwald.

My life, therefore, was more than just a dream.

Yet although the newsreel footage confirmed the truth of the actual experience (which was sometimes difficult for me to grasp and situate among my memories), at the same time these images underlined the exasperating difficulty of transmitting this truth, of making it, if not absolutely clear, at least communicable.

Even though they showed the naked obscenity, the physical deterioration, the grim destruction of death, the images, in fact, were silent. Not merely because they were filmed without live sound recording, which was standard practice at the time. They were silent above all because they said nothing precise about the reality they showed, because they delivered only confused scraps of meaning. One would have had to work on the body of the film, on its very cinematic material: stopping the sequence of images occasionally to freeze a frame, offering close-ups of certain details, sometimes showing the action in slow motion, speeding it up at other moments. What was really needed was commentary on the images, to decipher them, to situate them not only in a historical context but within a continuity of emotions. And in order to remain as close as possible to the actual experience, this commentary would have had to be spoken by the survivors themselves: the ghosts who had returned from that long absence, the Lazaruses of that long death.

One would have had to treat the documentary reality, in short, like the material of fiction.

The newsreel had lasted three or four minutes, at the most. Long enough to plunge me into a whirlwind of thoughts and feelings so upsetting that I'd remained sunk in anguished reverie throughout much of the film that followed, to which I was able to pay only sporadic attention.

But when I came out of the movie theater, there was Lorène. She'd happened to notice me going in, it seemed, and after finding out when the film would be over, had returned to wait for me.

I felt drawn to her by a kind of desperate gratitude.

"Locarno!" I'd exclaimed, two days earlier. "Then you must know Bakunin!"

I'd wanted to disconcert her, naturally. To attract her attention, provoke her curiosity—her charmed astonishment, in the end, after she'd been dazzled by my casually knowledgeable and witty remarks about Bakunin in Locarno.

Nothing doing. Lorène had nodded, unruffled.

"Yes, indeed," she'd replied, as though this went without saying. "We even have his umbrella in our house!"

I'd been dumbfounded.

We'd come to the end of a meal that had proved quite enjoyable, in spite of my initial misgivings. The restaurant car was three-quarters empty, but she had sat down across from me, deliberately. She'd needed company, had felt like talking, she told me later.

I'd have preferred to have the table to myself.

I'd decided to have a copious, substantial lunch, to relish it at my leisure. I'd intended to eat and drink my fill, with the respect and enjoyment that Swiss cooking deserves.

Before, there had always been an end to food. No matter how slowly you chewed the slice of black bread you'd cut into minuscule pieces, there always came a moment when it was finished. It was almost as though nothing had happened: black bread gone, mouth empty, stomach hollow. Nothing but the immediate return of hunger. In the restaurant car of the Swiss train, it would be different: there was no limit imaginable to the food on offer. There could only be a limit on hunger. The word, moreover, was inappropriate, unsuitable: hunger had become ordinary appetite.

That day, however, the old obsession had returned. On a moral rather than a physical plane, actually. It was the idea of hunger, its exhausting memory, that suddenly took hold of me, in an entirely different context. I knew that I could satisfy this hunger: it had become appetizing once more.

I'd therefore ordered a gin fizz as an aperitif, with the firm intention of following that with a bottle of Pontet-Canet 1929 and organizing my meal around that admirable wine.

I'd discovered the existence of Pontet-Canet on my first trip between Locarno and Berne—there and back on the same day—in the restaurant car of the Swiss train. Once a month, as it happened (Lorène appeared during my third trip, in December), I was obliged to have my residence permit visaed in Berne by the federal police. It had proven impossible to arrange with the said police to have my Swiss residence permit stamped in Locarno, the city closest to where I was staying that winter. I don't know what obscure and obtuse bureaucratic reason obliged me to go all the way to Berne. And so, instead of simply taking the tram from Solduno to Locarno, I then took an express—a "light" train, as it was called in the French-speaking cantons—and made the round trip during the day.

So, that time, on my third and final trip (my residence permit was to expire in January of 1946), I treated myself to a solitary meal: the bottle of Pontet-Canet, with a meal chosen to do honor to this sumptuous wine.

Under these circumstances, you can see that the unexpected company of this young woman was somewhat irritating. There would have to be a minimum of conversation. And then, above all, if there's a stranger looking on, one doesn't eat in the same way. With the same freedom, the same relaxed enthusiasm. You feel constrained, in front of a stranger—and a woman, besides. You watch yourself, you mind your manners and behave yourself. But what I particularly wanted was to let myself go, to be greedy and gluttonous if I felt like it, to gobble up the dishes I'd picked out.

She was disturbing me, true, but she was ravishing. Self-confident, with her bronzed complexion and the soft, lustrous look of her skin. At ease in her clothes, their quality a discreet but unmistakable reflection of good breeding. That's what was most striking: the tradition apparent behind so much composure, so much airy grace. The weight of inheritance, the extensive lineage behind such obvious poise. She was clearly the almost perfect product of several generations of Palmolive, cashmere, and piano lessons.

This appearance was not deceiving. Lorène turned out to be the heiress of a patrician family with a name as famous in the Swiss chemical industry as it was in the patronage of the arts.

"What are you celebrating?" she'd asked as she sat down at my table, noticing the bottle of wine the sommelier had just uncorked in an unctuous manner and presented for my approval.

"Nothing!" I'd replied. "Life!"

She ordered a light meal, with mineral water.

"And what do you do in life?" she added.

"Nothing, yet. . . . I just live!"

My laconic answers had not discomfited her, still less discouraged her. She continued to question me, without great success. Most of the information she succeeded in extorting from me was false, beginning with my first name: Manuel, I'd told her. Tiring of her inquiry, she talked to me about herself. It was touching, but banal. Besides, whenever strangers tell us their life stories in trains, these tales are always touchingly banal. Lorène had only just broken free of a disastrous marriage. Six months of nightmare, according to her. A costly divorce had recently put an end to this conjugal hell.

I listened to her with only half an ear, but contemplated her with delight. Her gestures were graceful, her voice melodious, her table manners exquisite and unaffected. A feast for the eyes while I was savoring various hearty or subtly flavored dishes.

At one point, I no longer remember why, she spoke of the family home in Locarno.

"Then you must know Bakunin!" I'd said.

Only to be flattened by her reply.

"Yes, indeed, we even have his umbrella at our house!"

It turned out that a cousin of Teresa Pedrazzini, the landlady of the Russian revolutionary, had worked for Lorène's great-grandparents in their home in Locarno, a house that had been in the family's possession throughout all patrician eternity, that eternity of patrimonies, entailed properties, and marriage contracts designed to safeguard real estate. One rainy day in the 1870s, this servant (whose name was also Teresa, like her cousin Pedrazzini, which singularly complicated the stories told by their ancillary but long-winded descendants, according to Lorène), her great-grandparents' Teresa, returning in the rain from an errand at her cousin's house, had borrowed a large black umbrella with a curiously carved handle, unaware that it belonged to Mikhail Alexandrovitch, that bearded and polyglot Russian refugee in Italian-speaking Switzerland who had rented a furnished apartment from Teresa Pedrazzini. Forgotten in the front hallway of Lorène's family home, the umbrella preserved its anonymity for a while. It was a forgotten umbrella, that's all. It happened to be there, without provoking either interest or disturbance. Until the day Bakunin in person arrived to reclaim it. Family legend presented this event in a particularly dramatic light: all the details—doubtless embellished with ornaments, additions, fioriture, and exaggerations during decades of oral transmission from one generation to the next—had been preserved, codified. Whatever its variants might have been, the end of the story was always the same: Lorène's great-grandfather refused to return the umbrella to Mikhail Alexandrovitch, on the pretext (morally futile, albeit legally impeccable) that the latter could not prove he was its owner. Furthermore, as a well-known anarchist, outlaw, and resolute opponent of private property, however did he dare invoke this sacred right in a personal affair as dubious as it was petty? It seems that this last argument had sent Bakunin into a resounding peal of laughter. After which he left Lorène's great-grandparents' house, abandoning his umbrella to the enemy, like a flag on the field of battle.

The story of Bakunin's umbrella and our laughter over it had brought us closer together. A kind of complicitous intimacy seemed to spring up between us. The possibility of a future meeting had hovered about our words, without becoming explicit. But we wound up driven politely from the restaurant car—where our conversation had threatened to go on forever— because, as they explained, they had to set the tables for dinner for the Lugano-Geneva night express.

Lorène looked up at me, in front of the movie theater in Locarno.

"Fine," I'd told her. "Let's go see Bakunin's umbrella!"

I wasn't thinking of Mikhail Alexandrovitch, however; nothing was farther from my mind.

I was thinking of Paul-Louis Landsberg. Of his wife, rather. I'd just discovered whom Lorène resembled. Even two days earlier, in the restaurant car, while I gazed at her with admiring interest, Lorène had reminded me of a woman I'd met at some other time, in some other place. I didn't know whom she reminded me of, but I was certain of the resemblance. I was also sure that it was a woman from my adolescence. But no matter how hard I tried to recall the women from that period of my life, I couldn't remember. The recollection, the resemblance, the memory remained enigmatic, evident yet indecipherable.

Everything had just become clear in an instant. It was the convertible that had provided the key to this obscure resemblance, making it abundantly obvious.

The woman Lorène reminded me of was the young wife of Paul-Louis Landsberg.

In the spring of 1939, during the Esprit conference I believe I've already mentioned, Jean-Marie Soutou and I had occasionally been given a lift by Landsberg's wife, who drove a cabriolet convertible. I rode in the rumble seat, the wind whipping my face. Once, over by Ville-d'Avray, I'd held the door open while she got out of the car. Rays of sunlight danced in the shade of the tree-lined avenue. Just as she stepped onto the pavement, her abrupt movement permitted a glimpse of her legs. All the way up to her garters and the milky skin of her thighs. The effect this had on me was increased by the memory of a book I'd read not long before, *La conspiration,* by Paul Nizan. Catherine Rosenthal's knee, revealed in similar circumstances: the power of the scene in the novel intensified my emotion.

As for Bakunin's umbrella, it was on display in a custom-built glass case in the huge anteroom of Lorène's family home in Locarno.

I had contemplated it almost blissfully. It was at that moment, while gazing in fond amusement at Bakunin's big, black umbrella, that I took the decision that would change my life.

My death as well, for that matter.

Or perhaps I should say that at that moment, I began to take this decision. Better yet: the decision began to be taken, to take itself, without my having to intervene to influence the course of events. It began to take, then, the way one says of a fire that it's "taking"; to crystallize, the way an impression is said to crystallize.

Lorène was leaning on my shoulder, but I had said nothing to her of all this. I couldn't speak of it without stirring up precisely those painful emotions my decision was designed to spare me.

It was as we were leaving the house—where an elderly maid had brought us some fragrant tea, before conveniently disappearing (I'd forgotten to ask if she was the descendant of Teresa, the cousin of the other one, la Pedrazzini, Bakunin's landlady!)—that Lorène had shown me the display case constructed specifically to preserve the spoils of victory represented by Bakunin's countrified black umbrella.

We had just walked through the library on our way back to

the anteroom. The library was enormous, full of books, with a lofty ceiling and a gallery that ran all along the walls, allowing access to the upper shelves. I don't remember many private libraries as beautiful as that one. Perhaps it was even the most beautiful of all those I've known. The only one—on a more modest scale, of course—that would bear comparison with it, though, would be the library of the Banfi family, in Milan, on the Via Bigli, which I was to discover quite a bit later. Perhaps, in fact, this library would be the only one imbued with the same luminous peace, the same aura of lively concentration. It was there, on the Via Bigli, a lifetime afterward, that Rossana Rossanda gave me the first books of Primo Levi to read.

I would probably not have been able to tear myself away from the contemplation and exploration of the library in Locarno, with all its foreseeable treasures, if we had begun our tour of the house there. In that case, it would have been impossible to get anything at all from me. But Lorène, guided by a presentiment, or quite simply by her impatience, had led me straight to her bedroom.

I looked at Bakunin's umbrella afterward, in a state of beatitude. I felt Lorène's weight on my shoulder. Suddenly, in the languid yet stimulating closeness of our two bodies, our feelings, our senses, a powerful illusion began to take shape.

Life was still livable. It was enough to forget, and to decide this with brutal determination. The choice was simple: literature or life. Would I have the courage—the cruelty toward myself— to pay this price?

"Careful, that's my bad ear!" I tell Lorène two weeks later.

She pulls away from me.

"You've got a good ear and a bad one?"

She seems to think I'm putting her on. I nod to show that I'm not.

"Show me," she says.

She leans toward me, pushing aside my hair, which I'm now letting grow too long, and discovers the bluish scar running along the upper part of my right ear, where it joins the scalp.

"But it's true!" she cries.

"I never lie about little things!"

We light cigarettes.

"Where'd you get that?" asks Lorène.

"I'd decided to cut off my right ear to offer it to a lady, but I couldn't go through with it. . . ."

She laughs, goes back to caressing the inside of my ear, my hair, the back of my neck. It bothers me, I'm looking at the scenery around Lake Maggiore.

Actually, I'd fallen off a train.

A rather wheezy train on a suburban line, even: nothing very adventurous, nothing exciting. But had I fallen from this ordinary, crowded commuter train, or had I deliberately thrown myself onto the tracks? Opinions differed; I myself had no conclusive view of the matter. A young woman claimed, after the accident, that I had jumped. The train was jammed with passengers; I was on the edge of the platform, between the two compartments of a car. It was very hot at the end of that August day, on the eve of Hiroshima. The door had remained open, and there were even a few passengers on the top step, which happened frequently, if not regularly, at that time of insufficient public transportation. At all events, the young woman was respectful—perhaps to a fault—of the freedom of others. Of mine, in this case. Having decided that I wished to commit suicide, she declared later, she moved aside to make it easier for me. She saw me hurl myself into the void.

I had no definitive judgment on the question.

I remembered my weariness, after a sleepless night. I remembered my feverish weakness, after the conversation with

Claude-Edmonde Magny, all those cups of coffee we drank together. The day spent with Laurence, afterward. I remembered
the dizziness, on the edge of the platform, squeezed among the
grumpy passengers.

But perhaps voluntary death is a kind of dizziness, nothing
else. A fainting fit isn't very glorious, true, but it's less trouble-
some to deal with.

So I had fallen on the tracks, somehow or other, and the
sharp edge of the steel transmission cable that ran alongside
the ballast on the roadbed sliced my right ear clean off. Well,
halfway off. They'd had to sew it back on. There's apparently
nothing easier, though, than reattaching an ear that's been half
torn off.

That was in August; now it's December, in the winter sunshine, in Ascona, on a café terrace overlooking Lake Maggiore.

"Manu," says Lorène.

"No," I reply.

"No what?"

"I hate pet names. They're too familiar," I add, as curtly as
possible.

She raises her sunglasses, takes a look at me.

"You hate me today," she says.

Not true—on the contrary, in fact. Anyway, that's not the
problem. I want to be alone, that's all. I need to be alone.

"Manuel isn't my real name. . . . So, 'Manu' doesn't make
sense!"

She shrugs. "I know . . . I checked up on you in Solduno, believe it or not! So what?"

So what indeed.

"Why do you hate me today?"

I don't answer; I look at the scenery. I'm not thinking of the
scenery, of course, I'm thinking about something else entirely.
There's nothing to think about this scenery, I might add. It's

quite lovely, and all you have to do is look at it, rejoicing in its loveliness as you contemplate it. Unmistakable beauty inspires not thought, but happiness: a kind of rapture, that's all. I'm sitting enraptured with this landscape in Ascona spread out before me in the December sunshine and I'm thinking of something completely different.

On the road to Brissago, the windshield of a speeding car catches the sun in a dazzling flash. I shut my eyes: shining white flakes swirl behind my closed eyelids. The way they often do, anytime, anywhere.

"Snow," I murmur, opening my eyes.

Snow at night in the beam of the searchlights.

I laugh, I can't help laughing. Because it's a farewell gesture, I can sense it. Farewell to the snows of yesteryear!

She has turned completely toward me, with her elbows on the table. Not worried yet, but intrigued.

"What snow?"

Off in the distance, the car has gone past the precise point on the road to Brissago, coming out of a curve, where the sun reflected off the windshield in a blaze of light. Everything in the afternoon is now back to normal: the lake, the sky, the trees, the mountains all around.

She doesn't give up in the face of my silence.

"Why snow? What snow?"

But she is the only one to whom I cannot, must not, explain. It's her ignorance that can save me, her innocence that sets me once again on the paths of life.

So: not one word about those long-ago snowfalls, not at any price. Then I turn toward her, I push her away from me with a determined gesture, a look stripped of all tenderness, even of all curiosity. It takes a while; she finally gives in. Raises a hand to her face, beaten.

"You want me to leave?" asks Lorène.

With one fingertip, I caress her eyebrows, the prominent cheekbone, the corner of her mouth.

"That's right," I tell her.

She stands up.

My right hand, stretched out, grazes her body as it unfolds. The charming breast, the flat, taut stomach, the soft curve of the hip. My hand comes to rest, gripping a round knee.

She's standing right next to me. I look at the scenery.

My hand slips lightly up her thigh, fingernails scratching faintly along the silk, up to the coolness of the bare skin above the garter.

"You're cheating," she says.

She moves away, gathers up her things from the table: sunglasses, cigarettes, a gold lighter, her scarf, a letter she hadn't opened, simply checking the return address instead. She puts it all into her purse.

She seems to hesitate, bobs her head, walks off.

I watch her as she goes.

"Lorène!"

She half turns.

"I'll catch up with you," I tell her.

She stumbles, smiles, moves off again.

On August 5, 1945, the day before Hiroshima vanished in an atomic firestorm, I fell from a commuter train. When I regained consciousness, I saw objects sitting on shelves: that's all I could have said about it. But I couldn't even have said that, being unaware that such a thing as speech existed. I knew only that there were objects and that I saw those objects. Although, now that I think about it, it would have been difficult for me to say "I," because self-awareness played no part in this situation. There was no consciousness of myself as a separate identity. There were objects, that's all, a world of visible objects in which vision itself belonged, and I did not yet realize that one could name these objects, to tell them apart. There were things that were there, and that's how everything began.

I didn't have the feeling you get when you awaken from sleep, when things fall back into place, in time and space. Very quickly, if you've woken up in a familiar room. After a moment's adjustment to reality, if you're in strange surroundings.

In either case, however, one's eyes open upon a world in which objects have some purpose, some decipherable meaning. A world immediately filled with traces of a past bespeaking an existence before sleep, a world where a certain implicit design of the future appears through the spontaneous return of one's awareness of everything that must be done, or else, on the contrary, of one's sense of being at leisure, a sense of what may seem, at that moment, like complete freedom, full of joyful prospects, if it's Sunday, for example, or if it's the holidays, a vacation at the shore: one can even fall back asleep assured of sand and sunshine later on.

But I was not emerging from sleep, I was emerging from nothingness.

And so, suddenly, there were objects. There had never been anything before *them*. Perhaps there would be nothing after them, either; the question did not arise, in any case. There were simply unidentifiable objects as yet unnamed, perhaps unnameable. The meaning and function of which were not obscure, not even opaque, but quite simply nonexistent. The entire reality of which was contained within their shape and color, easily differentiated.

There was no possibility of saying "I" in that instant, which was primordial, in a way. I did not exist: he, this "I," this subject who would have been looking, did not yet exist. There was the world, a minute fragment of the world making itself visible: that was all. Only then could I look at it. It was the visibility of the world that allowed me to see. Made me a voyeur, too, of course.

"Feeling better?" someone asked.

A physical happiness welled up inside me, an extraordinary happiness, when I heard the sound of that voice and discovered that it made sense, that I understood perfectly what it meant. The actual reasons behind the question were unclear, leaving it floating on a fog of ignorance. But the question had a specific meaning, which could be grasped with precision.

"Do you feel all right?" the voice asked intently.

For one second, I'd feared that the first words were only some kind of lightning flash in a night of silence. A few words and then nothing more: a dark ocean of mute objects. But no, other words had followed, which also had meaning. New words, just as easily comprehensible. So I hadn't understood the first ones just by accident. There was no reason for there to be limits on language. Perhaps one could say everything.

"I'm fine," I said.

The reply had come all by itself, without effort. I hadn't searched for the words.

I tried to sit up, but my head ached. A sharp, stabbing pain on the right side of my head.

"Don't move," someone said. "You're hurt!"

I sat up anyway, painfully. I saw a man wearing a white coat, observing me carefully.

It's at this precise moment that I began to exist. That I began to realize once more that it was my gaze that contemplated the world around me: this tiny fragment of the universe where there were colored objects and a person in a white coat. I became "me" at this very instant, beneath the watchful eye of that man. Before, there had been visible objects: from now on they were visible in my sight, for me. The universe was visible to me, in the tiny fragments that surrounded me. The world and my gaze faced each other, they coexisted—better yet, neither of them was anything without the other. It was the world that lent stability to my gaze; it was my gaze that gave the world its radiance.

Despite the joy of this discovery, I began to feel a vague irritation. A sense of uneasiness, of discomfort, at hearing that I was hurt. I had just realized that I existed, had just established my own identity (at least as someone other than the world, if not as myself: I knew that I was, without knowing who), and now I had to accept this peremptory affirmation that I was hurt. It was exasperating: it coursed through my entire body, this malaise, like a symptom of my still-mysterious wound.

But then there was a faint draft, bringing snatches of new sounds to my ears. Music, to begin with, above all the other noises. Tinny, high-pitched music, probably from a barrel organ. Or the music played by those primitive little wooden merry-go-rounds, turned by a hand crank, that you sometimes see on a village square. And inside the airy edifice of that music, an entire range of different noises: voices, some of them laughing and childish; hammer blows; a bicycle bell; and, piercing this dense yet porous mass of sound, a train whistle, quite close, and the hiccuping of a steam locomotive getting under way.

I tried to forget the irritation produced by the announcement that I was hurt, in order to let myself flow into the refreshing gust of sounds, music, train whistles: noises from the world beyond a door that must have opened. I tried to concentrate on this presentiment of a vivid, animated world, with children on bicycles and men working with heavy materials, hammering on wood, on metal, and trains that were departing, moving away into a space that must extend somewhere, behind a door that had opened: a world as unknown as the being I was for myself, sprung from nothing, but existing.

The noise died away abruptly—someone must have shut the door to the outside—and a new voice spoke up.

"The ambulance is here!"

Back came the anxiety. It really was important to learn more about what was happening.

"Tell me . . ."

But the strangeness of what I had to ask made me hesitate. My question should have been, "Who am I?" But my words sidestepped that vast issue.

"Don't be surprised at my question. . . . What day is today?"

The man in the white coat observed me, interested but visibly perturbed.

"What?" he exclaimed. "What day, you said?"

Suddenly I felt like laughing. I would have smiled if I hadn't hurt so much throughout my body, which had become present through pain, burdening me with that presence. I would have smiled because I had just discovered the word to identify that man wearing a white coat. And at the same time, the word to name the place where I found myself, as well: those shelves, those boxes, those multicolored bottles.

So: the pharmacist observed me.

"It's Monday," he said.

I thought it wonderful that it was Monday, but that wasn't at all what I was after.

"No, what day of the month, I mean . . . and what year. . . ."

There was a friendly, but pitying, gleam in the pharmacist's eye. He understood that I no longer knew where I was, who I was, what was going on.

He spoke slowly, pronouncing each syllable precisely.

"Today is Monday, the fifth of August, nineteen hundred and forty-five."

What struck me first was not this precision, which hadn't suggested anything to me. Nothing enlightening, at least, about myself. What had struck me, touched me to the heart, was this one little word, "August," which had exploded in me and immediately reproduced itself, becoming the word *agosto*.

I repeated this word in the silence of my thoughts: *agosto*. My mouth watered from turning the word over on my tongue. There were perhaps two words for each of the realities of this world. Almost feverishly, I tested this theory. There were "August," and *agosto*, and yes, "wound" and *herida*, "Monday" and *lunes*. Growing bolder, I searched out words further removed from immediate experience: it still worked. There were always two words for each object, each color, each feeling. Another word for "sky," for "cloud," for "sadness": *cielo, nube, tristeza*.

The words appeared in pairs, ad infinitum.

"And we're in the pharmacy in Gros-Noyer-Saint-Prix, next to the station," said the pharmacist.

This was information that should have been reassuring, because of its precision. Because of its innocuous nature, as well—its banality. A pharmacy, a station, such a traditional village name: all that should have been reassuring.

But I was seized with a new anxiety.

Words continued to pop into my mind, in twin streaks of light. The same gladness still filled me: the happiness of living. The purest, most overwhelming happiness at being alive. Because it wasn't based on the memory of former joys, or on the premonition—still less the certainty—of future felicity. It was based on nothing. On nothing else but the very fact of existing, of knowing myself to be alive, even without memories, without plans, without a foreseeable future. Perhaps this very absence of memory and future was the cause of my happiness—a kind of crazy happiness ungrounded in reason: wild, gratuitous, inexhaustible in its emptiness.

But within this radical, exorbitant joie de vivre, so naked and irrational, a new misgiving had begun to well up silently, carried along by the flood of words gushing forth in twin currents.

The word *nieve* had suddenly appeared. Not the word "snow," appearing first and then splitting up to produce *nieve*. No, this time the second form came first, with a meaning I recognized: snow, precisely. A meaning I also suspected of being original, of being not just the translation of the word "snow," but its oldest meaning. Its most primitive one, perhaps. Was that why the word *nieve* was unsettling? Because it was the original word?

I didn't know, but the uneasiness this word provoked began to muddy the irrational clarity of my happiness at being alive, a happiness based on nothing more than life itself.

"You've had an accident," the pharmacist explained. "You fell from the Paris train just as it was entering the station. . . . You've been injured!"

Memory returned all in a rush.

The sudden knowledge of who I was, where I was, and why.

I was in a train that had just halted. There had been a jolt, in the grinding noise of locked brakes. There had been cries, some of anger, others of despair. I was trapped in the crush of bodies that swayed back and forth, tightly pressed against one another. I saw a face turned toward me, mouth agape, trying to breathe. The young man with the expression of suffering, his face turned toward mine, was begging me, "Don't leave me, Gérard, don't leave me!" The sliding door of the freight car opened; there was the loud, savage barking of dogs. The harsh glare of spotlights illuminated a station platform. The nocturnal landscape was blanketed with snow. There were shouts, brief, gutteral orders. And still those dogs: a dark horizon of dogs howling in front of a curtain of snow-covered trees. We jumped down onto the platform in a confused, clumsy throng. Ran barefoot across the snow. Helmets, uniforms, blows with rifle butts. And always the dogs, hoarse, slavering with murderous rage. We left the station in ranks of five, on the double. We were on a broad avenue lighted by tall lampposts. At regular intervals there were columns crowned by Hitlerian eagles.

That was how I found out, in the abrupt flash of this resurgent memory, who I was, where I'd come from, where I was really going. This memory was the source of my recovered life, as I emerged from the void. From the temporary but complete amnesia caused by my fall onto the track bed.

That was how—by the return of this memory, of the sorrow of living—I was driven from the mad bliss of oblivion. From blessed nothingness to the anguish of life.

"Someone on the train recognized you," said the pharmacist, in conclusion. "You have family up in Saint-Prix. You'll be taken there by ambulance."

"Yes, Forty-seven Rue Auguste-Rey!" I said, to show that I really was myself again.

I pretended to be anyway, so as not to cause that nice pharmacist any more worry. Because I hadn't simply fallen on my head in the station at Gros-Noyer-Saint-Prix, in a northern suburb of Paris. That wasn't the main problem, anyway. The important thing was that I'd jumped down, amid the uproar of dogs and the shouting of the SS, onto the station platform of Buchenwald.

That's where everything had begun. Where everything always began again.

"You're leaving me, aren't you?" said Lorène.

With a sudden movement, she had just pulled down the bedspread in the room she'd rented in Ascona to make it easier for us to be together. Now the whiteness of the sheets stood out in the dim light, with the curtains drawn against a setting sun.

"I'm leaving Switzerland," I replied. "It's not the same thing. . . . But you knew!"

Lorène nodded, she knew, of course. She had always known. She held out her hand, drew me to her.

"What snow were you talking about?" she murmured in my ear, later on.

She was a stubborn young Swiss woman. Affectionate, head-strong, passionate, but stubborn. It was impossible to avoid pointed questions, the desire for details. I'd mentioned snow— what snow?—earlier. She wanted to know.

I could not possibly tell her the truth, however.

"Les Glières," I replied.

She didn't understand; neither did I. . . . What I mean is, she didn't understand what I had told her. And I didn't understand why I was telling her. No matter—I continued. I told her about the battle on the plateau of Les Glières, as though I had been there. It wasn't I, as you know, but Morales. I recounted the battle of Les Glières as Morales had remembered it. The snow, the flight through the deep snow, in the icy cold of winter, in the crossfire of the machine guns.

Night fell on my story, in Ascona. On Morales's story, actually. Lorène listened to me, enthralled. She listened to the narrative of an unknown dead man, with the impression that she was learning, finally, something about me. Something that truly belonged to me, was essential to me.

So, the snow, in Ascona, the snow in the epic of Les Glières in the deathly cold memory of Morales. The snow of yesteryear, as a parting gift to Lorène, unforgettable mistress of oblivion.

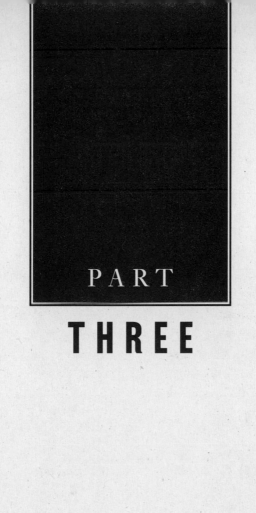

PART

THREE

8

THE DAY OF PRIMO LEVI'S DEATH

Years later—a lifetime, several lifetimes later—on a Saturday in April 1987, toward the end of the afternoon (at five-fifteen, quite precisely), I realized that I would not be keeping the pages written that day. That I would not be keeping them in the novel I was working on at the time, at least.

Yet they had been written with a disconcerting happiness (what I mean is, I'd felt a disconcerting felicity in writing them, however felicitous their style may have been), a happiness I felt each time I returned to this past. As if memory, strangely enough, quickened and grew green again, and the writing flowed easily (even though there might be a heavy, perhaps an exorbitant price to pay later on), the words falling more deftly into place, as soon as that everlasting death recovered its indefeasible rights, invading the most ordinary of present moments, on absolutely any occasion.

In the first draft of the novel I was writing (provisionally entitled *Un homme perdu* [*A Lost Man*], and published as *Netchaïev est de retour* [*Netchayev Is Back*]), in the narrative structure already worked out, Buchenwald was not supposed to be dwelt on at length. I'd felt that three or four pages would be enough to evoke Roger Marroux's journey across a defeated Germany in April 1945 in search of Michel Laurençon, a comrade in the Resistance who had been deported.

Here's how the text went, at first.

> On the morning of April 12, 1945, Marroux got out of the car in front of the offices of the *Politische Abteilung,* the Gestapo headquarters in Buchenwald. A few dozen yards away were the wrought-iron gates of the monumental entrance at the end of the long avenue, bordered with columns crowned by Hitlerian eagles, that linked the train station at Buchenwald to the camp itself.

I reread the sentence; it didn't say anything to me.

It contained nothing except information. Necessary information, no doubt, but that sort of thing, even when vital to the clarity of a narrative, has never interested me.

I wasn't thrilled with the way I was introducing Roger Marroux, a character in a novel, to this area of reality.

A vague, fleeting, and all too familiar uneasiness plunged me into bitter reflection. One cannot really write without experiencing such moments of confusion. When you step back from your own writing like that, this distance—sometimes tinged with disgust, or at least with dissatisfaction—reproduces, in a way, the insurmountable gulf between what you envision and its narrative realization.

Time passed: a minute, an hour, an eternity, in the solitude of wounded pride. Memories began to stir. Mine, of course, not just Roger Marroux's.

I was writing early on a Saturday morning in the seventh arrondissement of Paris, on the second floor of a turn-of-the-century house that looked out onto a vast private garden. Or perhaps it belonged to some governmental ministry. Closed to the public, at any rate.

Rereading the sentence in question, with an eye to getting around its informative dullness, I suddenly noticed the date I had written: April 12, 1945. It wasn't a date I had selected, obviously. I'd written it down without thinking about it, a simple fact of historical record. The arrival of Roger Marroux, a character in a novel, at the real entrance to the concentration camp of Buchenwald, could only occur on that date, or after that date, after the liberation by the American troops of Patton's Third Army.

Yet a strategy of the unconscious mind—subtle and sly in its methods, brutal in its exigency—had led me to describe that arrival on the very anniversary of this event, forty-two years later, to the day.

It was indeed Saturday, April 11, 1987.

I felt buoyed by a somber joy.

Once again, without having planned it, at least not as far as I knew, I'd faithfully kept that April rendezvous. Or rather, in spite of myself, some stern, inmost part of me had faithfully kept the appointment of memory and death.

In Ascona, in the winter sunshine of Ticino, at the end of those months of my return (recounted somewhat elliptically in these pages), I'd decided to abandon the book I was trying in vain to write. *In vain* does not mean that I couldn't manage it; it means that I could do so only at excessive cost. At the cost of my own survival, in a way, for writing was constantly returning me to the barrenness of a deadly experience.

I'd overtaxed my strength. I'd thought myself capable of returning to life—of forgetting those years in Buchenwald in the course of everyday existence, of no longer taking those years into account in my conversations, my friendships—and yet carrying out the writing project so dear to my heart. I'd been arro-

gant enough to think that I could control this studied schizo-
phrenia. But it became clear that by writing, in a certain way, I
was refusing to live.

So, in Ascona, in the winter sunshine, I decided to choose the
rustling silence of life instead of the murderous language of
writing. I made this radical choice; it was the only thing I could
do. I chose to forget: I set in place—without much consideration for my own identity, which was based essentially on
the horror, and no doubt the courage, of the experience of
Buchenwald—all the schemes inherent in the cruelly systematic
strategy of voluntary amnesia.

I became someone else, so that I might remain myself.

From then on, after that spring of 1946, having willingly
joined the collective anonymity of a postwar life glittering with
all sorts of possibilities for the future, I lived more than fifteen
years, the historic span of a generation, in the blissful fog of this
amnesia. Rarely did the memory of the camp suddenly shatter
my hard-won peace of mind: a temporary mastery, constantly
renewed, of the share of darkness that had fallen to my lot.

But after the publication of my first book, *Le grand voyage,*
everything changed. The anguish of former days returned to
haunt me, especially in April. Various circumstances make it
difficult to escape this month unscathed: the deeply affecting renewal of nature, the anniversary of the liberation of Buchenwald, the commemoration of Deportation Day.

And so, although in 1961 I'd succeeded in writing the book
abandoned sixteen years before (in writing one, at least, of the
possible accounts of that earlier experience, which was essentially inexhaustible), I paid for that success, which was to change
my life, with the brutal return of past despair.

In any case, nothing in the novel I was working on in April 1987
pointed to a drift toward that mortal darkness in which—no

matter what I do, no matter what ruse or reason I employ to avoid it—my desire to live is rooted. As well as my utter inability to be truly alive.

Actually, *Netchaïev est de retour* dealt with a completely different subject: the passage from militant action to its militarist, terrorist perversion. This theme had already been touched on in the screenplay for *La guerre est finie,* written in 1965. In a scene shot on the Boulevard Edgar-Quinet, in a studio with a clear view of the Cimetière Montparnasse, some young Leninists on the point of taking up arms argue against the strategy of peaceful mass struggle, a position defended by Diego, a militant Spanish Communist played by Yves Montand.

On the same Boulevard Edgar-Quinet, in front of the setting for that cinematic fiction, killers from the terrorist group Action Directe would later assassinate Georges Besse, the director of Régie Renault, and boast about the murder openly, ignobly, as though it were a revolutionary deed, in the verbal delirium of an autistic and bloodthirsty theoretical arrogance.

In writing *Netchaïev est de retour,* I was fully aware of its distant origins. I knew that the scene in the film, after wandering for a long time through the nebula of my projects, had finally attracted other themes, other bits and pieces of imagination or reality, crystallizing at last into the core of a new book.

I understood this so clearly that I returned in the novel to the urban landscapes of the Montparnasse neighborhood that had appeared in the scenario of *La guerre est finie.* Landscapes that had been, by the way, favorite haunts of my adolescence.

Looking up, I contemplated the garden spread out before me, deserted at that early hour, beneath an April sky streaked with small, fleecy clouds.

I'd just seen through the little games of the literary unconscious. I'd guessed whom Roger Marroux would meet at the entrance to Buchenwald: myself. The real memory of the three

Allied officers that could be glimpsed behind the fiction now
began to take shape, like images emerging from the initial haze
of a Polaroid photograph.

I returned to my writing with fresh enthusiasm.

> A young guy—hard to say exactly, though; about
> twenty, he figured—was standing guard at the door
> to the Gestapo barracks. The guy wore Russian boots
> of soft leather, and mismatched, cast-off clothing.
> His hair was cut short. But a German machine gun
> was slung across his chest, an obvious sign of author-
> ity. The American liaison officers had told them, at
> dawn, that the antifascist resistance in Buchenwald
> had managed to arm a few dozen men, who had par-
> ticipated in the last phase of the liberation of the
> camp, after the breakthrough of Patton's motorized
> advance guard. He was probably one of them, this
> young guy. Who watched them get out of the jeep,
> stretch in the spring sunshine, in the strange, dense si-
> lence of the beechwood at the edge of the barbed-
> wire fence encircling the camp. Marroux felt trapped
> by the icy devastation in those eyes glittering in a
> bony, haggard face. He felt as though he were being
> observed, sized up, by a look from the beyond, from
> outside of life. As though the flat, neutral beam of
> this gaze were coming to him from a dead star, from
> a vanished existence. As though this gaze had traveled
> to him across the steppes of a desolate mineral land-
> scape, reaching him permeated with a savage cold-
> ness. With an irremediable solitude.

And so, on April 11, 1987, on the anniversary of the liberation
of Buchenwald, I'd wound up meeting myself once again. Re-

covering an essential part of myself, of my memory, which I had been—and was still—obliged to repress, to restrain, in order to go on living. To simply be able to breathe. Stealthily, turning up by chance in a work of fiction that had not initially seemed to require my presence, I was appearing in the novel, equipped only with the stricken shadow of that memory.

Actually, I was even invading the narrative.

In fact, from that moment on, the writing turned toward the first person singular. Toward the extreme singularity of an experience that was difficult to share. I wrote for a long time, with impatience. With ease, for it seemed to me that the right words came effortlessly to mind. With the bracing pain of an inexhaustible memory, in which each new sentence revealed to me buried, obliterated riches.

Toward the end of the afternoon, however, at a quarter past five on the dot, I realized that I would not be keeping the pages written that day following my sudden, insidiously contrived appearance in a narrative that did not care about this presence, could have done without it, should do without it.

I set those pages aside. I expelled myself from the story. I returned to my previous plan, to the narrative structure I had already worked out. I returned to the all-purpose third person: to that "he" employed by the god of novels and mythologies.

This way:

> The young guy had noticed the tricolor badge, surmounted by the word "France," on Marroux's uniform jacket. He spoke to him in French.
>
> "You look stunned. . . . What is it? How quiet this place is? There are never any birds in this forest. . . . The smoke from the crematory chased them away, it seems. . . ."
>
> He laughed shortly.

"But the crematory stopped running yesterday. . . .
There won't ever be smoke again. . . . No more smell
of burning flesh over the countryside. . . ."

He laughed again.

I laughed, too, so many years later.

In spite of the tricks and detours of the unconscious, the deliberate or involuntary repressions, the strategy of forgetting, in
spite of memory's ducking and dodging, in spite of so many
pages already written to exorcise this experience, to make it at
least partly livable—in spite of all that, the snow and the smoke
were still as present in the past as they had been on that first day.

I laughed mirthlessly, but wholeheartedly, with a kind of insane pride.

No one can put himself in your place, I thought, or even
imagine your place, your entrenchment in nothingness, your
shroud in the sky, your fatal singularity. No one can imagine
how much that singularity rules your life: your weariness with
living, your voracity for life; your unflagging astonishment at
the gratuitousness of existence; your rapture at having returned
from the dead to breathe the salt air of certain seaside mornings,
to dip into books, to caress the hips of women and lightly touch
their eyelids closed in sleep, to discover how vast the future is.

There was plenty to laugh about, really. So I laughed, reim-
mersed in the gloomy pride of my solitude.

I'd set aside the pages written that day. I reread the first lines.

They stand amazed before me, and suddenly, in that
terror-stricken gaze, I see myself—in their horror.

For two years, I had lived without a face. No mirrors, in Buchenwald. I saw my body, its increasing
emaciation, once a week, in the shower. Faceless, that

absurd body. Sometimes I gently touched the jutting
bones of the eye sockets, the hollow of a cheek.

Another book had just come into being. Had begun to come
into being, at least. Perhaps it would take years more to mature,
which sometimes happens. I'd seen it happen, I mean: books
taking years to ripen. Never reaching full maturity, either. I'd always felt that their publication, determined by external, objective circumstances, was somewhat premature. I'm talking about
books that deal directly with the experience of the camps, of
course. The others—even if they allude to this experience as
part of the life of a character in a novel—do not ripen so slowly.
So painfully slowly. Ever since *Le grand voyage* (written all at one
go, in a few weeks, under circumstances I will describe when
the time comes), the other books concerning life in the camps
have drifted about for a long while in my imagination. In the actual work of writing. I persist in abandoning them, in rewriting
them. They persist in returning to me, to be written out to the
very end of the suffering they impose.

That's what happened with *Quel beau dimanche!* [*What a Beautiful Sunday!*]. I had the feeling it would happen again.

Anyway, I set these pages aside, in a cardboard folder of a
pale, washed-out blue, on which I immediately wrote the title
of the new book. This was not my usual habit. Ordinarily, my
books take their time finding titles. This book got its title right
away. I wrote it with a thick marker: L'ÉCRITURE OU LA MORT
[LITERATURE OR DEATH]. To these fifteen or so pages written
and clipped together that Saturday, April 11, 1987, pages that
would wait in their folder until such time as I could get back to
them, I added a note. A name, rather. A single first name in capital letters, underlined several times: LAURENCE, written on a
white index card.

Laurence?

Yet I'd forgotten her. That morning, when I'd begun describing Roger Marroux's arrival at the entrance to Buchenwald, in a novel that wound up entitled *Netchaïev est de retour,* I hadn't thought about Laurence. I knew (vaguely—I didn't try to clarify this memory while writing, I felt no need to) that Marroux's arrival at the entrance to Buchenwald, at the end of the Avenue of Eagles, had its origins in my own memory.

I had already alluded, in *Quel beau dimanche!,* to my encounter with the officers in British uniform, a few hours after the liberation of the camp. A brief allusion that skipped over the most important point, which wasn't relevant to my concerns at the time. I'd left out the French officer and the book of poems by René Char, *Seuls demeurent.*

And yet, on the morning of April 11, 1987, in describing the arrival of Roger Marroux at the entrance to Buchenwald and his encounter with a young Spanish deportee, I'd unconsciously fallen back on the words of the French officer—whose first name was Marc—to describe myself. The words he'd used in the long letter sent to Laurence the day after that encounter. The same words, one by one, word for word.

This is what I'd written:

> Marroux felt trapped by the icy devastation in those eyes, glittering in a bony, haggard face. He felt as though he were being observed, sized up, by a look from the beyond, from outside of life. As though the flat, neutral beam of this gaze were coming to him from a dead star, from a vanished existence.

They were the words of the French officer's long letter to Laurence, in which he described our meeting, spoke of the conversation about Char, told her about his visit to the camp.

Laurence had read me this letter on May 8, 1945, when I'd gone to the Rue de Varenne to return the French officer's copy of *Seuls demeurent.*

"Beauté, je me porte à ta rencontre," I'd thought, when I saw her appear at the door. She had snatched the volume of René Char from my hand.

Laurence had been moody, that first time we met. Sometimes distant, sometimes hostile, as though she reproached me for being alive, when Marc was dead.

"The look in your eyes—it's not at all the way Marc described it, he was wrong," she told me scathingly. "Instead, it shows a hunger for life!"

I pointed out to her that this wasn't a contradiction. But she insisted.

"A lustful look," she said.

I burst out laughing, making fun of her. "Don't be pretentious!"

She became irritated, flushing angrily.

"Anyway," I added, "you're right: lust is an ugly thing, according to Saint Augustine."

Her eyes widened. "You've read Saint Augustine?"

"I've read just about everything," I told her loftily. "By the way, I cannot recommend too strongly that you read his treatise *De bono conjugali.* It's ideal reading for a young woman in your position. It teaches us that procreation is the only reason for marriage, its very foundation. But it also teaches us all the ways to satisfy our lust without risking procreation. Of course, it's in Latin. . . . But judging from this apartment, I'm sure your family was able to afford a fine classical education for you!"

This left her speechless, torn between cold fury and hysterical giggles.

And then, at other moments, she'd been less tense, more vulnerable, seeking comfort in my arms. But that first day, she sent me away with angry tears.

It had taken other meetings, laughter, music (Mozart and Armstrong: I'd foisted my tastes on her, that summer), books read together, poems murmured in the mild air of the Jardin du Luxembourg, in the cool of the evening on the quays of the Seine, before she closed the shutters of her bedroom one sunny afternoon. She'd given herself the way one jumps into water, eyes closed, with movements of a resolute precision due neither to skill nor deceit, but to a desperate haste to affirm once again her incapacity for pleasure, sometimes grazed, never really grasped.

In spite of this, in spite of the frustrating aspect of our relationship, an episodic, discontinuous succession of passionate impulses and quarrels, of soulful communions and bitter conflicts, it was with Laurence and with her alone that I was able to speak about my years in Buchenwald, that summer of my return. Doubtless because of Marc, the French officer. Because of the long letter he'd written to her about our encounter. The words of a dead man had brought us together in life, Laurence and I, for a little while.

The evening of Saturday, April 11, 1987, was the way evenings are when memories take over and proliferate, devouring reality through a process of lightning-quick metastases. The way evenings have been, at least, ever since writing made me vulnerable once more to the pangs of memory. That evening was split into an outward happiness—I was dining that night with dear friends—and the inner anguish that imprisoned me. It was a brutal division into two territories. Two worlds, two lives. And at the time I could not have said which was the real one, which the dream.

I probably drank more than usual, that evening. Perhaps even more than was wise. Without any noticeable results: alcohol does not heal the wounds of death.

There's nothing special about such miseries. In one form or another, we've described them all. They figure in all accounts by former deportees, whether written in the white heat of immediate testimony—which runs out of breath and sometimes bogs down in the scrupulous reconstruction of a past that is hardly believable, positively unimaginable—or much later, with the perspective of the passage of time, in the endless attempt to explain an experience receding into the past, in which certain contours grow nevertheless more and more distinct, and certain areas gleam with a new light amid the mists of oblivion.

> *È un sogno entro un altro sogno, vario nei particolari, unico nella sostanza . . .*

No doubt: a dream, always the same one.

A dream within another dream, varied in detail but one in substance. A dream that can awaken you anywhere: in the serenity of a green countryside, at a table with friends. Why not with a lover, shall I add? Sometimes with a lover, at the very moment of love. Anywhere, in short, with anyone, suddenly: a diffuse and deep despair, the anguished certainty of the end of the world—of its unreality, at any rate.

Primo Levi speaks of this on the last page of *La tregua* [*The Reawakening*]. He speaks of it concisely, without raising his voice, with the simplicity of the plain-spoken truth.

Nothing can stop the course of this dream, says Levi; nothing can relieve the secret agony it causes. Even if you turn to a loved one, even if a friendly—or a loving—hand is held out to you. "What's the matter with you? What are you thinking of?" Even if they guess what's happening to you, overwhelming you, annihilating you. Nothing, ever, will deflect the course of that dream, the flood of that river Styx.

> *Tutto è ora volto in caos: sono solo al centro di un nulla gri-gio e torbido, ed ecco, io so che cosa questo significa, ed an-che di averlo sempre saputo: sono di nuovo in Lager, e nulla era vero all'infuori del Lager. Il resto era breve vacanza, o in-ganno dei sensi, sogno: la famiglia, la natura in fiore, la casa.*
>
> [Now all has changed to chaos: I am alone in the cen-ter of a gray and turbid nothing, and now, I know what this thing means, and I also know that I have al-ways known it: I am once more in the Lager, and nothing was true outside the Lager. The rest was a brief pause, or a deception of the senses, a dream: family, nature in bloom, home.]

No one could say it better than Primo Levi.

It's true that everything becomes chaotic, when that anguish reappears. You find yourself in the middle of a whirlwind of nothingness, a nebulous void, murky and grayish. From that moment on, you know what this means. You know that you have always known. Always, beneath the glittering surface of daily life, this terrible knowledge. Close at hand, this certainty: nothing is true except the camp, all the rest is but a dream, now and forever. Nothing is real but the smoke from the crematory of Buchenwald, the smell of burned flesh, the hunger, the roll calls in the snow, the beatings, the deaths of Maurice Halbwachs and Diego Morales, the fraternal stench of the latrines in the Little Camp.

It was in 1963 that I read Primo Levi's *La tregua*.

I'd known nothing about him until then. I hadn't read his first book, *Se questo è un uomo* [*If This Is a Man* or *Survival in*

Auschwitz]. It's true that I'd deliberately avoided reading the firsthand accounts of the Nazi camps. That was part of a strategy of survival.

I read Primo Levi's *La tregua* in Milan, on the Via Bigli, in the library of the Banfi family. The windows opened onto an interior garden where birds sang, where the foliage of an ancient tree was beginning to take on the colors of autumn.

It was Rossana Rossanda who urged me to read Primo Levi's book, which had come out some time before. I read it in one go, the way one takes a drink of cool water in the summer. Because by the autumn of 1963, the time of silence and oblivion had passed. The time of deafness to myself, as well: deafness to the most melancholy but truest part of myself.

A few months earlier, I'd published *Le grand voyage*.

That night, snow had fallen on my sleep.

I was living on the Calle Concepción-Bahamonde, in Madrid, not far from the arena in Ventas: the outskirts of the city, in those days. In the evening, when it was time to return to this safe house, I'd get off at the Goya subway station. It wasn't the closest station, of course, but I was taking my time, keeping an eye out behind me: I'd stroll along, stopping in front of the shop windows, abruptly crossing the street, walking through a supermarket, leaning on the counter in bistros while I had a strong black coffee or a cool draft beer, depending on the season. At all events, when I turned onto my street, I was sure I hadn't been followed.

But there had been snow, that night, in my sleep.

A sudden snow squall. It was on a public square, where avenues converged. A place not immediately identifiable, but familiar. There was the vague feeling, in any case, that the dreamer could certainly identify this dream landscape. An effort of will was perhaps all that was required. A square, some avenues, the crowd, a parade. Snow swirled in the rays of a setting sun that soon grew dim. Then elsewhere, without any apparent transition, yet in a different dream, there was deep snow, muffling footsteps among the beeches of the forest.

Snow blanketing my sleep, after so many years.

In those days, I was sticking close to home on the Calle Concepción-Bahamonde. There had been arrests, rather a lot of them. Whole sections of the underground apparatus seemed to be collapsing. I was in charge of the outlawed Communist organization in Madrid and had given instructions to the cadres at risk: cut all contact with the sectors hit by the wave of arrests, move as little as possible, change the mail drops, passwords, meeting places. In short, play dead for a while. Then, pick up the threads one by one, with extreme prudence. Do not venture out on ground that has not been cleared of any delayed-action traps set by Franco's police.

I hardly ever left the Calle Concepción-Bahamonde, during that time, while I waited for the dust to settle.

That's how I came to be taking my meals with Manuel and Maria A. They were militants, and had bought the apartment on behalf of the party. Franco's police knew nothing about the couple, whose only mission was to maintain that apartment. Manuel worked as a private chauffeur, Maria kept house. Two of the rooms in the apartment were at my disposal. Rather, at the disposal of the leadership of the underground organization, whoever they were. To put up a front for the neighbors, Manuel and Maria pretended to have a lodger: they would place an ad in the paper, and that did the trick. For several years, I used that apartment on the Calle Concepción-Bahamonde while doing clandestine work in Madrid. After 1962, when I was suspended from activity in Spain, prior to my expulsion from the party, it was Julián Grimau who lived in that apartment; he was still living with Manuel and Maria A. the following year, when he was arrested and shot.

During the time I was lying low, then, I used to eat with this couple. The midday meal was a speedy affair, as Manuel didn't have a long lunch hour. In the evening, we might linger at the table in conversation. That's probably not the right word—it was mostly a monologue by Manuel while Maria cleared the table and washed up. We'd smoke, have a drink together. Manuel would talk about his life, and I'd listen. I kept quiet, listening. First of all, I've always enjoyed hearing militants talk about their lives. And then, I couldn't tell him about mine, in polite reciprocation: the less they knew, Maria and he, the better. Actually, they knew almost nothing. They knew the name on my fake identity card: that was necessary, since I was supposed to be their lodger. They knew that I was one of the party leaders, of course. But they had no idea of my exact role in the underground organization, or even that I was using the alias of Federico Sanchez.

So, after dinner, when it was time for the cigarillo from the Canary Islands and a drop of brandy, I would listen to Manuel A. tell me about his life. Well, as it happened, he'd been deported to Mauthausen, a Nazi camp in Austria, an extremely harsh one. One of the harshest in the concentration camp system, with the exception of those in the Auschwitz-Birkenau complex, especially geared to the mass extermination of the Jewish people.

As a young soldier, Manuel A. had experienced the refugee camps of Roussillon after the defeat of the Republican Army. In 1940, like thousands of other Spaniards, he had been drafted into a labor gang under the firm command of the French Army. After Pétain's armistice, Manuel had wound up in a German stalag, mixed in—along with all his compatriots in the same situation—with French prisoners of war. Later, when the German command sorted out the mass of prisoners in its power, the few thousand Spanish in the work groups were transferred from the stalags to Mauthausen as political deportees.

Manuel A. was a survivor of this camp. A revenant, like myself. In the evenings, after dinner, over a small brandy and a little cigar from the Canary Islands, he would tell me about his life in Mauthausen.

But I didn't recognize anything, I couldn't get my bearings.

Obviously, there were differences between Buchenwald and Mauthausen: the deportees experienced very specific circumstances in each of the Nazi camps. In its essence, however, the system remained the same. The regimentation of daily life, the tempo of work, the hunger, the lack of sleep, the constant persecution, the sadism of the SS, the madness of the veteran detainees, the knife fights over control of personal fiefdoms of power: essentially the same. Yet I couldn't make sense of what Manuel A. had to say.

It was disorganized, confused, too wordy, mired in details: there wasn't any overall vision, everything was seen in the same light. In sum, a firsthand account that was rough, unpolished. A jumble of images, an avalanche of facts, impressions, pointless commentary.

I champed at the bit, unable to intervene with questions, to make him bring order and meaning to the chaotic nonsense of his torrent of words. His undeniable sincerity had been reduced to rhetoric, his truthfulness no longer even seemed convincing. But I couldn't say anything to him, I couldn't help him give shape to his memories, since he was not supposed to know that I, too, had been deported. Since I could not possibly share this secret with him.

Then, one night, after a long week of such stories, snow had fallen on my sleep.

The snow of yesteryear: snow deeply blanketing the forest of beeches around the camp, sparkling in the beams of the searchlights. Snow flurries on the May Day flags, on my return, a troubling reminder of suffering and courage. The snow of memory, for the first time in fifteen years. In Ascona, on the shore of Lake Maggiore, one limpid winter day, in December 1945, I'd closed my eyes, dazzled by the reflection of a ray of sunlight on the windshield of a car on the Brissago road. I'd closed my eyes: delicate, stubborn snowflakes had glistened in my memory. I'd opened my eyes: a young woman was there, Lorène. The snows of yesteryear, in Ascona, for the last time. I'd abandoned my plan to write. Lorène had helped me, without knowing it, to hang on to life.

For fifteen years, snow had never fallen on my sleep. I'd forgotten it, repressed it, censored it. I mastered my dreams, cleansing them of the snow and smoke over the Ettersberg. Sometimes, it's true, I felt a pang in my heart. An instant of anguish tinged with nostalgia, with a strange joy—who knows? How can I describe that absurdity, the uncanny happiness of that memory? Sometimes, a pain as sharp as a lancet stabbed my heart. When listening to a solo by Armstrong, perhaps. Once in a while, when biting hungrily into a piece of black bread. Smoking a Gitane down until it burned my lips. Someone would express astonishment at seeing me smoke my cigarette down to the butt like that. I couldn't explain this habit: it's just something I do, I'd say. But sometimes, abruptly, deliciously, the memory would wash over me: the cigarette butt of *makhorka* shared with pals, passing from hand to hand, mouth to mouth, the sweet drug of brotherhood.

But the snow had disappeared from my sleep.

I awoke with a start, after a week of Manuel A.'s stories about Mauthausen. It was in Madrid, on the Calle Concepción-Bahamonde, in 1961. But now that I think about it, "with a start" is not the right choice of words. Because I did wake up all at once, and felt immediately lucid, alert. But it wasn't anxiety or distress that awakened me. I was strangely calm, serene. Everything now seemed clear to me. I knew how to write the book that I'd had to abandon fifteen years before. Rather: I knew that I could write it, now. Because I'd always known how to write it: what I'd lacked was courage. The courage to confront death through writing. But I no longer needed this courage.

Dawn was breaking; oblique rays of sunshine grazed the windows of the little room with whitewashed walls on the Calle Concepción-Bahamonde. I was going to get started right away, taking advantage of the circumstances that were forcing me to stay at home, avoiding the dangers of the street.

I was going to write for myself, of course, for myself alone. There was no question of publishing anything, in fact. Publishing a book was unthinkable as long as I belonged to the clandestine leadership of the Spanish Communist Party.

At dawn on a spring morning on the Calle Concepción-Bahamonde, I sat down at my table, in front of my typewriter. It was an Olivetti portable, with a Spanish keyboard. Too bad: I would just have to do without the circumflex and grave accents.

"There is this crush of bodies in the boxcar, this throbbing pain in my right knee. The days, the nights. I make an effort and I try to count the days, to count the nights. . . . "

At the last page of Primo Levi's *La tregua*—so familiar, although his experience had been so much more terrible than mine; so fraternal, like the gaze of Maurice Halbwachs, dying on the bunk in Block 56 in Buchenwald—I closed my eyes.

> "È un sogno entro un altro sogno, vario nei particolari, unico nella sostanza . . . "

A dream within another dream, unquestionably. The dream of death within the dream of life. Or rather: the dream of death, sole reality of a life that is itself but a dream. Primo Levi expressed that anguish we all felt with incomparable precision. The camp was indeed our only truth. The rest—family, nature in flower, home—was no more than a brief interlude, an illusion of the senses.

That evening, on April 11, 1987, I remembered Primo Levi. And Rossana Rossanda, who had introduced me to his books. I also recalled Juan Larrea, who had read them, too. At dawn, Larrea had walked to the Seine, over by Freneuse. The river water was dark. He had stood motionless, gathering the last strength of his life to end it all.

Juan Larrea had just stopped for a moment on the grass that sloped in gentle undulations down to the river. The pink chestnut tree would soon be bursting into bloom. He had contemplated the tree, which stood off by itself in a morning twilight barely touched by the warmth of the sun's first rays. He had smiled sadly: he would not see the tiny pink flowers of Franca Castellani's chestnut tree that year. His death, the fact that he could not appreciate the flowers, would not prevent Franca from admiring them. The tree would bloom in spite of his fatal absence. The world would continue to exist, beneath the gaze of Franca Castellani.

Then he had continued on his way down to the river, the dark water, the end.

On the previous day, April 24, 1982 (it's not impossible to date precisely the events described in the novel), he had recalled the smell from the crematory oven drifting over the Ettersberg.

In February 1986, when *La montagne blanche* [*The White Mountain*] appeared, I had occasionally been asked some foolish questions. Foolish or pointless. In what way did Juan Larrea resemble me? Had I identified with this character?

It's already hard enough to identify with oneself, I'd offered by way of an answer (an evasion, rather)—too hard for any identification with one's own fictional characters to be plausible. Or even advisable. No, no identification with Juan Larrea, in spite of things we had in common: being Spanish, writers, former deportees. On the other hand, I was a bit jealous of him. I would really have liked to have known Franca Castellani. Or to have written the plays Larrea had produced, according to the novel. I would have liked to have written *Le tribunal de l'Askanischer Hof,* in particular.

In the first scene, Franz Kafka would indeed sit bolt upright in his seat. Openmouthed, gasping for breath, he wouldn't say a word. It's Grete Bloch who would speak, with the vehemence of despair. Warm weather: it was in July. A great war would soon break out. A waiter in a white jacket would appear, stage left, with refreshments.

It would be absurd for me to try rewriting *Le tribunal de l'Askanischer Hof.* I'd have the same misadventure that befell Pierre Ménard when he rewrote *Don Quixote:* I'd wind up with the same text as Larrea, word for word.

But Larrea had left behind an unfinished play, on which he was still working on the very eve of his suicide, along with notes, drafts, all sorts of papers that were found in his room in Freneuse. It was an untitled play—no title was found among the papers left behind, at least—based on the life of Britain's Lord Curzon, a fascinating historical figure of this century. Of the beginning of this century and the end of the old world.

In any case, I'd had the time (to say the least!) to read Larrea's rough drafts, and Ronaldshay's monumental biography of George Nathaniel Curzon, first Marquis Curzon of Kedleston, which Larrea had used in his work. I'd been able to dream about the dramatic construction that might have been assembled from all these elements.

And so Juan Larrea's tastes in literature, the plans I'd attributed to him—derived from his own psychological makeup, from the concrete circumstances of his imaginary life—these tastes and plans reverted to me as something personal: a future in which I might have invested on my own account, nurturing it with my doubts and my desires.

On Saturday, April 24, 1982, the day before his suicide, Juan Larrea had suddenly remembered. He'd believed, however, that he would manage to deal with it himself, once again. He'd decided to say nothing, at least. To keep the nauseating anguish to himself when the smoke from the power station of Porcheville, in the Seine Valley, had reminded him of the crematory smoke above the Ettersberg long ago. To keep quiet, bury, repress, forget. To allow that smoke to go up in smoke, saying nothing to anyone, not a word about it. To continue pretending to exist, the way he had done all along for all those long years: moving around, going through the motions, drinking, making scathing or witty remarks, loving young women, and writing, as though he were actually alive.

Or else quite the contrary: as though he'd died thirty-seven years before, in a puff of smoke. As though his life, from then on, had been only a dream in which he had been dreaming everything that was real: the trees, the books, the women, his characters. Unless they were the ones dreaming him.

Exactly: unless Juan Larrea dreamed me up himself. Unless Juan Larrea were a survivor of Buchenwald telling part of my life story in a book signed with a pseudonym: my own name. Hadn't I, for my part, given him the name Larrea because it was once one of my underground aliases in Spain?

"What do you want to call yourself this time?" the guy who made our false identity papers had asked me. A nice guy, by the way, and a brilliant counterfeiter. We were in a painter's studio, over in Montparnasse, where he'd set up one of his shady workshops. I'd thought of Juan Larrea that day: a little-known writer of refinement, a member of that flamboyant generation of the thirties that made the twentieth century a golden one for Spanish literature. And bilingual, too, this Juan Larrea, like his friend the Chilean Vicente Huidobro.

"Larrea," I told my counterfeiting pal. "Make me papers under the name of Larrea!"

A few months later, after a police sweep through the academic milieux of Madrid, someone proved unable to keep his mouth shut. Franco's police found out about this alias I'd used for certain contacts. The Department of the Interior then published a notice in the newspapers calling upon one Larrea (whose remarkably accurate physical description was provided) to present himself to the competent authorities.

Too competent, no doubt.

But Juan Larrea had escaped Franco's police. He committed suicide, dying in my place, a few years later, in the pages of *La montagne blanche*. The round of lives and deaths, real or fictitious, thus seemed to come full circle.

It was in Milan, on the Via Bigli, in the library of the Banfi family, that I read *La tregua* by Primo Levi. Out in the courtyard garden, the sky, the light, the foliage on the trees were all the color of autumn.

I'd closed my eyes, at the last page of the book. I'd remembered Lorène in Locarno, and my decision to abandon the manuscript I was working on, in 1945.

It was Rossana Rossanda who had given me Levi's book to read, as well as his first one, *Se questo è un uomo*. She offered to introduce me to him, to arrange this meeting.

But I felt no need to meet Primo Levi. I mean: to meet him *outside,* in the exterior reality of this dream that life had become ever since our return. I felt that between us, everything had already been said. Or had now become impossible to say. I found it unnecessary, perhaps even improper, for us to have a conversation between survivors, a dialogue of the rescued.

And anyway, had we really survived?

On April 11, 1987, at all events, the Saturday when the ghost of the young deportee I once was had appeared—without warning, at the turn of a page—in a novel where he was unexpected, unforeseen, to sow confusion there, looking on with a troubled eye, Primo Levi chose to die by throwing himself down the stairwell of his house in Turin.

It was the first news I heard on the radio on Sunday, the next morning.

It was seven o'clock; an anonymous voice was giving a rundown of the news. Suddenly, Primo Levi was mentioned. The voice announced his suicide, the previous day, in Turin. I remembered a long walk beneath the arcade in the center of the town, one sunny day, with Italo Calvino, shortly after the publication of *Le grand voyage*. We'd talked about Primo Levi. The anonymous voice on the radio recalled the titles of his books, which had recently become the subject of critical praise in France, with the customary delay that affects all discoveries in the Hexagon.

The voice mentioned Primo Levi's age.

Then, with a trembling of my entire soul, I told myself that I had five years left to live. Primo Levi was indeed five years older than I was. I knew that this was absurd, of course. I knew that this chilling certainty was unreasonable: there was no fate obliging me to die at the same age as Primo Levi. I might well die younger than he was. Or older. Or at any time. But I understood almost immediately the meaning of this insane premonition, the significance of this ridiculous certainty.

I realized that death was once again in my future, on the horizon.

Ever since my return from Buchenwald—and still more precisely: ever since I'd abandoned my plans to write, in Ascona—I'd lived by leaving death behind. Death was in my past, farther away with each passing day, like childhood, one's first books, and first loves. Death was an experience of which the memory was growing dim.

I lived with the carefree immortality of the revenant.

This feeling later changed, when I published *Le grand voyage.* From then on, death was still in the past, but was no longer receding, fading away. Quite the contrary: it was reasserting its presence. I was beginning to go back upstream in the course of my life, toward that source, that original void.

Suddenly, the news of Primo Levi's death, of his suicide, had radically reversed my perspective. I became mortal once more. Perhaps I did not have only five more years to live, years that would make me as old as Primo Levi, but death was once again marked down on my future. I wondered if I were going to begin having more memories of death. Or else just presentiments, from now on.

Be that as it may, on April 11, 1987, death had caught up with Primo Levi.

In October 1945, though, after the long odyssey of his return from Auschwitz subsequently described in *La tregua,* he had begun writing his first book, *Se questo è un uomo.* He'd written it in haste, feverishly, with a kind of happiness. "The things I had suffered, lived through, were searing my insides," he wrote later. "I felt closer to the dead than to the living, I felt guilty for being a man, because men had built Auschwitz and Auschwitz had swallowed up millions of human beings, many of my friends, and a woman close to my heart. I felt as though I were cleansing myself by telling my story, I felt like Coleridge's Ancient Mariner."

Indeed, a quotation from Coleridge's poem serves as an epigraph to Levi's last book, *I sommersi e i salvati* [*The Drowned and the Saved*], which title he also gave to a chapter in *Se questo è un uomo.*

Since then, at an uncertain hour,
That agony returns:
And till my ghastly tale is told
This heart within me burns.

"I wrote," continued Levi, "concise poems tinged with blood, I told my story with a kind of dizzying compulsion, aloud or in writing, so often and so thoroughly that a book gradually came of this: through writing I recovered scraps of peace and became a man again, a man like anyone else, neither martyr nor wretch nor saint, one of those who start families and look to the future as much as back at the past."

Primo Levi spoke on several occasions about his feelings during this period, about the austere joys of writing. It was through writing that he felt himself returning, literally, to life.

Yet when it was finished—a masterpiece of restraint, an account of incredible honesty, lucidity, and compassion—this incomparable book found no takers. Every major publishing house turned it down. It was finally brought out by a small press and passed completely unnoticed. Primo Levi then abandoned all literary aspirations and concentrated on his career as a chemical engineer.

And so a dream he had described, a deportee's nightmare, seemed to come true: you go home and tell everyone in your family, passionately and in great detail, about what you have gone through. But no one believes you. In the end, your stories create a kind of uneasiness, provoking a deepening silence.

Those around you—even the woman you love, in the most agonizing variations of the nightmare—finally rise and turn their backs on you, leaving the room.

History, therefore, appeared to be proving him right: his dream had become reality. It was only long years later that his book, *Se questo è un uomo,* abruptly obtained an audience, won a huge public, began to be translated throughout the world.

It was this belated success that led him to write a new account, *La tregua.*

My experience had been different.

While writing may have torn Primo Levi from the past, assuaging the pain of memory ("Strangely enough," he wrote, "my baggage of ghastly memories became a fruitful store of riches: I felt, when writing, as though I were growing like a plant"), it thrust me back into death, drowning me in it. I choked in the unbreathable air of my manuscript: every line I wrote pushed my head underwater as though I were once again in the bathtub of the Gestapo's villa in Auxerre. I struggled to survive. I failed in my attempt to speak of death in order to reduce it to silence: if I had continued, it would have been death, in all probability, that would have silenced me.

Despite the radical difference in the course of our lives, in our experiences, there yet remains one coincidence, and a troubling one. The time span between Levi's first book—a masterful piece of writing; a complete flop in reaching its audience—and his second, *La tregua,* is in fact the same as that separating the failure in 1945 of my attempts to write and *Le grand voyage.* These last two books were written in the same period, published almost simultaneously: Levi's in April 1963, mine in May.

As though an ability to listen had developed on its own, beyond all the petty circumstances of our lives, within the almost unfathomable progress of history. A development all the more remarkable and fascinating in that it coincides with the first accounts of the Soviet Gulag that managed to surmount the West's traditional barrier of distrust and misunderstanding: Aleksandr Solzhenitsyn's *One Day in the Life of Ivan Denisovich* appeared in that same spring of 1963.

In any case, on April 11, 1987, death had caught up with Primo Levi.

Why, forty years later, had his recollections ceased to be a rich resource for him? Why had he lost the peace that writing seemed to have restored to him? What cataclysm had occurred in his memory that Saturday? Why did it suddenly become impossible for him to cope with the horrors of remembrance?

One last time, with no help for it, anguish had quite simply overwhelmed him. Leaving no hope of any way out. The anguish he described in the last lines of *La tregua.*

> *Nulla era vero all'infuori del Lager. Il resto era breve vacanza o inganno dei sensi, sogno . . .*

Nothing was real outside the camp, that's all. The rest was only a brief pause, an illusion of the senses, an uncertain dream. And that's all there is to say.

9

"Ô SAISONS, Ô CHÂTEAUX . . ."

Why had this young woman reminded me of Milena?

These days, whenever I happen to look at one of the photos taken in Salzburg that year, in far-off 1964, the resemblance doesn't seem striking, to say the least.

The young woman is in profile, sitting at a table at the gala dinner. Dressed in black, a lock of hair falling over her forehead, her right hand lying on the tablecloth, delicate fingers slightly curled, lace at her wrist. The left hand in the air, holding a cigarette.

The barest hint of a smile on her lips.

There are several of us around the table, in that photograph. It's the end of the meal, that's clear. We're having coffee, and the gentlemen, cigars. That young woman, a few more young women, two men, and me. I don't recognize one of the men, whose face means nothing to me. The other man is George Weidenfeld.

But perhaps he was already Lord Weidenfeld, in 1964. I have no idea anymore.

The young woman who reminded me of Milena belonged, I seem to recall, to Weidenfeld's group, whether he was a lord or not. In this old photograph, the London publisher is beaming at her with a smile of indulgent beatitude. Or complicity, perhaps.

Actually, we're all smiling.

The photograph has captured a light moment of relaxed, convivial companionship. Were we merely pretending, putting on a show for the photographer? There's no way of knowing. The semblance would be the truth of this image, in that case. The false pretense or the real semblance. It's the end of the formal dinner, just before the presentation of the Formentor Prize. Everything is going well. The publishers of the international prize jury will soon stand up, one after another, so that each of them can present me with a copy of his publishing house's translation of *Le grand voyage*.

But this isn't the moment when the anonymous young woman made me think of Milena Jesenskà. In the picture the woman is sitting there calmly; neither her face nor her placid, smiling immobility could give her even a passing resemblance to Milena.

Before the dinner, however, when I hadn't known that she would be seated at my table, I'd seen her making her way through one of the rooms in the castle in Salzburg where the Formentor Prize ceremony was being held. There was something in her bearing, her profile, the way she carried her head, that had made me think of Milena Jesenskà.

Or rather, to be completely accurate: I was reminded of something Kafka wrote about her. I hadn't really thought of Milena, after all—she'd only come to mind around a turn of phrase by Kafka.

Es fällt mir ein, dass ich mich an Ihr Gesicht eigentlich in keiner bestimmten Einzelheit erinnern kann . . .

"It occurs to me that I truly cannot remember your face in any particular detail. Only your form, your dress, how you left the café, wending your way among the tables: this I can still see . . ."

That is how Franz Kafka ended his second letter to Milena, written from a sanitarium in Merano in April 1920.

We have all of us, on occasion, been struck by the graceful carriage, proud bearing, and softly flowing garments of a woman whose face we cannot see as she moves through a crowded café. Or a theater lobby. Or even a subway car.

In 1942, in the Café de Flore, it was the walk and silhouette of Simone Kaminker that I'd noticed. She, too, was threading her way among the tables, and I was unable to catch a glimpse of her face that day. I really didn't see her face until three years later, in 1945, the summer of my return, on the terrace of that same café. The Kaminker girl had a new name by then, but her expression perfectly suited the regal bearing and light step that made the space through which she moved dance with light and silence, and which had been the first things I'd noticed about her.

So Kafka's remark is quite reasonable. Even banal. He remembers the way Milena moves, the way she walks among the tables of a café in Prague. He reminds her of this memory in one of the first letters he writes to her. It's what comes next that makes no sense. What's insane is that, without waiting to see Milena's face, to look into her eyes, without even feeling the desire or the need to do this, Kafka managed—deliberately, with desperate tenacity, with the obstinacy of an incredible moral aggressiveness beneath his apparent helplessness, his show of complaisant dereliction—to awaken and crystallize an obsessive, demanding love (a love made wretched, however, by his inability to back up his stakes, still less his promises, to face up to them, to pay the carnal price they implied) in response to this one sign, this vague token: the figure of a woman moving among the tables of a café.

Nur wie Sie dann zwischen den Kaffeehaustischen weggin-gen, Ihre Gestalt, Ihr Kleid, das sehe ich noch . . .

A love-until-death unfolds, feeding solely on its disembodied substance, on its autistic violence, in which the face of the Beloved (her expression, her gaze, the fluttering of her eyelashes, the sudden curve of her mouth, a pale shadow of sorrow, the light of a dawning pleasure) plays no role, counts for nothing. A love whose sterile strength springs from the single memory of a body in movement, an image no doubt obscurely empowered by the taboo in Hebraic law against representation, an image transcended by the arrogance of an abstract will to seduce, a desire for spiritual possession.

If I weren't sitting at a table during a gala dinner in Salzburg in 1964, just before the presentation of the Formentor Prize, and if I weren't engaged in elucidating the connection between writing and the memory of death (an enterprise for which the publication of *Le grand voyage* provides an ideal occasion), I would eagerly play hooky with a digression on Kafka and women: his love for women, or rather, his self-love—although he claimed not to love himself—through his love of the love of women. A digression on Kafka and seduction, in short. Who seduces, who is seduced? Put another way, who suborns? Who soils?

But I'm in Salzburg: the formal dinner is drawing to a close.

Ledig Rowohlt, as ebullient as a character from one of Brecht's early plays (before the pedagogical glaciation of Communism set in), has just stood up. He is the first of the twelve publishers who will be giving me a copy of *Le grand voyage:* in this case, the German translation.

The young woman whose name I won't be able to remember, of whom I know only that she was born in Czechoslovakia and that she is part of Weidenfeld's entourage, the woman whose walk, a bit earlier, made me think of something Kafka once wrote, the young woman whom I shall call Milena, for convenience's sake, watches Ledig Rowohlt come toward me after he has said a few kind words about my book.

I remember *Briefe an Milena* [*Letters to Milena*].

The volume had been on display in the window of a bookstore on the Bahnhofstrasse, in Zürich, a few years earlier.

To pass the time—or rather, to make it pass—I was strolling along that main thoroughfare, a commercial street, in both directions: from the station to the lake and back again. I was on the return trip, walking toward the station, on the left sidewalk of the Bahnhofstrasse (if your back is to the lake).

In the spring, in the summer, I would probably have passed the time in Zürich by taking a tour of the lake on one of those white excursion boats. At the quay at Wädenswil, I would have been reminded of Parvus, a wonderfully romantic character. Trotsky's companion at the Saint Petersburg soviet in 1905, organizer of Lenin's 1917 return to Russia in the sealed German railway carriage, he came here to die, in this Swiss village as peaceful as a Swiss village on a lake can be.

But it wasn't springtime. Or summertime, either. It was the month of January in the year 1956. Cold, dry air enveloped the city with impalpable crystals of ice that seemed to swirl in the limpid and chill atmosphere.

Arriving from Paris that same morning, I had changed identities in the lavatory of a café on the Paradeplatz, a square bordered by the severe but prosperous-looking facades of Swiss banks. I had placed my Uruguayan passport in the false bottom of a traveling case from which I had already removed French identification papers. Enough to muddle my trail, cover my tracks at the various police checkpoints in the airports.

I'd arrived from Paris and would be flying to Prague in a few hours. I was killing time and keeping an eye out behind me between the landing of the flight from Paris and the departure of the one to Prague. Between my identity as a well-to-do Uruguayan and my cover as a French businessman.

It now makes me feel vaguely uneasy (and slightly disgusted) to talk about this past. The secret journeys, the illusion of a future, the political commitment, the real fraternity of Communist militants, the counterfeit coin of our ideological discourse: today all that—which was my life and which turned out to be the tragic horizon of this century—seems shabby, dusty, and absurd.

Yet I must recall this past, however briefly, to clarify the moral dimension of this story. And there's no better moment to do so than now.

Because I find myself going back and forth in my memory between May 1964, in Salzburg, and January 1956, in Zürich: the connection here is the image of Milena Jesenskà that Kafka evoked in his letters to her. Soon after that January 1956, the Twentieth Congress of the Soviet Party would turn history on its ear. Or at least start slowly tipping it over. In Spain, too. It was in February, after my return from Prague and Bucharest (about which I'll say a few words), that the outlawed Communist student organizations—which I had been helping, no doubt decisively, to keep alive for the past two years—managed to shake up the University of Madrid with a wave of protest that then spread to the streets, provoking the first serious crisis of Franco's regime.

So this is an excellent moment, you will agree, to speak of this political prehistory, this last period of apparent immobility in the Cold War: a frozen ice bank beneath which flowed a rushing current already swollen by the thaw.

From another point of view, the very moment of this writing—the immediate present of words and phrases written down, crossed out, uselessly repeated, hopelessly mixed up—is quite timely as well. This book was born of a spontaneous, breathtaking plunge into memory on April 11, 1987, a few hours before I heard the announcement on the radio of Primo Levi's suicide, and I am now going over the last version of the text seven years later, almost to the day, in that anxious state of mind that April has awakened in me once again.

The sky is stormy over the plains and forests of the Gâtinais. From my window, I see the shimmering surface of a pond. Tree branches sway in the rising wind. A wind from the northwest, today. The wind that has finally risen over the dismembered empire of Communism. A single human lifetime will have been enough to witness the rise, zenith, and fall of the Communist Empire.

Even Goethe, who lived long enough to see the end of the Ancien Régime, the ferment of postrevolutionary Europe, the rise and collapse of the Napoleonic Empire, could not boast of experiencing such an event. However charming his conversation, we shouldn't be taken in by it: Napoleon's empire cannot compare to the Soviet one.

The history of this century has thus been scarred with deadly strife by the murderous illusion of the Communist adventure, which has aroused the purest of emotions, the most idealistic devotion, the most fraternal enthusiasm, only to end in the bloodiest failure, the most unfathomable and abject social injustice of History.

But I was in Zürich, at the end of January 1956, the bearer of an urgent message.

In the upper echelons of the Spanish Communist Party, to which I belonged at the time, a rather bitter debate had just begun on a question of political strategy. I'll spare you the details. Which would seem futile at this point, in any case, or incomprehensible: palimpsests of a forgotten text. Futile though these matters may have been, the stakes were high: a power struggle was going on within the leadership.

But struggles are always over power, as we all learn in the end.

Here's the gist of it: a disagreement over strategy had led to a division between the group working in Paris, headed by Santiago Carrillo (who was in charge of underground organizations in Spain itself, the main focus of my activity), and the party veterans in Prague and Bucharest who rallied around Dolorès Ibarruri, "La Pasionaria." Carrillo was sending me to the East to explain our position to the Old Guard, to try and persuade them to convene a larger assembly so that the problem might be debated more thoroughly.

In Zürich, for the moment, on the sidewalk of the Bahnhofstrasse, I'm not thinking about this delicate task. I know that Carrillo has perhaps sent me off to the slaughter, that he may be sacrificing a light horseman on this mission, a newcomer to the upper ranks, someone who doesn't belong to the inner circle. I also know that this singular position gives me distinct advantages: I'm disinterested, uninvolved in the obscure power plays among the various Communist generations. I'm interested only in ideas and will thus be more convincing—because more convinced—than an old apparatchik. Carrillo has not chosen his emissary foolishly.

But I'm not thinking about that at all for the moment.

I'm in front of a bookstore window on the Bahnhofstrasse staring in astonished delight at the white cover of a book by Franz Kafka. *Briefe an Milena.*

My heart is racing, my hands are trembling at the sight of it.

I push open the door. The lady who takes care of me has a lovely smile, an unlined face, a halo of gray hair. She is clearly surprised by the warmth of my thanks when I take the book she holds out to me. "No, don't wrap it, thank you, I'll take it like this, thanks again!" She smiles at me as I walk away from the cash register with my purchase.

On the sidewalk of the Bahnhofstrasse, I wonder briefly what the accountant will say when he sees the price of this book by Franz Kafka on my list of expenses for the trip. When he sees the name of the author, actually, rather than the price, which is negligible. I probably won't mention Kafka's name, and will doubtless claim that these few Swiss francs have been spent on a volume of Marx.

That's definitely the simplest solution.

In any case, it was in Zürich that I met Milena Jesenskà, in January 1956. She kept me company throughout the entire voyage.

But Ledig Rowohlt has just risen to his feet.

Silence has fallen over the room where the gala dinner for the Formentor Prize is being held. Rowohlt says a few kind things about me, then walks toward me carrying a presentation copy of the German translation of *Le grand voyage*.

I should be deeply moved, it's a historic moment. I mean: for me, in my personal history, this is a special moment. But instead of paying attention, I'm thinking of lots of other things; so many faces are suddenly appearing in my memory, it's distracting, I can't manage to concentrate on this momentous occasion. And after Ledig Rowohlt will come Claude Gallimard. And then Giulio Einaudi. And Barney Rossett. And George Weidenfeld. Twelve of the most important publishers in the world will each come up to me in turn to present a copy of *Le grand voyage* in their respective languages.

I still cannot manage to focus on this historic moment. I can tell that I'm going to miss it, that it will pass, vanish, before I've become fully conscious of it. Before I've savored the substantive and succulent sap of it. I guess I have no gift for historic moments.

Just in case, to keep from having my head turned by the intoxicating flattery, the applause, the radiant smiles of my friends in the room, I recite to myself in a low voice the text of Jean Paulhan's report on the manuscript of my novel.

Which doesn't take me long: it's quite a short reader's comment. So short that I remember it perfectly, that I know it by heart. So succinct that Paulhan did not require a whole sheet of paper to write it. Thrifty with his time, his words, and his paper, Paulhan cut a regular sheet of paper into quarters and wrote his reader's comment on *Le grand voyage* on one of these pieces. It's easy to see that it was cut with scissors, carefully, it's true, but with the inevitable irregularities this kind of cutting creates.

At the top of this quarter sheet of paper, Jean Paulhan wrote my name, the title of the manuscript: *Le grand voyage*. He underlined this information; then, in his neat, rounded, perfectly legible handwriting, he recorded his opinion of the book:

> It's the journey into Germany of deportees who are crowded, crushed up against one another. The conversations of the author with his neighbor, the "guy from Semur," are excellent. Unfortunately, the guy from Semur dies before their arrival, and the rest of the story is more lackluster. Nothing very remarkable. Nothing execrable, either, in this honest story.

There's a number at the end of this note, a rather large *2* which probably corresponds to some in-house code I don't understand. Does the *2* mean this book should be published? Or neither yes nor no? Does it mean they can easily do without it?

I have no idea. But silently, to myself, in the midst of all the applause at the ceremony, I repeat the words of Jean Paulhan. Just to keep from getting a swelled head, just to keep my feet on the ground. This exercise in modesty won't keep me from pointing out, however, that the conversations between the author and the guy from Semur are excellent, Paulhan *dixit*. And that the guy from Semur doesn't die until the end of the book, so Paulhan's regret ("Unfortunately, the guy from Semur dies before their arrival, and the rest of the story is more lackluster") thus applies only to a few pages.

The Paulhanian compliments are all the more comforting in that the guy from Semur is a character in a novel. I invented the guy from Semur to keep me company, when I took this same journey again in the imagined reality of literature. To spare myself the loneliness I'd felt during the real journey from Compiègne to Buchenwald, no doubt. I invented the guy from Semur, I invented our conversations: reality often needs some make-believe, to become real. In other words, to be made believable. To win the heart and mind of the reader.

The actor who played the guy from Semur in the television film Jean Prat made of *Le grand voyage* would have preferred portraying an actual person. He was disconcerted, almost saddened, to hear the character was an invention. "I would've liked to have really kept you company during the journey," Jean Le Mouël told me, mixing reality and fiction. But fraternity is not simply a fact of reality. It is also, perhaps above all, a craving of the soul: a continent to discover, to invent. A meaningful and impassioned fiction.

Still, it's not Jean Paulhan who's distracting me at this historic moment, just when I'm about to receive the twelve editions of *Le grand voyage*—that would be all I need!

What is distracting me—and it's the young woman of Czech origin in George Weidenfeld's party who is indirectly responsible—is the memory of a journey with Milena in January of 1956. Or rather, with Franz Kafka's *Briefe an Milena*.

In Prague that year I'd explained our disagreements with the old Guard to Vicente Uribe and Enrique Lister, two veteran leaders, two dinosaurs of Spanish Communism. Amazed to find that the Paris group disapproved of a political text that they had personally drawn up with la Pasionaria, and taken aback by my insistence, which they must have considered quite arrogant, they decided to defer to the incontestable authority of Dolorès Ibarruri: she would make the final decision on how to deal with this dispute.

It just so happened that Dolorès would be passing through the station in Prague the very next day, on her way back from some congress or other in East Berlin, on the special train of the Romanian delegation returning to Bucharest, where she had her winter quarters that year. It was therefore decided that I, too, would take this official train, if the Romanians gave their permission, and accompany La Pasionaria to Bucharest, explaining the objections of Carrillo's group to her during the trip. I would then await her decision or verdict, which I would communicate to the Parisian leadership of the political committee of the Spanish Communist Party upon my return.

Which was done.

If I were not at this moment in Salzburg, on May 1, 1964, at the gala presentation dinner for the Formentor Prize, watching Giulio Einaudi come forward in turn, after Ledig Rowohlt and Claude Gallimard, bearing a copy of the Italian edition of *Le grand voyage,* I would certainly take advantage of this opportunity to tell you about the trip from Prague to Bucharest. But I won't make this digression, brilliant though it might have been, any more than I made an *excursus* on the subject of Kafka, a little while ago.

One must know how to hold back, sometimes, leaving the reader hungry for more.

I will say simply that the trip was interminable, as the average speed of the special train was not more than sixty kilometers an hour. I will say simply that the trip was fascinating. That is, from a certain point of view it was a deadly bore, but I learned some fascinating things about how the Communist Nomenklatura functions.

In the luxurious private stateroom placed at my disposal on the special Romanian train, I had time to read the letters of Franz Kafka to Milena Jesenskà at my leisure.

Later, whenever I happened to think about the reasons why I didn't succumb to the idiocy of Communism (not completely, anyway), I always felt that my reading of Kafka played a part in this, and not a small one. Not only the reading of Kafka, of course. Reading in general. Certain frowned-upon works in particular. Including those of Franz Kafka.

It was neither by chance nor by despotic caprice that the reading of Kafka was forbidden—at least made suspect or rendered practically impossible because of the scarcity of his works in print—during the entire Stalinist period in Czechoslovakia. Nor was it an accident that the first timid signs of what would become the short-lived Prague Spring appeared at the international symposium on Kafka organized in that city in 1963, after so many years of official disfavor.

Because Kafka's fiction—untouched by grandiloquence, almost impenetrable in its transparence—brings us constantly back to the realm of social or historical reality, revealing its true face with implacable equanimity.

Kafka lived from 1883, the year of Karl Marx's death, to 1924, the year Lenin died. He never dealt directly with the historical events of his time. His *Journal,* in this respect, is stunningly vacuous: not one echo of the sound and fury of the world can be heard there. Yet all his works (written with his back turned on the problems and crises of the historical environment, works painfully chipped, bit by bit, from a glacial block of unnatural coherence—unnatural in its essence, at least, and whatever its misleadingly naturalistic form might be) revolve, in fact, around the density, the opacity, the uncertainty, the cruelty of this century, which they illuminate with decisive clarity. And not—or not simply—because Kafka manages, in the disarming modesty of his narrative endeavors, to get at the very heart, the metaphysical core, of the human condition, its timeless truth.

Kafka's oeuvre is not timeless in the sense that it rises above the hurly-burly of the times; it is eternal, and written with eternity in mind, which is something else entirely. But it is indeed of our time, which it yet constantly, overwhelmingly transcends, and would be otherwise unthinkable.

While Kafka's works belong to the field of literature, not sociological analysis, they are clearly contemporaneous with the writings of Max Weber or Robert Michels, to mention only two authors who devoted themselves to the study of bureaucratized society.

And so, all during that time, Franz Kafka's works of fiction brought me back to reality, while the reality constantly evoked in the political or theoretical discourse of Communism was only a fiction: repressive, certainly, and sometimes stifling, but also increasingly devoid of any foundation in concrete reality, in everyday life.

Anyway, during the endless journey of the special train from Prague to Bucharest, I spent a great deal of my time with Kafka and Milena, in that January 1956, a few weeks before the Twentieth Congress of the Russian Communist Party began to reveal, and only in part, with the utmost dialectical prudence, the Kafkaesque reality of the Stalinist universe.

I left my stateroom several times a day. Meals were served in the elegant dining car, where I would join La Pasionaria and her Romanian hosts, the most powerful and highest-ranking of whom was a certain Chivu Stoica, an almost completely bald man who seemed down-to-earth, or rather, unpolished, yet was surrounded by a circle of slimy flatterers. All the Romanians at his table laughed uproariously at every one of his drearily banal anecdotes, going into ecstasies over his memories as a militant worker.

I must say that La Pasionaria observed all this with a disenchanted air, and the way she kept fiddling with her hair clearly betrayed her impatience. But it probably wasn't the obsequious ritual of these endless meals with their parade of fancy dishes and strong drink that irritated her so much. No doubt it was that she didn't consider Chivu Stoica worthy of such fussing and fawning. Indeed, as soon as she became the center of attention—which she often was—and had a chance to reminisce about the Spanish Civil War, when she'd been world-famous, La Pasionaria recovered her smile, her spirits, and her garrulity, reeling off picturesque or heroic anecdotes, all starring herself, of course.

But I mustn't keep talking about this trip across Central Europe by train with a Romanian Communist delegation in January 1956.

In the dining room of the castle in Salzburg, Carlos Barral has just risen to present me with a copy of the Spanish edition of *Le grand voyage*. Taking advantage of the fact that Barral's table is some distance from mine, which means that it will take him a few seconds to cross the enormous dining room, I will wind this up for the time being.

By saying that the most important thing about that journey, the only important thing about it, actually, was the discovery of Milena. Or rather, to be specific, the discovery of Milena through Kafka's mad obsession with her.

Es fällt mir ein, dass ich mich an Ihr Gesicht eigentlich in keiner bestimmten Einzelheit erinnern kann . . .

"It occurs to me that I truly cannot remember your face in any particular detail. Only your form, your dress, how you left the café, wending your way among the tables: this I can still see . . . "

On the foundation of that fleeting glimpse of a form moving through the noise and bustle of a café in Prague, Franz Kafka fabricated the literary structure—illusory, poignant, superb—of a sterile, destructive love feeding exclusively on absence and separation, falling miserably to pieces, sadly, at each real encounter, each moment of physical presence. A literary creation so poignant and superb that generations of readers—particularly women, since well-bred, cultivated women too often have the disastrous habit of devaluating carnal pleasure, of considering it to be inferior, if not vulgar, while at the same time exalting the spiritual pleasure of an intense but painful relationship transcended through the dubious bliss of failure and inadequacy—and a long line of stuffy scholiasts have mistaken this literary exercise or exorcism for the real thing, holding up as a sublime example of true love this insanely narcissistic, disincarnate passion, brutally indifferent to its object, insensible to the other's gaze, to her face, her pleasure, her very life. . . .

But Carlos Barral has arrived at my table. He holds out to me a copy of the Spanish edition of my book, *El largo viaje.*

I return to the pleasant reality of the gala dinner held in Salzburg on May 1, 1964, to celebrate the presentation of the Formentor Prize. I forget Milena Jesenskà for a moment. I stand up to welcome Carlos Barral, to take him in my arms, to receive a copy of my book from him.

I'm not happy, however.

What I mean is, beneath the obvious joy of this moment, a profound sadness is welling up in me. Perhaps "sadness" isn't the right word, though. I know that my life is changing in this instant, that I am changing lives. This isn't a theoretical proposition, a conclusion drawn through psychological introspection. It's a physical impression, a bodily certainty. As though I were taking a long walk and were suddenly to emerge from the darkness of a forest into the sunshine of a summer's day. Or the other way around. In short, I'm changing my life the way one steps from shadows into sunlight, or from sunlight into shadows, at a precise moment that establishes a physical difference—skin-deep, subtle, but radical—between before and after, between past and future.

By the time Barral has given me the Spanish copy of *Le grand voyage,* when I hold the book in my hand, my life will have changed. And one does not change one's life without risk, especially if one is aware of the change, acutely conscious of the event: the advent of a different future, one that represents—no matter what it has in store for you—a profound break with the past.

A few weeks before this Formentor Prize ceremony, in fact, in another castle (once owned, not by the Hohenlohe, like the one in Salzburg, but by the kings of Bohemia), the leadership of the Spanish Communist Party had held a long meeting that had ended with my expulsion from the Executive Committee. Actions had been taken that would lead inevitably to my definitive expulsion from the party.

But I won't go into that.

It's not for lack of time that I pass over that episode, even though Carlos Barral has already reached my table and is holding out a copy of my novel. Because I am the one who is writing, I am the omnipotent god of the narrative. If I so pleased, I could freeze Carlos Barral in his current position, immobilizing him in a present I could draw out for as long as I liked. Barral would stay there, without moving, with a frozen smile that would begin to look silly, awaiting the narrator's pleasure. Waiting until

I'd finished my account of that meeting of the Executive Committee of the Spanish Communist Party in a castle that once belonged to the kings of Bohemia.

But I shall do nothing of the sort. I will not recount this episode of my life that changed my life. That restored me to life, in a way. In the first place, I've already done so: anyone interested can read about it in my *Autobiographie de Federico Sanchez*. And then, most importantly, no one would be interested anymore. Myself first of all, I take no further interest in that episode. The fact of having been right in 1964, as History has largely proved, is of no interest anymore: being right had no effect on History. Even if I had persuaded them during our discussions that I was right, even if I had won my case, even if the majority of the Executive Committee—an utterly absurd hypothesis—had decided in favor of Fernando Claudín and me, it would have served no purpose. Except to have been right, to be able to console or satisfy ourselves with this fact. But History would not have changed one whit for all that. Well, losing that argument in 1964 and being expelled, hurled into the outer darkness, spared me years of unproductive delusion, years of fruitless struggle to renew and reform Communism, which is in its essence, in its historical manifestation, incapable of renewing itself, impossible to reform.

Carlos Barral stands before me. He holds out a copy of my book in Spanish, *El largo viaje*. He tells me something that I don't understand right away. That I don't quite grasp. I'm still deeply immersed in my memories of Prague, in those private images of my last stroll through Prague a few weeks before.

When the Executive Committee of the Spanish Communist Party had finished its deliberations, Dolorès Ibarruri, La Pasionaria, returned the verdict. With a few sentences, she well and truly executed Claudín and me. Her final pronouncement—

which she probably considered an adequate explanation for our erring ways—upbraided us for being *intelectuales con cabeza de chorlito*: feather-brained intellectuals.

Carrillo then suggested that the two of us remain in Czechoslovakia or in another Eastern European country. That way, while we waited for the Central Committee to study the issues that had been debated and approve the actions taken against us, we might devote our time to self-critical reflection, in a suitable environment.

We refused, of course. For one thing, we were not likely to be inclined to self-critical reflection, given the terms of our disagreement. For another, we didn't consider the environment of real socialism to be suitable in any way. For my part, I added that I was expected in Salzburg in a few weeks for the presentation of the Formentor Prize, and that my absence would create a certain stir.

Our refusal was met with vexed silence. But times had changed, it was impossible to impose blind disciplinary obedience on us, *perinde ac cadaver*. Despite the implosion of the reform movement instituted by the Twentieth Congress of the Soviet Party, certain things were no longer possible.

Unable to prevent my departure, the apparatchiks took their petty revenge: I was given a plane ticket to Rome, no farther, and nothing in the way of travel expenses. As for going on to Paris, I was left to manage for myself. I managed quite well: I had enough friends in the upper circles of the Italian Communist Party to ensure that the rest of the trip would be no problem.

In Prague, that last day, I'd gone to all my favorite places in the city, with the anxious fear that I might never see them again.

I visited Franz Kafka's tomb, in the new Jewish cemetery in Strasnice. I went to look at a Renoir painting hanging in the National Gallery, within Prague Castle. I'd often contemplated this portrait of a laughing and rosy young woman. I'd been captivated by the line of her neck, a fold in the material on her shoulder, the imagined whiteness of this shoulder, the firm curve of her bosom beneath the fabric.

Once, in 1960, during one of my stays in Prague, I'd suddenly had the idea, as I gazed at that Renoir painting, that Milena Jesenskà must surely have gazed at it, too. This memory of Milena cropped up again, four years later, during my last visit to Prague. I remembered the shiver that had come over me at the idea that Milena must have stood more than once in that same place, motionless, contemplating the Renoir. I recalled a memory of snow glittering in the beams of searchlights, a wrenching memory that had just shattered the memory of Milena herself like frosty fire: Milena Jesenskà, dead in the Ravensbrück concentration camp. I'd recalled this memory of snow falling on the ashes of Milena Jesenskà. I'd thought once more of Milena's beauty, whirled away by the wind, with the smoke from the crematory.

And then, to wind up this long tour through my memories of Prague—I had no idea when, if ever, I might return there—I'd gone to revisit the old Jewish cemetery and adjoining synagogue in Pinkas.

There, amid the jumbled tombstones, in the silence of this immemorial place, I'd thought back to that distant August dawn in 1945, at the home of Claude-Edmonde Magny, on the Rue Schoelcher. Nearly twenty years later, I'd recalled our conversation, the long letter she'd read to me about the power to write. There among the tombstones of Pinkas, I'd reflected that in a few weeks, in Salzburg, I would be receiving the Formentor Prize for the book we had talked about so long ago, and which I had put off writing for almost twenty years.

But I won't keep Carlos Barral waiting any longer.

He has been standing next to my table for a while now, holding that copy of my book in Spanish. A smile frozen on his lips. I will give life, color, movement back to Carlos Barral. I will even listen to what he has been trying—in vain, until now—to tell me. I'm being quite magnanimous: a god of narration doesn't often allow the minor characters in his story to speak, for fear that they'll seize the opportunity to do as they please, take themselves for protagonists, and thus disrupt the course of the narrative.

Carlos Barral explains to me what is so special about the book he holds in his hand, the book he is about to present to me.

As it happens, Franco's censors prohibited the publication of *Le grand voyage* in Spain. Ever since the announcement a year ago that I'd won the Formentor Prize, General Franco's Minister of Information, M. Fraga Iribarne, has led a campaign against me, attacking the publishers on the international jury—in particular the Italian Giulio Einaudi—for having honored an opponent of the regime, a member of the "Communist diaspora." Barral has been obliged to have the book printed in Mexico, bringing out a coedition with Joaquin Mortiz. This edition is not yet ready, so there will be no copies available for another few weeks.

In order to be able nevertheless to present the ritual copy of the prizewinning novel to the author, Barral has had a single copy of my novel made up. The format, binding, number of pages, jacket illustration—everything matches what the Mexican edition will look like. Except for one detail: the pages of my presentation copy are blank, without a single printed character.

Carlos Barral flips through the pages in front of me, so that I can see their immaculate whiteness.

Finally, I feel moved.

The unique moment I feared I had missed, the significance of which I had thought myself unable to grasp, the moment that had slipped through my fingers like water, sand, smoke, now recovers its full, sparkling density.

It becomes once again a unique moment, in truth.

On May 1, 1945, a snow squall had fallen upon the red flags of the May Day parade at the precise moment when a group of deportees in striped uniforms had swung out into the Place de la Nation. At that instant, on that first day of renewed life, the swirling snow had seemed to remind me that it would always bring with it the presence of death.

Nineteen years later, the span of a generation, on May 1, 1964, in Salzburg, the snow of yesteryear had once again fallen on my life. It had erased the printed traces of the book I'd written in one headlong stretch, in a safe house on the Calle Concepción-Bahamonde in Madrid. The snow of yesteryear blanketed the pages of my book, burying them beneath a powdery shroud. The snow had erased my book, at least in its Spanish version.

The sign was easy to interpret, the lesson easy to draw: I had not yet accomplished anything. This book it had taken me almost twenty years to be able to write was vanishing once more, practically as soon as it had been finished. I would have to begin it again: an endless task, most likely, transcribing the experience of death.

Of all the copies of *Le grand voyage* that I've been given so far this evening, and that I will yet receive, the Spanish copy is the most beautiful. The most meaningful to me, because of its dazzling emptiness, the innocent and perverse blankness of all those pages to be rewritten.

Carlos Barral has just walked away from my table. It's Barney Rossett's turn to bring me a copy of the American edition of the novel, published by Grove Press.

While Barney Rossett approaches, I turn over the blank pages of the Spanish volume with delight.

The snow of yesteryear has not fallen on any text at random, I tell myself. It hasn't buried any language at random from among all those represented here. Not English, German, Swedish, Finnish, Portuguese, what have you, up to a dozen. The snow erased the original language, the mother tongue.

Of course, by suppressing the text of my novel in its native tongue, Franco's censors merely duplicated a fait accompli. Because I hadn't written *Le grand voyage* in my native tongue.

I hadn't written it in Spanish, but in French.

Yet I'd been living in Madrid during most of that time. I'd found once more, in the language of my childhood, all the complicity, the passion, the wariness, and the taste for defiance that foster the intimacy of writing. And besides, I already knew (even though the little poems that had so charmed Claude-Edmonde Magny were nothing more than a memory, and barely that, surviving only as an allusion in the text of her *Lettre sur le pouvoir d'écrire* that I took along with me on my travels and sometimes reread; even though the play I'd written in the late forties, *Soledad,* had been simply a personal exercise to prove to myself that it wasn't laziness or inability that prevented me from writing, but a deliberate decision)—I already knew that on the day when the power to write would be restored to me, when I resumed possession of it, I would be able to choose my mother tongue.

French was just as much my mother tongue, in fact, as Spanish. It had become so, at least. I hadn't chosen the place where I was born, the native soil of my native language. Nationality: this thing, or idea, or reality for which so many have fought, spilling so much blood, is the thing that least belongs to you, the most accidental, the most dangerous part of one's self, and the most senseless, too. Senseless with stupidity and brutality. So I hadn't chosen my nationality, or my native language. Or rather, I had chosen one: French.

You could say that I'd been forced to do so as a result of exile and deracination. This is true only to an extent, to a very small extent. How many Spaniards have refused the language of exile? Have they kept their accents, their linguistic foreignness, in the pathetic, irrational hope of remaining the same? In other words, different? How many deliberately use correct French only for practical purposes? For my part, I'd chosen French, the language of exile, as another mother tongue. I'd chosen a new nationality for myself. I'd made exile into a homeland.

In short, I no longer really had a native language. Or else I had two of them, which is a delicate situation as far as affiliations go, you must agree. Having two mothers, like having two countries, doesn't really make life easier. But I'm probably not partial to things that are too simple.

In any case, I hadn't written *Le grand voyage* in French for the sake of convenience. It would have been just as easy (if one can apply such a frivolous adjective to that kind of work), or just as difficult, to write it in Spanish. I'd written it in French because I'd made that language my native tongue.

One day, I thought, after that evening in Salzburg, one day I'll rewrite this book on the blank pages of that single copy. I'll rewrite it in Spanish, disregarding the existing translation.

"That's not a bad idea," Carlos Fuentes told me, not very long afterward.

We were in Paris, in a café on the Boulevard Saint-Germain-des-Prés.

"Anyway, you should have done the Spanish version yourself. You wouldn't have simply translated, you'd have been able to transform. To transform your original text, to try to go farther with it. This would have created a different book, which you could have turned into a new French version, a whole new book! You say so yourself: this experience is inexhaustible. . . . "

His conclusion had made us laugh, on a day of Parisian spring showers that might have come from a poem by César Vallejo.

"And so," Carlos Fuentes concluded, "you will have realized

every writer's dream: to spend your life writing a single book, endlessly renewed!"

We laughed. The downpour battered the windows of the café where we'd taken refuge.

But I didn't carry out this plan. The pages of the single copy Carlos Barral presented to me in Salzburg on May 1, 1964, have remained blank, untouched by writing. Still available, then. I love the promise and symbolism of it: that this book yet remains to be written, that the task is infinite, the tale never-ending.

For a little while now, however, I've known what I'm going to do, how I'm going to fill those pages. I will write on those blank pages, for Cécilia Landman, the story of Jerzy Zweig, a little Jewish child in Buchenwald.

When Cécilia was three, I'd hold her in my arms, I'd recite poetry to her. It was the best way to quiet her in the evenings, soothe her nightly anxieties, overcome her resistance to the oblivion of sleep.

I would recite Ronsard, Apollinaire, Aragon. I also recited Baudelaire's "Le voyage," it was her favorite poem. With time, she learned it by heart, repeated it along with me. But I'd always stopped before reaching the line that begins, *"Ô mort, vieux capitaine . . ."* Not only to avoid any questions prompted by her curiosity. Above all because it was this particular verse I'd murmured to Maurice Halbwachs as he lay dying on that bunk in Block 56 in Buchenwald.

I'd hold the little girl in my arms and she'd gaze at me with an attentive, trusting eye. For Halbwachs, Baudelaire's lines had been a kind of prayer for the dying. When he'd heard them, a smile had played about his lips. But when I held Cécilia in my arms, I'd recite Baudelaire to her, and this memory would grow dim. Would be transfigured, rather. The stench, the injustice, the horror of that ancient death faded away, but not the compassion: a piercing, irresistible feeling of the brotherhood of man.

I'd recite to the little girl these verses that were an invitation to the voyage of life, and I'd seem to see an expression of peace come over Halbwachs's face. In my memory, his eyes seemed to shine with a great serenity, on that Sunday long ago. I'd cradle Cécilia Landman in my arms, my radiant little Jewish quadroon, through whose veins flowed the blood of Czernowitz, the birthplace of Paul Celan, and the pain of those wrenching memories seemed to subside.

I will write down for her, in the blank pages of *El largo viaje,* the story of Jerzy Zweig, the Jewish child we saved, whom I met years later in Vienna, in another life: life.

10

RETURN TO WEIMAR

"No, that's not what he wrote!"

Although the man speaks firmly, even emphatically, his voice is not strident, but almost low. As if the truth he is stating does not require a raised voice, a trenchant tone, to affirm its incontestability.

We turn toward him.

The man is about forty years old, has a reddish beard, an alert but reticent expression. Shy, almost. Until now, he's been more or less quiet.

In the cross fire of our astonished looks, he speaks up again.

"He didn't write down 'student,' but something completely different!"

The man uses the German word, *Student,* because he's speaking German. The whole conversation is in German. Which is normal, after all, since we're in Germany.

The man gestures vaguely, as though he were going to reach into his inside jacket pocket. Perhaps he's going to pull out the proof of his assertion, that's exactly what it looks like.

We stare at him, transfixed.

———

It was on the roll-call square of Buchenwald, one Sunday in March. In 1992: forty-seven years after my last day in the camp.

Several weeks earlier, a German journalist, Peter Merseburger, had called me on the phone. He was going to do a program on Weimar, a center of culture with a concentration camp. He wanted me to be one of the principal participants in this exploration of the past. In the concentration camp department, of course. He suggested filming an interview with me at Buchenwald itself.

I had refused immediately, without even thinking about it.

I had never gone back to Weimar, had never felt any desire to do so. I had always refused, whenever the occasion offered.

But the next night, I'd dreamed about Buchenwald again. A voice awakened me in the night. Rather, a voice burst into my sleep. I hadn't woken up yet, I knew that I was sleeping, that I was having that recurrent dream. A sinister, angry male voice was about to say, as usual, *"Krematorium, ausmachen!"* But not at all. The voice I expected—I was already trembling, already gripped by fear, just as I was passing from deep sleep into this anguished dream—was not the voice I heard. Not at all: it was a woman's voice. A lovely, feminine voice, iridescent, a bit husky: the voice of Zarah Leander. She was singing a love song. That beautiful, coppery voice of Zarah Leander's never sang anything but love songs, anyway. At least not in Buchenwald, over the loudspeakers of Buchenwald, on Sundays.

> *So stelle ich mir die Liebe vor,*
> *ich bin nicht mehr allein . . .*

In my dream I heard the voice of Zarah Leander instead of the one I'd expected, the usual SS *Sturmführer*'s voice demanding over and over that the crematory oven be shut down. I heard her

sing her love song, the way she did on so many Sundays long
ago in Buchenwald.

Schön war die Zeit da wir uns so geliebt . . .

Then I woke up. I'd understood the message I was sending to
myself through this transparent dream. As soon as I could, I tele-
phoned Peter Merseburger in Berlin to accept his offer. To tell
him I was willing to return to Weimar, to give him the interview he wanted.

All in all, in this roundabout way—a German television program that was neither my idea nor my doing, a dream that was
almost too easy to interpret—I was telling myself to finish the
book I had put off so often, for so long: *L'écriture ou la mort* [*Literature or Death*] . . .

It had sprung from a hallucination of my memory, on April
11, 1987, the anniversary of the liberation of Buchenwald. The
day of Primo Levi's death: the day death caught up with him. A
year later, when Felipe González asked me to accept a post in his
government, I'd been happy to abandon the book. After this
ministerial interlude was over, I'd gone back to work for a while
on my book only to abandon it again in favor of an account of
my experience in the Spanish Ministry of Culture, entitled *Federico Sanchez vous salue bien* [*Federico Sanchez Sends You His Best*].
This last was an unforeseen development. I hadn't even intended
writing on this subject, actually, until a few years later.

But Zarah Leander's voice was calling me to order, drawing
me back to Buchenwald. It was an intelligent voice, although it
came from beyond the grave. For the only way, in fact, to force
me to finish the story I had repressed for so long was to lure me
back to Buchenwald.

On the day I left for Berlin, I ran into Dany Cohn-Bendit in the airport at Roissy. A good omen, I thought. Dany was born in April 1945, at the very time when I was returning from the dead. His life began when mine was beginning all over again: the days that took me farther and farther away from death, week after week, year after year, were days that became a part of his life. Besides, Dany Cohn-Bendit was born in Montauban, a town where foreigners found refuge, during the dark years under Pétain, thanks to a leftist mayor. Manuel Azaña died there, in Montauban: the last president of the republic, one of the greatest Spanish writers of the twentieth century. All that death, all that life had clearly created bonds between us, Dany and I.

So it was a good omen, our meeting.

I was traveling to Weimar with Thomas and Mathieu Landman, my grandsons through ties of affection. Ties as strong as any others, that may even come before all others. But I think I've said that already. Have I also said why I'd chosen them to accompany me?

With them, it had become possible to talk about that distant time, the experience of that ancient death, without feeling that my words were improper, or that I was speaking in vain. It probably seems shocking to say the "experience" of death, it sounds so strange. In German, it would be brilliant, no matter what Ludwig Wittgenstein might have thought of it: *das Erlebnis dieses Todes*. In Spanish as well, I might add: *la vivencia de aquella antigua muerte. Le vécu de cette ancienne mort:* French has no active noun to express the experience of life. Someone should look into that, one day.

Was it because Thomas and Mathieu had been well brought up? I don't mean, as I should hope you'd realize, brought up to have good manners. I'm talking about the elevation of the spirit, an open mind, something taught by example, tenderly, with long-suffering parental patience. Well brought up, then, to be on the qui vive, taught not to take life as it comes but to seize it with both hands. Was it because they were—providentially— one quarter Jewish, with the Jewish blood of Czernowitz in their veins? Enough Jewish blood to be curious about the world, its misery and grandeur, as this century draws to a close? Or was it simply because their age and relationship with me—a relationship full of needs and demands, but unfettered by any obligations—allowed them to ask questions that a son would never have ventured (or even wanted, naturally) to ask? The fact is that Thomas and Mathieu Landman both felt the need, when they reached that questioning age of adolescence (each in his turn, for there were ten years between them), to know more about my past. About my past experience of the camps.

So, they came with me, in that month of March in 1992. On that Saturday in March 1992.

At the airport in Berlin, a car was waiting to take us to Weimar, where we were to meet with Peter Merseburger, his wife Sabine, and their television crew.

It wasn't long before the poor condition of the roadway and the increasing number of buildings undergoing repairs revealed that we had entered the former German Democratic Republic.

I looked at the countryside, the names of the towns and villages on the signs marking the exits along the highway. At some point, I began to feel anxious, uneasy. I didn't know why, but for a while, each time I glimpsed the name of a town on one of those exit signs, my anxiety deepened. Suddenly, I understood: each of these towns had been the site of an outside *Kommando* or secondary camp under the central administration of Buchenwald. Working at the *Arbeitsstatistik,* I recorded all the data that came in from these outlying subcamps in the central card index. Forty-seven years later, the names were coming back to me. These towns scattered across the plain or nestled in the greenery all bore the names of former subcamps of Buchenwald.

So we were approaching Weimar. We were entering the territory of ancient death.

"Das hat er nicht eingeschrieben, Student. . . . Etwas ganz anderes hat er geschrieben."

The man seems to be about forty years old, at first glance. His beard is somewhat reddish, the look in his eye is attentive yet melancholy. He has broken the silence to which he had accustomed us, since the beginning of our visit to Buchenwald, to speak these words, in a low but firm voice. "He didn't write down 'student,' but something completely different!"

A Sunday in March. A beautiful Sunday in March, sunny and cool. A Sunday in Buchenwald, once again. The wind blows on the hill of the Ettersberg, as on those Sundays long ago. The wind of eternity on the eternal hill of the Ettersberg.

On the previous day, the car had dropped us off, Thomas, Mathieu, and I, on the market square of Weimar, in front of the Elephant Hotel, where Peter Merseburger was waiting for us.

I'd stepped out onto the sidewalk, stretched my legs a bit, taken a look around. The square slumbered in provincial quiet with its trim facades. It was lovely and strangely familiar: it resembled all kinds of marketplaces that I'd already seen in old Central European towns.

I was gazing at the urban landscape, taking in the details with a sense of familiarity, of déjà vu that was troubled, nevertheless, by a vague feeling of discomfort, a touch of dismay, when my heart began pounding wildly.

Of course it was déjà vu!

I'd come here in an earlier life, one April day in 1945, with Lieutenant Rosenfeld. I'd forgotten that escapade in Weimar with Rosenfeld. I'd forgotten it so completely that in the first version of this book I hadn't said one word about it. I would have to give Lieutenant Rosenfeld his place in my account of those former days. I'd have to reinvent Rosenfeld, in a way: make him rise again from the confused obscurity of my clouded, tattered memory.

I looked at the Marktplatz of Weimar with new eyes. I understood why everything had seemed familiar, yet strange and upsetting. Almost half a century later, the square looked newer and neater than it had to my twenty-year-old gaze. In 1945, with the entire north side destroyed by Allied shelling, the square had been partly buried beneath dust and rubble.

I then summoned the spirit of Lieutenant Rosenfeld to my side. I was going to try to spend the coming days with him. With the memory of my younger self, in short. Because now I knew the hidden purpose of this return to Weimar. It would allow me to recover, for a short while, the strength, energy, and will to live of my youth. And in thus finding myself once again, I would doubtless—perhaps—find the strength, energy, and will to persevere until the end of this writing that constantly eluded me, avoided me. Or rather: that I constantly eluded, that I avoided on the slightest pretext.

Accompanied by Thomas and Mathieu Landman, and by the spirit of a young German Jew, Lieutenant Rosenfeld of the American Army, I crossed the threshold of the Elephant Hotel.

After settling into my room, and before joining my grandsons for lunch, I placed the three books I'd brought with me on my bedside table.

The first was a novel by Thomas Mann, *Charlotte à Weimar,* published in Paris in early 1945 by the NRF in their *collection blanche,* translated from the German by Louise Servicen. This novel was the first book I'd bought after my return from Buchenwald. I'd gone into a bookstore on the Boulevard Saint-Michel one ordinary day that May. I wanted to see if the literary landscape was indeed as the French officer had described it. To see if Marc had forgotten or ignored some new author. Laurence was with me, actually. Which means this ordinary day in May when I stepped inside a bookstore on the Boulevard Saint-Michel was after the eighth, the date on which I met Laurence.

I must admit that at the time, it was Laurence who went to bookstores with me, while Odile went to bed with me. It wasn't a choice, it just happened that way. I'm not sure that I would have preferred the contrary, I simply regret not having had the opportunity to go occasionally from bookstore to bedroom, or vice versa, but life isn't perfect, as we know. It can be a path to perfection, but is far from perfect.

On some ordinary day in May—after the eighth—I'd gone into a bookstore with Laurence, and I'd bought Thomas Mann's *Charlotte à Weimar.* Partly because of Thomas Mann. Mostly because of Weimar. I knew that the Charlotte in question was Goethe's Charlotte, from Johann Wolfgang von Goethe's *Werther,* and Goethe had been a part of my life in Buchenwald. Because of his walks on the Ettersberg with Eckermann, and because of Léon Blum.

But I did not know, when I bought the novel, that the place where Charlotte Kestner—née Buff, from Hanover, *Werther's* Lotte—stays in Weimar is the Elephant Hotel. I didn't realize this, but that detail stuck in my memory.

So when I received Merseburger's itinerary for our filmed interview at Buchenwald and learned that we'd be staying at the Elephant, I'd immediately gone looking in my library for the volume of Thomas Mann. Which I'd found, perhaps not exactly where it ought to have been, if my library were arranged in a more logical fashion, but found nonetheless. Among certain other books that had nothing to do with Thomas Mann, or even with Goethe, but which had some connection to Buchenwald, as though an obscure premonition had led me to include the novel within a context that would become clear many years later.

I finally found *Charlotte à Weimar* next to a book by Serge Miller, a comrade of mine from our quarantine days in Block 62 in the Little Camp: *Le laminoir* [*The Steamroller*] (with a preface by François Mitterrand, incidentally, since Serge had belonged to the MNPGD, a movement for former French prisoners of war organized by Mitterrand in the forties). Next to Eugen Kogon's *L'enfer organisé* [*The Theory and Practice of Hell*], too, probably the most objective and exhaustive report—even though it was written immediately after the liberation of the camp—on the conditions of life, work, and death in Buchenwald.

The copy of Thomas Mann I'd found again in such strange but significant company was not the same one I'd bought in May 1945 (after the eighth of the month). It was a copy from the fourteenth edition, published in October 1948. Which proves that I've always felt strongly about keeping the book close by me, and that after losing the original copy, very likely during one of my many changes of residence (if one can call them residences, all those places where I used to alight for a while at that time), I'd gone out and bought another. The one I'd brought to Weimar, in March of 1992.

The Elephant had obviously changed considerably since the autumn of 1816 when Charlotte Kestner—née Buff—visited Weimar, judging from the description of the hotel in Thomas Mann's novel. In 1938, in particular, the interior had been redecorated in the taste of the period, which was anything but innocent. Hitlerian, rather: German neatness warped by showy affectations of grandeur.

Lieutenant Rosenfeld hadn't taken me to see the Elephant Hotel during our escapade in Weimar on Saint George's day in 1945. I could imagine the talk he would have given about it if he had, however. He would have told me its history since 1696, the year it was built. He would have told me about the lives and work of all those who had come here, at one time or another, from Goethe and Schiller, Bach and Wagner, to Tolstoy and Gropius. Not forgetting Adolf Hitler, of course, or the French writers of the dark years who came to those *Propagandastaffel* conferences to discuss the new Europe, a few kilometers away from the crematory ovens of Buchenwald.

Although Lieutenant Rosenfeld had not had the opportunity to tell me the history of the Elephant Hotel, with his sparkling and witty erudition, I am certain nevertheless that he would have approved my choice of book-companions for this trip. *Charlotte à Weimar,* that goes without saying. But he would have been equally satisfied with the two others. The second contained the correspondence between Martin Heidegger and Karl Jaspers from 1920 to 1963, published by Klostermann and Piper.

I had begun discussing *Sein und Zeit* with Claude-Edmonde Magny in 1941. Around the same time, Heidegger was also the subject, at least occasionally, of my conversations with Henri-Irénée Marrou, who was known in particular for his music criticism, written under the pen name of Davenson. Marrou was a gentle giant of vast learning: pedagogic, when appropriate, but never pedantic, because his knowledge was tempered by irony and tolerance, two cardinal virtues of great minds. He would arrange to meet me at the Dauphine, a pâtisserie and tea salon on the Boulevard Saint-Germain that offered only ersatz fare, during that period of restrictions under the Occupation, but offered it with elegance and savoir faire. From there we'd set out for long walks to the outskirts of the city (my thorough familiarity with the gates, posterns, fortifications, and less verdant suburbs of Paris dates from this time), and he would stride on, with that tireless gait typical of mountain people, while he talked to me of Aristotle and Saint Augustine. And Heidegger, on occasion.

But it was with Lieutenant Rosenfeld that I'd begun thinking about the philosopher of Todtnauberg's relations with Nazism. Another endless analysis.

I'd brought along the volume of correspondence between Heidegger and Jaspers—in the background of which figured four decades of tragic and decisive German history—because I'd felt it appropriate to reread these letters in the lucid emotion of my return to Buchenwald. A return to the only place in the world where both totalitarianisms of the twentieth century, Nazism and Bolshevism, have together left their mark. (Islamic fundamentalism will wreak incredible havoc in the next century if we do not pursue a politics of reform and justice throughout the world.)

The third book I'd chosen for this trip would also have met with Lieutenant Rosenfeld's approval, I was certain of it. If Rosenfeld had continued on as he was then, still resembling the young man I had known, no doubt he would have one day discovered and loved the poetry of Paul Celan.

My third choice was a volume of Celan's poetry. A somewhat special volume: a selection of poems in a bilingual edition— German and English—translated by Michael Hamburger. After long years of patiently deciphering Paul Celan's poems in the original German—which he, a Romanian poet, intended at least to be originative, even unprecedented—and comparing those translations available in languages accessible to me, I've concluded that English is the one that best lends itself to a convincing likeness.

Before leaving my room to rejoin Thomas and Mathieu, I'd opened the volume of Celan at random, at one of the pages with its corner turned down to mark the poems I reread most often. Once again, luck was with me: I'd chanced upon "Todtnauberg."

As far as I know, this poem is the only trace left to us of the conversation between Celan and Heidegger in the latter's cabin hideaway in the Black Forest. Enigmatic—his poetry is here at its densest strength, brilliantly hermetic—and yet chillingly transparent. What Paul Celan wanted from Martin Heidegger, you may recall, was a clear statement of his position on Nazism. And on the extermination of the Jewish people in Hitler's camps, specifically. As you doubtless also recall, Celan was unsuccessful. He found only that silence some have tried to fill with empty chatter, or to erase from memory: Heidegger's definitive silence on the question of German culpability. A silence Karl Jaspers speaks of with devastating philosophical rigor in some of his letters, despite the politeness of his remarks.

We do have this one trace, however, and it is stunning. A few lines from Paul Celan.

die in das Buch
—wessen Namen nahms auf
vor dem meinen?—
die in dies Buch
geschriebene Zeile von
einer Hoffnung, heute,
auf eines Denkenden
kommendes
Wort
im Herzen . . .

And so, in Martin Heidegger's guest book (what name is written there before his? Celan asks, or pretends to ask), the poet has written a line expressing his hope for the day in question.

einer Hoffnung, heute . . .

Hope for a heartfelt word from the philosopher. About what, this hoped-for word, spoken from the heart? About the subject of their conversation, which has just ended, probably. Which has just ended in the silence of the heart. Of the mind as well, of course, but it was to the philosopher's heart that Paul Celan had spoken. A heartfelt word about the unsaid in that conversation, in short. The Heideggerian unsaid par excellence: the unsaid of German guilt. With which Martin Heidegger resisted, underhandedly, but with remarkable tenacity and obvious constancy throughout the years of their correspondence, the courteous efforts of Jaspers to obtain Heidegger's opinion on his essay on the question of German guilt, *Die Schuldfrage*. An opinion the thinker of Todtnauberg refused to give, no more to Jaspers than to Paul Celan. Leaving its negative reflection for us, the trace of its absence, in the former's letters and the latter's poem, "Todtnauberg."

In my room at the Elephant, I recite aloud the lines of Paul Celan.

> *einer Hoffnung, heute*
> *auf eines Denkenden*
> *kommendes*
> *Wort*
> *im Herzen . . .*

The words of a Jewish poet from Czernowitz. I recite Celan's poem out loud to myself and I think about the destiny of the German language: language of barked SS commands (*"der Tod ist ein Meister aus Deutschland,"* Celan could write: "death is a master from Germany"), and language of Kafka, of Husserl, Freud, Benjamin, Canetti, of Paul Celan himself—of so many other Jewish intellectuals who created the grandeur and richness of German culture during the 1930s. Language of subversion, therefore: language of the universal affirmation of critical reason.

einer Hoffnung, heute . . .

The hope inscribed that day in the guest book of Martin Heidegger was not fulfilled. No heartfelt word had come from the philosopher to fill this silence. Shortly afterward, Paul Celan drowned himself in the Seine. No heartfelt word had held him back.

It was the following day, Sunday, on the roll-call square of Buchenwald.

We'd all turned in amazement toward the thoughtful, taciturn bearded man who had accompanied us throughout our visit to the camp.

The same wind, the everlasting wind, was blowing across the eternity of the Ettersberg.

We had arrived by car, with Sabine and Peter Merseburger, to find the television crew waiting for us. We walked down the Avenue of Eagles that leads to the entrance to Buchenwald. But there were no more Hitlerian eagles, no more tall columns lofting them into the sky once darkened by the smoke from the crematory. There was the road, and a few barracks remained in the SS quarters. The massive entrance still stood, surmounted by the watchtower. We walked through the gate, accompanied by the bearded guide who had awaited us there. I brushed my hand across the letters of the wrought-iron inscription on the gate, JEDEM DAS SEINE: to each his due.

I cannot say that I was moved; that word is not strong enough. I realized that I was coming home. It was not hope I had to abandon, at the gate to that hell; on the contrary. I was abandoning my old age, my disappointments, the mistakes and failures of life. I was coming home. What I mean is, home to my world when I was twenty: its angers, passions, laughter, curiosity. Above all, its hope. I was abandoning all the deadly despair that accumulates in the soul, throughout a lifetime, to rediscover the hopefulness I knew at twenty, surrounded by death.

We had stepped through the gate; the wind on the Ettersberg hit me full in the face. Unable to speak, I felt like running madly at full tilt across the square, rushing down to the Little Camp, to the site of Block 56, where Maurice Halbwachs had died, to the infirmary hut where I'd closed the eyes of Diego Morales.

I couldn't say a word, I stood motionless, struck by the dramatic beauty of the open space spread out before me. I placed a hand on the shoulder of Thomas Landman, who was by my side. I had dedicated *Quel beau dimanche!* to him so that later, after my death, he might remember my memories of Buchenwald. It would be easier for him, now. Harder, too, probably, because less abstract.

I placed a hand on Thomas's shoulder, as though calling him to witness in his turn. A day would come, relatively soon, when there would no longer be a single survivor of Buchenwald left. There would be no more immediate memory of Buchenwald. No longer would anyone be able to say, with words springing from physical recollection and not some theoretical reconstruction, what it was like: the hunger, the exhaustion, the anguish, the blinding presence of absolute Evil—precisely insofar as it lies hidden in all of us, as the condition of our freedom. No longer would anyone be indelibly marked, body and soul, by the smell of burning flesh from the crematory ovens.

One day I put these words into the mouth of Juan Larrea, a character in the novel *La montagne blanche,* whom I sent to his death in my stead:

> I reflected that my most personal memory, the one
> kept most to myself . . . the one that makes me what

I am ... that distinguishes me from other people,
at least, from everyone else ... that cuts me off
from the human race—with only a few hundred ex-
ceptions—even as it establishes my identity ... that
burns in my memory with a flame of abject horror ...
and pride, too ... is the undying, stifling memory of
the smell from the crematory: stale, nauseating ... the
odor of burned flesh on the Ettersberg hill.

A day is coming, though, when no one will actually remember
this smell: it will be nothing more than a phrase, a literary reference, an idea of an odor. Odorless, therefore.

I'd thought about all that, as I approached the center of the
roll-call square of Buchenwald one March Sunday in 1992. I'd
thought of Juan Larrea, who had taken the place death had always reserved for me by its side. And I had laid my hand on the
shoulder of Thomas Landman.

A hand as gentle as the affection I felt for him, as weighty as
the memory I entrusted to him.

One August morning, almost a half-century earlier, on the
eve of the destruction of Hiroshima, I'd left Claude-Edmonde
Magny's studio on the Rue Schoelcher. I'd walked toward the
Rue Froidevaux, toward one of the side entrances of the
Cimetière Montparnasse. I had to spend a few moments in quiet
reflection at the tomb of César Vallejo.

... *no mueras, te amo tanto!*
Pero el cadáver ¡ay! siguió muriendo ...

I'd barely had time to remember Vallejo's words, three months
earlier, in a ward in the Buchenwald infirmary, when Diego
Morales had died in my arms.

> *. . . do not die, I love you so!*
> *But the corpse, alas! continued dying . . .*

The Peruvian poet rested in peace, as they say, in his grave in Montparnasse. Where one could leave flowers, now and then: Claude-Edmonde Magny had done so while I was gone. Where one could visit, to meditate at the grave. In all senses of the term, including the strongest: a meditation that would transcend and gather together all the scattered, distracted fragments of oneself.

But as for Diego Morales, the Spanish Red, brother to those who haunt the last poems of Vallejo—he rested nowhere in peace. He hadn't gone up in smoke over the Ettersberg forest, though, like so many thousands of other fighters: the sky had not been his shroud, because the crematory oven was no longer in service. Morales had been buried in one of the common graves dug by the Americans to bury the hundreds of corpses stinking up the Little Camp. And so he would rest nowhere, in no man's land, a place for which there is no word in French. *Niemandsland,* in German. *Tierra de nadie,* in Spanish.

I needed to meditate for a moment at the tomb of César Vallejo.

Just before she walked me to her door, Claude-Edmonde Magny had flipped one last time through the typed pages of her *Lettre sur le pouvoir d'écrire.* She had found the sentence she was looking for.

"I would even say that no one can write unless his heart is pure: in other words, unless he has sufficiently cast off his own personality. . . . "

She had looked at me in silence.

There would certainly have been much to say on that subject. How can a writer attain that purity of heart she spoke of—except through writing? Isn't the only possible ascesis for a writer to be found by seeking precisely through writing, without shame, the diabolical joy and radiant sorrow that are of one substance with writing itself?

There would have been much to say on the subject, but I no longer had the strength for it, that day. In any case, the phrase had to be considered within the context of the *Lettre*. And in that context, the meaning was clear: writing, if it claims to be more than a game, or a gamble, is but a long, endless labor of ascesis, a way of casting off one's self by keeping a firm hold on oneself. Becoming oneself through recognizing and bringing into the world that *other* one always is.

On the square of Buchenwald, one Sunday in March, so many years later I remembered Claude-Edmonde Magny's words.

I'd halted, startled by the spectacular beauty of the vast space that lay before me.

I knew that the authorities of the German Democratic Republic had erected a huge memorial complex on the slope of the Ettersberg overlooking the city of Weimar. I'd seen photographs: it was ghastly. A tower, groups of sculptures, an avenue flanked by walls covered with bas-reliefs, monumental steps. "Disgusting" would be the most appropriate way to describe it: the style of Arno Breker compounded by Socialist Realism. Or vice versa. Although it just might be that both styles are essentially identical, and therefore superimposable.

I didn't know, however, what had been done with the camp itself, with the monotonous rows of huts and concrete barracks. So I was completely surprised.

They'd kept the barbed-wire fence, the observation towers set at regular intervals along this perimeter. The watchtower over the entrance gate was still there, just as I'd remembered it. As well as the crematory, the washhouse, and the store for prisoners' belongings. Everything else had been leveled, but as at an archaeological excavation site, the positions and foundations of each wooden or concrete hut were indicated by rectangles of fine gray gravel, edged with stone, with a marker at one corner bearing the number that had once identified the vanished building.

The effect was unbelievably powerful. The empty space thus created, surrounded by barbed wire, dominated by the crematory chimney, swept by the wind off the Ettersberg, was a place of overwhelming remembrance.

I stood motionless.

Mathieu took photos; Thomas had moved slightly off to one side, understanding my need to be alone.

Would my heart be pure, from now on? Had I cast off enough of my former self? I thought so, at that moment. My whole life had become clear to me, in a sort of blissful giddiness. Here, I'd been twenty years old; here, my life was coming full circle, with this return to the time when my whole life lay before me.

It was then that I heard the myriad murmurs of the birds. They had returned to the Ettersberg, after all. The rustle of birdsong surrounded me like the voice of the ocean. Life had returned to the slopes of the Ettersberg. I dedicated that news to Lieutenant Rosenfeld, wherever he might be in this wide world.

We had all turned, mesmerized, toward the taciturn and bearded quadragenarian who had accompanied us throughout our visit to Buchenwald.

From time to time, when our eyes met, I'd detected a somewhat admiring astonishment in his expression. He was doubtless amazed at the precision of my memories. He would nod, silently approving my explanations.

The man had already been working at Buchenwald under the previous regime, which had made the camp into a political tourist attraction. A museum had been installed there, on the ground floor of what had been the *Effektenkammer,* the main clothing store.

So this forty-year-old man, bearded, pensive, and probably a former Communist, had let me do the talking, while we walked around the camp. I'd tried to be as objective as possible, avoiding adjectives and adverbs, keeping my feelings at a distance.

At the end of our tour, back on the square, I'd told Thomas, Mathieu, and the Merseburgers the story of the night I arrived in the camp, in January 1944.

The bearded forty-year-old with the sad eyes had listened to me attentively.

Half a century earlier, more or less, I'd already recounted that episode to Lieutenant Rosenfeld. The exhaustion, the thirst, the shower, the disinfection, the dash—stark naked—through the underground passage connecting the washhouse and the building containing the *Effektenkammer,* the ill-assorted items of clothing tossed at us across the long counter. And lastly, the German detainee who hadn't wanted to register me as a student, who'd wanted so much to give me some other profession.

Lieutenant Rosenfeld had thought it was a good beginning. Beginning of what? I'd asked. Beginning of this experience and the account I could give of it, he'd replied.

Almost a half-century later, I was just telling the end of that same story, while the bearded man looked on watchfully.

"Then, probably fed up with my stubbornness, he waved me aside, to make way for the next in line. . . . And he wrote 'student' on my card, rather angrily, I think."

That was when the guide spoke up, calmly, evenly, but firmly.

"No," he said, "that's not what he wrote!"

We turned toward him, transfixed.

"He didn't write down 'student,' but something completely different!"

The man had reached into his inside jacket pocket and pulled out a piece of paper.

"I've read your books," he told me. "You mentioned this

episode already, in *Quel beau dimanche!* So, knowing that you were coming today, I went looking for your registration card in the Buchenwald files."

He smiled, briefly.

"You know how Germans love order! So I found your card, just as it was filled out on the night you arrived."

He held the piece of paper out to me.

"Here's a photocopy of it! You can see for yourself that the German comrade did not write down 'student'!"

I took the paper with trembling hands.

No, he hadn't written *Student,* the unknown German comrade. No doubt guided by some phonetic association, he'd written *Stukkateur.*

I looked at the card, my hands were shaking.

44904

S e m p r u n , George　　　Polit.
10. 12. 23 Madrid　　　　　　Span.
Stukkateur
29. Jan. 1944

That's what was on my registration card, filled out the night I arrived in Buchenwald.

44904 was the preprinted identification number assigned to me. I mean: assigned to the deportee, whoever he was, who would turn up at that particular moment in front of the man in charge of filling out that card.

By chance, it turned out to be me. By good fortune, I should say.

The simple fact of having been registered as a stucco worker probably saved me from the massive transports being sent at that time to Dora, the construction site of an underground factory where the V-1 and V-2 rockets were to be assembled. A hellish

place, where the exhausting labor in the dusty tunnels was over-
seen by the SS *Sturmführer* bullies themselves, with no other in-
termediaries between them and the deportees than common
prisoners, who consolidated their own power through even
more stupidity and brutality. Avoiding Dora, in other words,
meant avoiding death. Avoiding increasing your chances of dying, at any rate.

I only found this out later, of course. Only afterward did I
discover how the system of massive transports to Dora operated
during January and February 1944. As soon as a new contingent
of deportees arrived in Buchenwald, in those months, a first selection was made among the men confined in the quarantine
huts of the Little Camp. The only deportees excluded from that
first blind selection were those possessing some qualification,
some professional experience that would be useful within the
Buchenwald complex.

He'd been right, that anonymous Communist who had tried
to make me understand this reality: to survive, in Buchenwald,
it was better to be a skilled worker, a *Facharbeiter*.

And stucco work was skilled labor. Stucco workers had come
from Italy, centuries earlier, during the Renaissance. They'd
brought with them their craft and the name by which they
would be known. They had decorated Fontainebleau and the
chateaux of the kings of France along the Loire.

So, on some bitterly cold day in February 1944, when snow
covered the camp, as it would later cover my memory, and
forced-labor conditions were atrocious, someone drawing up
the list for a transport to Dora probably skipped over my name
because I was a stucco worker. I could decorate, if not the
châteaux of the kings of France, the luxurious villas of the leaders of the SS *Totenkopf* Division, at least.

I held my registration form in my hand, a half-century later.
I was shaking. The Merseburgers, Thomas and Mathieu Land-

man, they'd all come over to me. Dumbfounded by this unexpected final twist to my story, they stared at that absurd and magical word, *Stukkateur,* which had quite possibly saved my life. I remembered the look in the German Communist's eyes— a look from the far side of death—as he'd tried to explain why it was better to be a skilled worker in Buchenwald. Everyone exclaimed over my card as they passed it around.

I looked into the sad eyes of the bearded forty-year-old man. They gleamed with a new light. In their depths shone a kind of virile pride.

"As far as survival is concerned," Primo Levi once said during an interview with Philip Roth, "I often wonder about it, and many people have asked me that question. I maintain that there was no general rule, except perhaps arriving at the camp in good health and speaking German. Aside from that, chance determined the rest. I saw cunning people and idiots survive, brave souls and cowards, 'thinkers' and madmen."

I was healthy when I arrived in Buchenwald. And I knew German. Actually, I was the only Spanish deportee who spoke the supervisors' language, and thus the only one able to be assigned to a *Kommando* in the camp administration.

To these objective elements, I would add—as Primo Levi also does, in his remarkable interview with Roth—a subjective factor: curiosity. It helps you to hang on in a way that is impossible to evaluate, of course, but is surely decisive.

"I remember living that year in Auschwitz," continues Primo Levi, "in a state of exceptional keenness. I don't know if that was due to my professional training, to some unsuspected resistance, or to a profound instinct. I never stopped observing the world and the people around me so intensely that these images still remain quite clear in my mind. I felt a deep desire to understand, I was constantly filled with a curiosity that someone later described, in fact, as nothing less than cynical."

To know German, be healthy, and feel curious about the world: chance would take care of the rest, true enough.

All my life—my survival—I'd thought that, too. Even when I wasn't talking about this experience. That's why I haven't ever been able to feel guilty. Guilty of being alive? I've never experienced that sentiment—or resentment?—even though I'm perfectly capable of imagining it, or admitting its existence. Of discussing it, consequently.

But that March Sunday in 1992, on the parade ground of Buchenwald, the registration card filled out the night of my arrival with that incongruous word, *Stukkateur,* forced me to rethink things.

Of course, it was chance that sent me to the German Communist with the cold, hard eyes, a survivor of the terrible years of Buchenwald. Some other German Communist—I've known many of them, too many of them, who would have acted this way—might have been irritated by my intellectual arrogance and written me down as a *Student.* Probably without even trying to give me the slightest explanation about what the camp was like. Exasperated beyond measure, and not bothered at all by sending a young bourgeois off to Dora. "He's on his own, the little shit! Let the sucker find out how to take care of himself! Anyway, they'll never know how it really was—the camps are nothing but health spas now!"

How many times, later on, did I hear veteran German detainees say things like that in similar, if not identical, situations!

And yet, my German Communist had acted like a Communist. What I mean is, in a manner befitting the idea of Communism, whatever its rather bloody, suffocating, morally destructive history has been. He had reacted according to an idea of solidarity, of internationalism. A generous idea of humanity. He knew nothing about me, he saw me for a few moments of his life, like so many thousands of other strangers who passed by during those awful years. Perhaps, afterward, he even forgot what he had done, that word he'd come up with through phonetic association. Perhaps he completely forgot about me.

All the same, because he was a Communist, that anonymous German saved my life.

I know—I guess or I suppose, actually, from my own experience, since the documents and factual accounts are not yet fully available to us—I can easily guess what a complex history the organization of the KPD, the German Communist Party, had at Buchenwald. How sordid and heroic this history was, how cruel and noble, how deadly and morally courageous.

Let's imagine, if only for a moment.

These men were arrested after the Nazis came to power in 1933. Arrested after a shameful political defeat for which they were greatly to blame. Truly, the main responsibility for this disaster and the demoralization of the militants lay with the absurdly inconsistent and sectarian political adventurism of Stalin and the Comintern. Later, most of these German Communists—one of the particularities of Buchenwald was the concentration there of Communist and Social Democratic cadres, which eventually allowed the politicals to wrest control of the internal administration from the common criminals—found themselves in 1937 clearing a slope of the Ettersberg as a site for the camp. Hardly had the buildings been finished, and the Communists' systems of resistance and survival put in place, when these prisoners were hit by the news of the Nazi-Soviet Pact. Can you try to understand what that meant, to be a loyal Communist, in Buchenwald, in 1939, at the moment of the accord between Hitler and Stalin?

What wrenching arguments, what agonizing realizations that event must have occasioned in the illegal organizations of Buchenwald!

It's not impossible to imagine what fearful history was both concealed and revealed by the hints, the silences, the glances of the German Communists I knew in Buchenwald. Whom I found hateful at times, admirable at others. But in whom I have always respected the burden of darkness, of appalling existential anguish even if this respect—I hope I've made this clear—does not mean that I have forgiven. And still less forgotten.

On that far-off night in January, it was chance that brought me before this anonymous Communist with eyes that looked at me from beyond all suffering, all death, all compassion. Perhaps it was chance as well that had made him a Communist. It was lucky for me that he was one, though. That he was able, at that moment, to be attentive to the Other: myself. Attentive to something in my face, my words. Attentive to the idea of humanity that had made a militant of him, in the past, in life outside: an idea that yet glimmered like a tiny, wavering flame in his spirit, an idea that nothing had been able to snuff out. Neither horror, nor lies, nor death.

An idea of fraternity still challenging the fatal advance of absolute Evil.

So, *Stukkateur:* this was the password that had reopened the gates of life for me.

In my room at the Elephant, that Sunday night, snow fell on my dreams once again.

Since the actual interview was not to be filmed until Monday, the following day, on locations in Buchenwald we'd visited that morning, I spent the afternoon wandering around Weimar with Thomas and Mathieu Landman.

The spirit of Lieutenant Rosenfeld kept us company. At some point during our stroll, I wondered if Rosenfeld had been familiar with the works of Jean Giraudoux. Had the two of us talked about Giraudoux, in those distant April days of 1945? I didn't remember that we had. It wasn't impossible, though. Rosenfeld was quite familiar with French literature, and we did discuss how French writers had reacted to the Occupation. Jean Giraudoux, in any case, had not come to Weimar, to the conferences of the *Propagandastaffel*. I thought of Giraudoux because he would have been able to write a lovely monologue for the ghost of Lieutenant Rosenfeld, who spent that afternoon with us.

In any event, Thomas, Mathieu, and I visited Goethe's *Gartenhaus,* on the other side of the Ilm, as well as his house in town, on the *Frauenplan*. We made a complete tour of the small city, stopping to look at the chief monuments and historic homes, to have a beer or a coffee, or to bargain for souvenirs in the few shops with decent merchandise.

Peter and Sabine Merseburger had invited us to a local restaurant for dinner that evening. The atmosphere was friendly, relaxed, convivial. The *Stukkateur* did not fail to make a brief appearance, however: the story had obviously impressed my German friends.

And snow had fallen on my sleep once more.

It wasn't the snow of former times. More precisely, it was the snow of yesteryear, but it had fallen today, on my last sight of Buchenwald. The snow had fallen, in my dreams, on the camp of Buchenwald as I had seen it that morning.

I'd been struck by one thing, right after hearing the variegated rustling of the birds that had come back to the Ettersberg: that the Little Camp of quarantine huts was no longer visible at the foot of the slope. It didn't surprise me that the barracks had been razed, as they had been throughout the camp. But this empty space had not been maintained: the forest had reclaimed the site of the Little Camp.

The forest now covered Block 56, where I'd watched Halbwachs and Maspero die. It had overgrown the site of Block 62, where I'd arrived on January 29, 1944, where I'd begun learning how to decipher the mysteries of Buchenwald. To discover the secrets of fraternity. To contemplate, face-to-face, the radiant horror of absolute Evil. The forest had overgrown the site of the collective latrines, that place of many liberties in the farthest circle of hell.

Only later did I learn the explanation behind this.

In 1945, just a few months after the liquidation of the Nazi camp (the last deportees, some Yugoslavs, had left there in June, it seems), Buchenwald had been reopened by the Soviet occupation authorities. Under the control of the KGB, Buchenwald had become a concentration camp again.

I already knew this, I was aware of the fact.

In 1980, in Hanover, during a discussion with readers of the German translation of *Quel beau dimanche!,* a young woman, a refugee from the East, had already told me. Later, in 1983, I was sent a short novel by Peter Pöttgen, *Am Ettersberg,* in which the history of the two Buchenwalds, the Nazi camp and the Stalinist camp, is presented through the story of a German family, the Steins.

What I did not know, however, was that during the five years or so of the Stalinist camp's operation (it was shut down in 1950, at the time of the creation of the German Democratic Republic, which erected the disgraceful memorial I've already mentioned), thousands of bodies were buried in common graves, at the foot of the Ettersberg. The return of the forest covered more than the former quarantine camp: it covered and concealed the corpses of these thousands of dead, these thousands of victims of Stalinism.

So on one side, on one of the slopes of the hill, a monstrous and pompous marble monument was supposed to remind the good people of the misleading (since it was purely symbolic) connection of the Communist regime to the anti-Fascist struggles of Europe's past. On the other side, a new forest had grown over the boneyards of Communism, to erase their traces in the humble and tenacious memory of the countryside, if not in that of men.

We had left the actual enclosure of the camp, that morning, along the sentinel's path that skirted what had once been the buildings of the DAW factory (*Deutsche Ausrüstungswerke*), now gone. We'd entered that forest of young trees hiding ancient Stalinist death. A little way into the wood, in a kind of clearing, a few families of those who had disappeared had erected crosses bearing the names of their relatives. A few dozen crosses for thousands of dead who had vanished into mass graves.

Mathieu Landman took photos of this clearing, of this moving assembly of mismatched crosses. I look at them, sometimes. It seems only proper to me that reunified, democratic Germany (one of the subjects on which Heidegger and Jaspers could not agree, in their correspondence, since Heidegger obstinately refused to consider the question of German guilt), the new Germany, born of the double tragedy of the twentieth century, anchored in Europe and a possible stabilizing force for its future, should make the Weimar-Buchenwald site a place of remembrance, an international center of democratic Reason.

Germany's special place in the history of this century is obvious: it is the only European country that has had to experience, suffer, and acknowledge responsibility for the devastating effects of both totalitarian movements of the twentieth century: Nazism and Bolshevism. I leave it to the learned professors of political science to point out or emphasize the indisputable specific differences between these two movements. That is not my concern at the moment, at this moment, as I remember, in my room at the Elephant, the snow that fell on my dreams. My point is that the same political experiences that have made the history of Germany a tragic history can also allow Germany to take its place in the forefront of a democratic and universalist expansion of the idea of Europe.

And the site of Weimar-Buchenwald could become the symbol of this idea, a place of remembrance and promise.

But snow had fallen on my sleep.

It blanketed the young forest that had sprung up where the Little Camp had been. Where the thousands of nameless corpses that had not gone up in smoke, like their brothers from years past, lay rotting in the Thuringian earth.

I was walking in the deep snow, through the trees, with Thomas and Mathieu Landman. I was telling them where Block 56 had been. I talked to them about Maurice Halbwachs. I explained where the latrines had been and spoke of our poetry reciting sessions, with Serge Miller and Yves Darriet.

Suddenly, they couldn't keep up with me anymore. They fell behind, floundering in the deep snow. All at once I was twenty years old and I was striding swiftly through the swirling snow, right here, but long years ago. On that distant Sunday when Kaminski had called me to the meeting where we listened to the survivor of the Auschwitz *Sonderkommando*.

I woke up, in the room at the Elephant.

I was no longer dreaming, I had returned to this dream that had been my life, that would be my life.

I was in the tiny glass-walled office of Ludwig G., the *Kapo* of the Contagious Ward, in the Buchenwald infirmary. I was alone there; all my pals had left.

Lamplight shone dimly on Ludwig's hands, lying flat on the table. We said nothing, in a silence still echoing with the voice of the survivor from Auschwitz.

This monotonous voice, with its irregular rhythm, now slow, painstaking, repetitious, and then hurried, as though driven by sudden overwhelming emotion (strangely, this would happen when he went into detail, noting for example the distraught glance of a woman at someone dear, someone familiar, from whom she had just been separated by the selection on the arrival platform, or someone's outburst of rebellion as the great crowd of those selected was herded ever closer to the disinfection building, as though this man or woman had a vague premonition of iminent danger, a revolt suppressed with a horrible, gentle reasonableness by the very companions of the rebel, who was finally urged—almost carried—along by helping hands, off to the unthinkable death of the gas chambers: it was in offering such details that his words would tumble out, while his voice remained even, precise, and neutral when he presented an overall view of this horror, a collective, abstract horror in which individuals disappeared, as if melting away in the flow of icy lava sweeping them toward programmed destruction), this voice of the *Sonderkommando* survivor still echoed dully in the deepening silence.

Shortly before, Kaminski had asked us sternly never to forget the testimony of the survivor from Auschwitz, never to forget Germany's guilt.

I'd murmured a few lines of Bertolt Brecht.

O Deutschland, bleiche Mutter . . .

It was Julia, the young Austrian Jewish woman in the military apparatus of the MOI, who had taught me this poem by Brecht.

"What was that?" asked Ludwig.

He didn't know that one, apparently.

Yet Ludwig G. had often talked about Brecht to me. He had recited some of his poetry for me. That's how I learned the *Eulogies* by heart. Eulogies of the party, of underground work, of the Marxist canon. But I hadn't known that these poems were extracts from *Die Massnahme,* one of Brecht's didactic plays, the most violent, the most lucid—or the most cynical?—work ever written about the totalitarian nature of Correct Thought.

> *O Deutschland, bleiche Mutter!*
> *Wie sitzest Du besudelt*
> *Unter den Völkern . . .*

But he didn't know that one, Ludwig G. He remembered another of Brecht's poems, from the twenties.

> *Deutschland, du Blondes, Bleiches*
> *Wildwolkiges mit sanfter Stirn!*
> *Was ging vor in deinen lautlosen Himmeln?*
> *Nun bist du das Aasloch Europas.*

So we talked about Germany, that pallid mother whose sons, according to Brecht, had made her the laughingstock or scarecrow of peoples. Or the blond, pale Germany evoked in the earlier poem, whose smooth brow was wreathed in storm clouds, the Germany that had become the carrion heap of Europe.

Shrill whistles had abruptly silenced our conversation in the half-light of the Contagious Ward. Time had passed: those whistles were sounding curfew.

I had to get back to my block in a hurry.

Outside, the night was clear, the snow squall was over. Stars glittered in the Thuringian sky. I stepped briskly across the squeaking snow, through the trees of the little wood surrounding the infirmary compound. In spite of the strident sound of the whistles, in the distance, it was a lovely, quiet night, full of peace. The world lay spread out before me in the luminous mystery of a darkling lunar clarity. I had to stop, to catch my breath. My heart was pounding. All my life, I thought, I'll remember this insane happiness. This nocturnal beauty.

I looked up.

On the crest of the Ettersberg, tongues of orange flame protruded from the mouth of the squat crematory chimney.